A DIGITAL GUIDE

INTERNET
FACTS

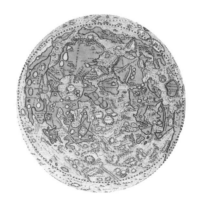

This is a Starfire Book
First Published in 2002

02 04 05 03

1 3 5 7 9 10 8 6 4 2

Starfire is part of
The Foundry Creative Media Company Limited
Crabtree Hall, Crabtree Lane, Fulham, London SW6 6TY

Visit the Foundry website: www.foundry.co.uk

Copyright © 2002 The Foundry

ISBN 1 903817 95 1

A copy of the CIP data for this book is available from the British Library

Printed in China

Special thanks to: Julia Rolf and Tom Worsley

A DIGITAL GUIDE

INTERNET FACTS

Roger Laing and Ian Powling

TECHNICAL CONSULTANT: MARTIN NOBLE

STAR
FIRE

CONTENTS

HOW TO USE THIS BOOK

This book is a mine of information for all internet users, regardless of their experience; so whether you are a beginner, relatively familiar with the Internet, an advanced user or are simply after some hot tips and hot web sites, this is definitely the book for you. You can also discover the technical aspects of using the Internet and learn all about the history of the Net.

By using the icons (illustrated in the blue box below), which tag each entry, you can read the entries that are specifically of interest to you.

1. Designed in an A–Z format for ease-of-use, you can simply look up the information that you are interested in by using the Contents List on page 6, or by flicking through the book. Please note that some entries are obvious (e.g. multitasking) but others, are more descriptive and may need some searching.

2. You can interrogate the book by use of the themes tagged throughout. We have provided seven categories: Basic, Intermediate, Advanced, Technical, History of the Net, Hot Tip and Hot Web Site, each represented by an icon (see below). So, if you are just beginning you can flick through the pages and read only the information which is tagged by the Beginners icon. If you already know more than the basics then you can read only the entries tagged by the Intermediate or Difficult icons. If you are an experienced user you can avoid wading through the unneccessary basics and concentrate on those entries tagged by the Difficult and Technical icons. The History of the Net, Hot Tip and Hot Web Site categories have been created for users of all levels. So whether you are a student writing an essay on the history of the Internet, or you simply want to find out about the latest sites and what they have to offer, by using the icons all the information that you need is at your fingertips.

Each A–Z entry is tagged by themes which can be followed as threads throughout the book

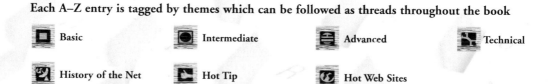

| Basic | Intermediate | Advanced | Technical |
| History of the Net | Hot Tip | Hot Web Sites | |

3. The pages at the back of the book provided you with further more detailed information to give you everything you need as an Internet user. Two of the most important sections are:

- **150 Useful Websites** In this section we have divided the web sites by interest areas. We've got everything covered: from the best search engines and directories, to online booksellers for bargain books. We've listed the best leisure and entertainment sites, where to find the latest news headlines and any reference information you may require for research purposes and also those sites offering up-to-the-minute travel information and bargain flights.

- **Top ISPs** Simply to make your life easier we have supplied you with everything you need to know about ISPs to allow you to choose one with all the right requirements for you, regardless of whether you want unmetered access or a pay ISP.

There are two types of pages throughout the book: the main A–Z entries and feature spreads (within the A–Z order), which focus on major topics and often present step-by-step information

Main A–Z entries

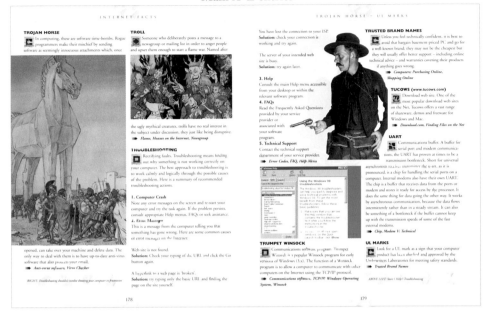

Feature Spreads

INTRODUCTION

So, what exactly is this thing called the Internet? It seems you cannot pick up a magazine, watch television or even walk down the high street without encountering some reference to it. The Internet, or 'Net' for short, is a global network of powerful computers connected together that allows millions of people to communicate with one another and share information. Although the population of North America led the way, the Internet's popularity is extending rapidly throughout the world.

The Internet contains the World Wide Web, a collection of millions of web pages with information on just about every subject you can think of. It allows people to shop online, enjoy entertainment, and get the latest news. It provides new ways for children to learn at school. The Net also helps friends to keep in touch and communities to interact.

In its embryonic form, the Internet was a cluster of military, government and educational networks, and specialized knowledge was required to use it. As a result of the technical advances of the 1980s and 1990s, we now have software programs for browsing web pages and using email that are quite easy to use. Quite easy, that is, if you happen to be a computer user already. If you're new to using a computer, and want to find essential facts about the Internet, we don't label you as a 'dummy' or an 'idiot' as some books imply, we simply give you the facts – in a concise, easy-to-read format.

The book you're holding now is not your standard step-by-step how-to book. We're not going to bore you with pages of point-and-click sequences. We don't think it's the right approach. Firstly, the technology changes so fast that what you've learned so diligently quickly becomes redundant. Secondly, we believe in empowering you. We think it's much more helpful to explain the concepts and principles of the Internet so you can apply them yourself, and not get lost when your carefully-learned step-by-step sequence no longer applies. That's why we compiled this book as a clearly-written compendium of essential nuggets of information, organized into a logical A-Z sequence.

We've shown every entry as belonging to one of seven themes: Basic, Intermediate, Advanced, Technical, History of the Net, Hot Tip and Hot Web Site. So when you find an entry you can see at a glance whether it matches your level of knowledge or interest. You'll find that certain important words such as 'modem' have multiple entries with different levels of complexity. This means that, first time around, you can find out what a modem is, and how to choose one. Then, when you have gained more experience, you might return to read about the more technical aspects of using a modem. Every entry is accompanied by numerous cross-references, so it is easy to follow your interest and go deeper into a subject or find out about related ideas. If you're a home user of a Windows personal computer, then our explanations of technical matters are primarily aimed at you. Both beginners and advanced users will find the book a handy resource for everyday reference.

So, what's in the book? Within the Basic theme, we tell you exactly what you need to know to get onto the Internet. 'Connecting to the Internet I' is a good starting point for information about connecting to the Net for the first time. Also within the Basic theme, you'll find entries explaining what a 'Browser' is, how to use 'Email', and why unwanted emails are given the curious name of 'Spam'. As well as giving information on 'Children and the Internet', we tell you what 'Bookmarks' are, and that they're the same thing as 'Favorites'. We tell you about 'Chat' for when you want to communicate, and about 'Privacy' for when you don't.

Entries within the Intermediate, Advanced and Technical themes cover all the important terms and concepts you'll need, everything from 'ActiveX' to 'Xmodem'. The History of the Net entries tell the story of how it all started, the unprecendented surges in technology and investment, the booms and the busts. Look out for Hot Tip entries covering a range of key topics and techniques, and check out the Hot Websites theme for our selection of prime sites catering for all tastes and interests. That's the beauty of the Internet, it's growing by the hour and there's so much to explore and discover.

This book is intended to be your everyday companion. Keep it by your computer – or by your bedside, if you're really keen! Whenever you hit a snag, or come across a concept you haven't encountered before, open this book and browse through the A-Z list. We had enormous fun putting this book together, and we learned new things, too! We hope you'll have the same experience reading it.

IAN POWLING

ACCESS PROVIDER

 See ISP

ACCOUNT

The relationship between a client and an Internet Service Provider (ISP). To be connected to the Internet, you need to open an account with an ISP, just as you would with a telephone company. The account specifies your username and your password and with some ISPs includes your tariff and billing arrangements.

))))▶ *ISP, OSP*

ACTIVE WINDOW

The active part of a computer screen. Browsing or email software lets you have multiple windows

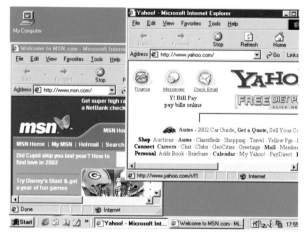

open at once. To make a window active, click on it and it will appear more distinctly defined than non-active windows. You can then click inside this window to use it.

))))▶ *Application, Auto-Hide, Browser, Esc Key*

ACTIVEX

Web page technology. A technology developed by Microsoft, which sets down rules for how applications share information. ActiveX controls can be embedded in web pages and automatically downloaded to a

computer. These mini programs can be used to play music or video clips, or for other methods of interaction.

))))▶ *Applet, Application, OLE, Web Page*

ADAPTER CARD

A plug-in board that extends a computer's functions. An adapter card adds a new function to a computer or allows it to communicate with other bits of hardware. For example, a sound card enables sound to be played back or recorded, while a network card enables a PC to link up to other computers.

))))▶ *Expansion Card, Expansion Slot Graphics Card, Interface*

ADDRESS BOOK

Email contact addresses. Just as their paper counterparts do, email address books range from the simple to fully fledged personal assistants. Whatever email client is used, the basic purpose of the address book is the same: to provide a directory of contacts together with their email addresses; what varies is the amount of information stored. Most have space for addresses along with telephone, fax and mobile phone numbers. The more sophisticated organizers allow detailed personal information, such as nicknames, birthdays or partner's names, to be entered. They also allow a user to group different contacts together under one name, so an email can be sent to several people by selecting a single address. Under some programs the full email address is automatically entered when you type in a name.

))))▶ *Composing Email, Email Address, Phone Dialer*

ADDRESS, INTERNET

A location on the Internet. An Internet address describes precisely where something is on the Internet; this can be a web page or even a picture

ABOVE: Desktop view of an Active Window
RIGHT: Internet addresses describe the exact location of a web page

BELOW RIGHT: *Some instant messaging programs allow you to use vocal communication*

within a page. This address is technically called an 'URL', pronounced 'earl' or 'U-R-L' (Uniform Resource Locator). A web site address typically starts with 'http://www.' followed by the name of the web site; for example: '*http://www.bbc.co.uk*'. However, often you need only type the web site name, as many web sites now work without the 'http://' or the 'www.'.

))))▶ *Com, EDU, Email Address, GOV, Home Page, MIL, Net, Org, URL, Zone, Web Page, World Wide Web*

ADOBE ACROBAT

An online document viewer. Acrobat is a software program devised by Adobe, which save files with text and graphics in such a way as to ensure they replicate the original, regardless of the computer or platform used to view them. Documents are saved as PDF files and need to be viewed through the Acrobat reader (available free from *www. adobe.com*).

))))▶ *Extension, Multi-Platform, PDF File, Viewer*

ADSL

'Asymmetric Digital Subscriber Line', a broadband internet connection. The great advantage of ADSL is that it provides a fast, permanent connection to the Internet. Because ADSL works at a higher frequency than normal voice traffic a telephone can be used on the same

line. It is asymmetric in that it delivers data such as web pages and downloads faster than it sends them.

))))▶ *Bandwidth, BPS, DSL, High-Speed Connection*

AIM

'AOL Instant Messenger', instant chat online. Instant messengers enable you to set up private chats with friends online, even when travelling, but this is limited by the need to use the same system. Instant messaging (IM) is the big growth area on the Internet. IM programs, such as AIM produced by AOL, enable users who are online to have real-time conversations. Unlike the public chat rooms, these are private communications. You can personalize your IM so you only chat with people you want to. By linking your IM to your address book, or 'buddy list' you can be alerted when friends come online and buzz them for a quick chat.

This is more than simple text messaging: as well as instant chats, the latest breed of IMs enable you to start voice conversations (to do so you will need a microphone and speakers or a headset). Once hooked on the ease and convenience of instant messaging, the facility to chat is not confined to your own computer. A traveller's version of AIM, called Quick buddy, lets you send instant messages from any computer that has a web browser. But there is a limit to free speech; there is no agreed standard, so several competing instant messaging systems have emerged. As a result if you want to send instant messages to a friend or colleague they need to use the same system.

))))▶ *AOL, ICQ, IM, MSN Messenger, Netscape Messenger*

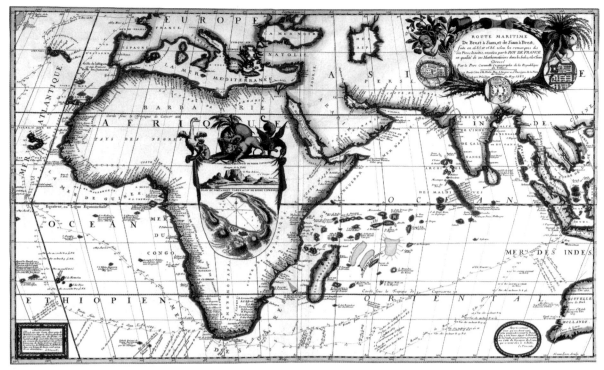

ALTAVISTA (*www.altavista.com*)

Search engine. AltaVista calls itself 'The Search Company' and is one of the oldest search engines on the Web, launched in 1995. With a large index of web pages and a wide range of powerful searching commands, it is one of the most popular web sites for searching on the Internet. As well as searches for images, video, MP3/Audio and news, a set of specialized search tools can also be found on the site:

Comparison Shop: For comparing prices on cars, home appliances and other goods
Yellow Pages: For finding businesses in the USA
Find a Person: A tool for finding people in the USA
Get a Map: Specializes in finding maps and atlases to locate places around the world
Translate: You can type up to 150 words into a box and select a language to translate into.

ABOVE: AltaVista has a special search tool for finding maps and atlases
RIGHT: Browser view of www.amazon.com

In addition to using its search features, you can browse through a directory of web sites organized into topics such as Shopping, Travel, Lifestyle, etc. AltaVista offers sites tailored to 21 countries around the world, for example Brazil, Germany and Korea.

))))➡ *Search Directory, Search Engine, Portal*

AMAZON (*www.amazon.com*)

Shopping web site. Amazon.com began selling books online in July 1995 and has since expanded

RIGHT: Animation brings action to the Internet

its product range to include CDs, videos, DVDs, toys and electronics. An estimated 29-million shoppers make Amazon probably the world's biggest shopping web site.

))))▶ **Books: Purchasing, CDs and Tapes, DVD, Video**

ANALOGUE

A continuous, wave-form signal. Computers are digital; machines can only distinguish between 0 and 1, nothing in between. The world outside, however, is mainly analogue, with smooth and continuous signals. Many processes in computing involve switching between the two, such as using a modem to convert digital data into an analogue signal in order to send it over a telephone line.

))))▶ **Digital**

ANIMATION

Any form of movement on the Web. Animated GIFs bring action to the Internet, but for interaction more complex programs are needed. The World Wide Web is an animated place, thanks mainly to the popularity of animated GIFs. These work by combining several still images and converting them into a single GIF file, cycling through them to produce the animation effect, much the same way as thumbing through the pages of a flip book. Animated GIFs are generally quite fast because of their small file size and they do not require any special viewers. However, they are silent 'movies' and they do not allow any interaction; for this you need to use more complex programs such as

Macromedia's Shockwave or Flash, both of which require a plug-in to view the animation.

))))▶ **DHTML, GIF, Macromedia Flash, Multimedia, Web Page**

ANONYMOUS FTP SERVER

FTP sites where users can log on anonymously to download files. FTP sites store files for users to download to their computer. Before they can do so they need to log on to the server with an account number (or username) and a password. Some sites let anyone enter and download files, but they still have to go through the signing-on process. Usually, anonymous is the username and their email address is the password. As a result, these file archives are known as anonymous FTP servers. In contrast, some FTP sites are private and only authorized users with a specific username and password can access the server.

))))▶ **FTP, FTP Search, FTP Server, WS_FTP**

ANTI-ALIASING

The process of tidying up images. This is a technique used to reduce the jagged look some lines or objects have on-screen, particularly when magnified. Anti-aliasing is used in many imaging programs – such as Adobe Photoshop – to compensate for the jagged lines. It works by blending the edges with dots of intermediate colours to give smoother-looking text and curves.

))))▶ **Graphics File, Picture Formats**

ANTI-VIRUS SOFTWARE

A program to detect viruses. Software is needed to hunt out and destroy malicious programs, known as viruses, that can unwittingly be downloaded from the Internet. Viruses are the scourge of this medium, and it is essential to have anti-virus software to remove them before they cause irreversible damage to a computer. Viruses are essentially mini-programs that 'infect' the computer by inserting themselves into files and then replicating. Most anti-virus software can be set to check the computer each time it is switched on. The software also watches for any suspicious activity suggesting virus attacks from infected files, downloaded from the Internet or copied to the computer from disks. Because new viruses are always appearing, manufacturers provide regular updates, usually downloaded automatically from the Web, to ensure the maximum possible protection.

))))➤ *Trojan Horse, Norton Antivirus, Virus Checker*

AOL (www.aol.com)

'America Online', an Online Service Provider (OSP). AOL is one of the world's two biggest OSPs; the other is Microsoft (*www.msn.com*). It has grown from providing limited online services in 1985 to serving a worldwide membership of 31 million. As well as giving its members internet access, AOL offers a host of other proprietary services. It has been a pioneer in simplifying Internet access for a wide audience and its software is designed so that members do not need any other software; a web browser for surfing the Net and an email function are built in. Although many of its features – such as chat

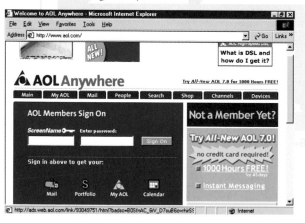

FAR RIGHT: Apple computers have come a long way; compare the new iMac to this original computer
BELOW: Browser view of www.aol.com
BOTTOM RIGHT: Browser view of applet of 3D rotating cube

rooms, shopping and message boards – can be found on other web sites, AOL offers a combination of services that put most rival ISPs in the shade.

))))➤ *AIM, ICQ, Macs: Connection to the Internet, MSN, Software Needed to Connect to the Internet*

APPLE COMPUTER (www.apple.com)

Computer manufacturer. This web site is a must for Mac owners everywhere. There is a store for buying the latest Apple Macs and associated software, areas dedicated to Apple technology such as Quicktime and Mac OS X and support for users and developers.

))))➤ *iMac, Localtalk, Macs: Connecting to the Internet, Operating System, Multi-platform, PC vs Mac, Quicktime*

APPLET

A mini-program designed to run within other programs. Because they are small and can work across different platforms, applets are widely used to add interaction to web pages. The Calculator and Character map available in the Windows' Accessories section are both examples of applets. They can be called up from within many applications.

Applets have particularly taken off on the Web, in the form of Java applets. These are self-contained mini programs, written using the Java programming language, which run right off the page. You do not have to do anything when you visit a web page that has a Java applet on it; it is automatically downloaded from the server and runs in the browser. Because it is a program like any other, it could carry a virus; to ensure it is clean the applet goes through a verification process when it is first downloaded to your computer.

The range of an applet's function is pretty well limitless. It can be used for everything from adding background music to simple animations and interactive games. In business, they can be used to provide spreadsheets, calculate delivery charges or even serve live data, ticker-tape style, with news headlines, sports results and stock prices.

As applets are small they download quickly. All that is needed to run them is a Java-enabled web browser, which is the form all major browsers take. Because the program runs within the browser – in what is called a Java virtual machine – it is secure and cannot directly access the user's hard drive. This also means an applet can run on any platform without the installation of a proprietary plug-in.

Whether you want to add chat or a search engine to your web pages, there are many sites, such as *www.free-warejava*.com, that have a huge array of Java applets available to download. This is a good way to add interactivity to your site, without knowing how to program. Most files come with documentation, which explains how to add the applet to your page using either the 'applet' or 'object' HTML tag.

ActiveX controls are similar to Java applets; they are mini-applications that can be downloaded to the computer. You will need a browser that supports ActiveX, such as Internet Explorer (some other browsers require plug-ins in order to support ActiveX). As the controls are built as components, you can put several together like building blocks to make a larger, more sophisticated program. In fact, several controls may be needed to run the control on a single page but only those that you do

not already have on your machine will be downloaded. Unlike Java applets, ActiveX controls can access the Windows operating system, so security can be a problem. One way round this is to have the ActiveX controls digitally signed by a certification authority, such as VeriSign, which shows that the control was written by the company named on it. With some browsers it is possible to set the security settings so that unsigned ActiveX controls will not be downloaded, or your permission will be asked first.

))) ➤ *ActiveX, Application, Java, Web Page*

APPLICATION

Any software program that performs a task. People often use the word 'application' as another way of saying 'software program'. More accurately, an application is a program that a computer user works with to perform a particular task or to produce a useful output. Microsoft's Internet Explorer, Word and Excel are widely used applications, as are QuarkXpress and Adobe Photoshop. By contrast, a utility is a software program that maintains or enhances the computer's operations, and an operating system is software that controls the computer and provides the environment in which applications work.

))))▶ *Operating System, Program, Software Guides*

ARCHIVE

A collection of files, often compressed and stored to save space. Groups of files, either on your computer or on the Internet, are often stored in archives. Some programs, such as the email client Outlook, back up material that is out of date, or not accessed recently, in an archive. This can be done automatically or at set periods. Online archives of files, music or software are commonly found on FTP sites. They can be accessed anonymously and downloaded, but as they are usually compressed, they will need to be extracted from the archive before they can be used.

))))▶ *Compression, Stuffit, WinZip*

ARPANET

The original computer network. ARPA (The Advanced Research Projects Agency) was formed by the US Department of Defence, partly in reaction to the then Soviet Union's launch of Sputnik in 1957. In 1969, the ARPAnet project was begun. It was intended to test the feasibility of linking together computers that were spread over a wide area, to form a network. This might seem logical, even easy, to us now, but the idea was revolutionary in the 1960s and many computer scientists had little faith in its development. At that time computers were generally regarded simply as arithmetic machines, not as communication devices. Despite its critics, the project was a huge success and marked the beginning of the Internet.

))))▶ *Internet in the 1950s: Prehistory, Network*

ABOVE: There are sites on the Internet for viewing, researching and buying art
LEFT: Thankfully, online archives can be compressed to save space

RIGHT: Browser view: smileys and emoticons at www.learnthenet.com/ English/html/25smile.htm

ART WEB SITES

Art on the Internet. The Web is a handy place to view, research and even buy art. A good starting point is the portal ArtNet (*www.artnet.com*), which has a searchable database for research, galleries and even an online magazine. Here, you can view works by more than 16,000 artists. By clicking on the thumbnails of the pictures you can download and print off a larger image. At *www.the-artists.org* you can find the best of twentieth-century art. There are also sites for less mainstream art – such as Art Crimes (*www.graffiti.org*), with its subtitle 'The Writing on the Wall', a showcase of graffiti as art. Ready to laugh? Then turn for a bit of light relief to the International Museum of Cartoon Art (*www.cartoon.org/ artists.html*). This shows examples from its collection of exhibits by luminaries such as Charles M. Schulz of Peanuts fame and Donald Reilly of the *New Yorker*.

))))▶ *Museum Web Sites, Photography, Pictures: Sources for*

ASCII

The standard code for representing text. ASCII, pronounced 'ass-key', is the acronym for the American Standard Code for Information Interchange. It is a seven-bit code for representing alphanumeric characters in binary format. Established in 1968 to achieve compatibility between various types of data-processing equipment, it is now employed throughout the computer industry and is commonly used to encode email messages. When people refer to an 'ASCII file', they usually mean a text only version of a word-processing file; this contains the basic text and punctuation but has all the formatting removed.

))))▶ *ASCII Art, Text File*

ASCII ART

Text as art. Just as the original cave dwellers crafted their paintings out of unlikely materials, plain text has now been developed as decorative art. The punctuation characters and spaces from ASCII have been crafted into illustrations to reflect the feelings of people writing in chat rooms, newsgroups or emails. The smiley face :-)

created using a colon, hyphen and closing bracket was the first, but now a whole dictionary of expressions has emerged. They have also gone from simply portraying emotion (emoticons) to physical description, e.g. (:-)</////////> someone wearing a tie, and even objects such as >[] to represent a television.

))))▶ *ASCII, Smileys and Emoticons, Text File*

ASKJEEVES (www.askjeeves.com)

Search engine. You can type your question to AskJeeves in plain English and it will answer with links to web sites chosen from their human-compiled database.

))))▶ *Portal, Search Engine*

ASPECT RATIO

The size of images. In graphics, the aspect ratio compares the width of an object to its height. For example, if a graphic is said to have an aspect ratio of 2:1 it is twice as wide as it is high. When resizing a graphic it is important to maintain the aspect ratio or the image will be distorted.

))))▶ *Graphics File*

ATTACHMENT

Any file attached to an email. The types of file commonly sent as attachments are word-processing files and graphics files. Such files are composed of eight bits and need to be encoded into a seven-bit form in order to be sent with an email message. When attaching a file to an email, select the encoding standard that suits your recipient's computer, e.g. Binhex (Mac), MIME (PC), or UUE (Unix).

))))▶ *Email, Receiving Email, Sending Email*

AUCTIONS ONLINE

Sites allowing the user to buy or sell items over the Internet. Not quite the Sotheby's experience, but virtually anything goes on sale at online auctions. There have been human body parts (withdrawn after protests) and even a blonde dotcom boss offering marriage. Auction sites to look out for include *www.qxl.com*, *www.ebay.com* and Yahoo. Most sites offer two types of services – auctions for new equipment, holidays etc., offered direct by suppliers – and person-to-person sales. The procedure is similar in both cases. You will need to register to get an account number and password that will allow you to bid. Bids are legally binding and cannot be retracted, although the seller does have the right to a reserve price below which the product cannot be sold. A site such as Auction Watch (*www.auctionwatch.com*) lets

you search for products across several sites and also has a community to chat about dark deeds in the sale rooms.

))))▶ *eBay, Yahoo Auctions*

AUDIO FILE

Files that store sound in the digital format. Audio files contain the digital data that represent a sound. To create an audio file, the computer has to convert the original smooth, continuous, analogue sound into the digital format used by the computer. This is done by an analogue-to-digital converter, which 'samples' the

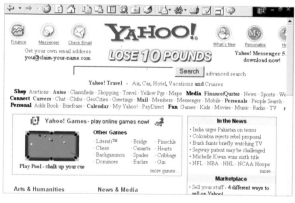

TOP: Computers convert analogue sound into digital format to create audio files
ABOVE: Browser view of www.yahoo.com *with Auto-Hide enabled*
LEFT: Auction sites allow you to buy and sell goods such as maps online

wave-form thousands of times per second and stores the information as numbers.

For a computer to produce the sound, it needs a sound card, which is fitted inside the PC and speakers. The sound card takes the digital information from the audio file and converts it back into analogue signals, which are then amplified and played through the speakers.

))➤ *Sound Card, Sound File*

AUTO-HIDE

Function that allows the user to maximize the view in the browser. To maximize the viewing area with Internet Explorer press F11. Press it again to restore the full browser. Previously, you would use the Auto-Hide feature, selected by clicking the icon on the toolbar.

))➤ *Active Window, Browser*

AUTOMATION

Automatic actions. Automation is the carrying out of tasks or processes by computers or electronic devices without human intervention. The software programs on a computer are capable of automation in a variety of ways: for example, a virus-checking utility can scan for viruses automatically.

))➤ *Robot, Wizard*

AVI

'Audio Video Interleaved', a multimedia file format. Video clips with sound are often stored in the AVI file format, but can be big files to download. A common format for animation files, AVI is used for storing video clips with sound. The true multimedia file, they are typically large and take a long time to download. Consequently, streaming video – in which files are downloaded into a buffer and then run, seemingly in real-time – is becoming more popular, particularly for people with broadband connections. There are other file formats for storing video files of which the best known is MPEG, but special media players are needed.

))➤ *Graphics File, Media Players, Movies, MPEG/MPG*

BACKBONE

The Internet's main network connections. These connections are very high-capacity, long-distance lines, which carry an enormous amount of Internet traffic across the world. They are funded by major corporations and Telcos, and some government agencies such as the National Science Foundation and NASA in the US.

))➤ *Internet Connections, ISP, Server*

BACKGROUND

The visual backdrop on a computer screen. The background can feature live content. When it comes to looking at a screen or web page, the background can, more accurately, be thought of as the backdrop. With Windows Active Desktop virtually anything can be set as the background: a picture of your pet, your favourite web page, or pictures from webcams

around the world that are constantly updated via a live internet connection. Through the Plus packs released with Windows you can co-ordinate backgrounds with system sounds and mouse pointers into themes as various as space travel or 1920s America.

))➤ *Tile, Wallpaper, Web Page*

BACKGROUND PRINTING

Print spooling. With today's multitasking computers there are some programs that run in the background while others are still active in the foreground. A classic example of this is background printing, also known as print spooling. While you carry on working, the computer can access the data you want and send it to the printer.

))))➤ *Printers*

BANDWIDTH

The rate at which data is transmitted. On the Internet this varies at peak times, according to demand. Bandwidth is used to show network capacity. The greater the bandwidth the faster data is sent, or the more data signals can be carried. For example, a broadband connection such as ADSL offers much faster speeds than a typical modem connection, which makes it ideal for viewing streaming media such as films or concerts. The Internet may react slower at peak times because the same amount of bandwidth is dealing with a higher volume of traffic. Bandwidth is usually shown as bits per second (bps).

))))➤ *Internet Connections*

BANKING AND FINANCE ON THE NET

Online financial services. Aggregation services can help you keep track of all your online bank and credit-card accounts. If time is money, the Internet can save you cash. Online banking gives you access to your accounts from the home or office, 24 hours a day. You can check balances, make payments and even arrange a loan. It is also possible to download statement details into financial software programs that will prepare reports on your profitability (or lack of it), budgeting, cash flow etc.

The likelihood is that you might have more than one bank account and most probably several charge or credit-card accounts. Keeping track of all of them – whether online or off – can be a daunting business. Aggregation sites, such as Citibank, take the leg work out of it by summarizing all the account information in one place. They cover thousands of different types of account, from credit cards to air miles. Such services have met with some resistance from financial authorities. There are concerns about security and privacy, as the user names and

passwords needed to log in to the various accounts are stored in one place. In the event of a security breach or fraud there are best-practice guidelines to determine who is liable for any losses incurred, but these are only voluntary.

))))➤ *Banking and Finance Web Sites, Credit Cards, Credit-Card Safety*

BANKING AND FINANCE WEB SITES

Web sites offering banking and financial services. Although probably every bank and financial services company in the world now claims to have a web site, the quality and competitiveness of their offerings varies considerably. The range of services available includes current (checking) accounts, loans, credit cards and mortgages. The most advanced sites allow customers to look at their transactions online, set up automated payments and move money between accounts. Major US banking web sites include Citibank (*www.citibank.com*), Bank of America (*www.bankofamerica.com*) and Wells Fargo (*www.wellsfargo.com*). For the UK market, new banking operations have been launched with 'Internet-friendly' brand names such as Egg (*www.egg.com*), Cahoot (*www.cahoot.com*) and Smile (*www.smile.co.uk*). There is also a wealth of sites geared to the online investor. Typical is the Australian investors' site The Trading Room (*www.tradingroom.com.au*), which offers real-time stock quotes, market analysis, tips and strategies for investors and a directory of stock-brokers.

))))➤ *Banking and Finance on the Net, Business Web Sites*

ABOVE: You can keep an eye on your money on the Internet

LEFT: Instead of visiting the bank, you can now do all your banking online
BELOW LEFT: Browser view of www.egg.com

increases their irritation factor and has led to a burgeoning demand for software that kills the ads.

))))➤ **Publicizing Your Site**

BARNES & NOBLE (www.bn.com)

 Shopping web site. The US bookstore chain Barnes & Noble have been trying to catch up with Amazon since 1995. It offers a similar mix of products to its competitor: books, music CDs, DVDs, and PC and video games. Some of its more distinctive lines include eBooks, Online Courses and Magazine Subscriptions.

))))➤ **Books: Purchasing, CDs and Tapes, DVD, Video**

BAUD OR BAUD RATE

A measurement of connection speed. The baud rate measures the speed of a connection. Modem speeds are sometimes described in terms of baud rate, but this is not the same as BPS (bits per second), which is the amount of digital data they can transmit. Modems can compress data as it is transmitted to allow more bits to the baud.

))))➤ **Bandwidth, BPS, Internet Connections**

BBS

See Bulletin Board Software

BETA SOFTWARE

The pre-release category of software; testing software before it is commercially released may uncover any problems it has. Beta software describes a program in the second phase of its testing. It follows the alpha version and is the first copy that is released to people outside the manufacturers for testing. Given the sheer complexity of modern programs and the various systems on which it is likely to be used, it is virtually impossible for vendor testing to cover all combinations and this makes beta software risky for the regular user. The intention is that any major problems or bugs will be uncovered by the beta testers, allowing it to be corrected before the program is released commercially.

))))➤ **Application, Program, Software: Purchasing**

BANNER AD

A promotional image found on a web page; the Internet's commercial breaks. Ads have their advantages but as they get more fanciful in their attempts to catch our attention, they also risk being zapped. Typically clicking on a link within a banner ad will take you through to the advertiser's web site. Originally the cost of a banner ad was based on page impressions, the number of people who could potentially see it. Now, they are more likely to be linked to the click through rate. To maximize the chances of catching a user's attention, banner ads have evolved from simple text and pictures to all-flashing, all-singing animations. For some, this merely

and binary files, which are coded and are only computer-readable. Multimedia files – sound, video, graphics and animation – will all be stored in the binary format and need special players or programs to view them. These binary files are often posted on newsgroups. Encoding and decoding such files used to be extremely complicated but most modern newsreaders, such as Outlook Express, are able to handle this automatically in the background.

))))➤ *Application, ASCII, Bit, Byte, Newsgroups, Program*

BINARY NEWSGROUP

Multimedia files posted to newsgroups. Complex multimedia files need to be specially coded and decoded for posting to binary newsgroups. Binary files, such as pictures, video, audio, even programs, can be posted in newsgroups. In fact, there are hundreds of groups dedicated to these that are known as binary newsgroups. Usually, they will have .binaries as part of their address, such as *alt.binaries.sounds.mp3,* which covers music files stored in the MP3 format. Binary files need to be encoded before they are posted to a newsgroup and decoded before they can run on a computer. This task is usually handled by the newsreader software.

))))➤ *Binary File, Newsgroups, Usenet*

BINHEX

A file-conversion format. An abbreviation of BINary HEXadecimal, this is a way of converting binary data, such as a graphics file, into ASCII characters. It is useful for transferring files from one platform to another, because all computers are able to read ASCII files. It is also the method many email programs use for handling attachments and is a particularly common format for Macintosh files.

))))➤ *Attachment, Apple Computer*

BIT

The smallest unit of information on a computer, short for binary digit. A single bit can have one of just two values: 0 or 1. The value of a bit represents a simple choice, such as on or off, true or false, black or white.

))))➤ *Byte*

BIGFOOT (*www.bigfoot.com*)

A web site for finding people online. If you want to find someone's email address, try Bigfoot – one of the Internet's best-known services for this task. The site also has tools for forwarding, filtering and distributing email, combating spam and auto-responding to email.

))))➤ *Directory Service, Finding People on the Net, Search Engine, Spam*

BINARY FILE

Multimedia files stored on the Internet. Binaries are only computer-readable and special players, readers or plug-ins are needed to view them. There are two main types of files on the Internet: text files (based on the ASCII characters), which can be read normally;

ABOVE: Bigfoot can find a person's email address, wherever they are

RIGHT: Netscape browser view showing Add Bookmark menu
BELOW: There is no need to let your money fly away; minimize your
connection time by Blinking

BITMAP

See BMP

BLINKING

A method of minimizing connection time.
Blinking, which is the name for writing and reading
email messages offline, is a good way to cut phone costs by
keeping connection time to the minimum. It involves
connecting to the Internet just long enough to send any
messages written and to receive any that have been sent.

))⮞ ***Internet Connections, Phone Bills: Cutting Down On***

BMP

'Bitmap', a graphics file format. Bitmap images are
represented by rows and columns of dots – or
pixels – and come in many file formats. For black and
white images one bit equals one dot. For colours and
shades of grey, however, each dot is represented by several
bits of data. The density of the dots (measured as dots per
inch or dpi) shows the resolution, which is the sharpness
of the image. To show the image on screen the computer
translates the bitmap into pixels. Also known as raster
graphics, bitmaps come in many file
formats including GIF, JPEG and
TIFF as well as BMP (which has
the filename extension .bmp).

))⮞ ***Graphics File, Picture Formats***

BOOKMARK

A quick method
for saving web site
addresses. If you visit a
web page and decide
you would like to return
to it, you do not have
to copy the web site
address – there is an
easy short cut. If your
browser is Netscape

Navigator, this short cut is called bookmarking. Choose
Bookmarks|Add Bookmark and the address of the current
web page will be added to your Bookmarks menu. Each
time you add a page, the page's title is added as a menu
item. Simply select the title to display the page on your
screen. The equivalent feature is called 'Favorites' in
Microsoft Internet Explorer.

))⮞ ***Favorites, Short cuts***

BOOKS: ELECTRONIC ON THE NET

Electronic publishing on the Net: whether for new
writers or established authors e-books give writers a
new channel for their work. There are many
books, classic texts and short documents
– some free and some for which a charge
is made – that can be downloaded from
the Web. These e-books (electronic
books) can be viewed in special
formats that make them easier to
read. Some are available in PDF
format and can be read on any
computer or PDA that has the right
plug-in. While most e-book authors
are unknown, some well-known
authors, such as Stephen King and
Michael Crichton, have
released e-book versions of
their novels on the Net.

))⮞ ***Ezines, Literature***
Web Sites, Publicizing
Your Site, Web Page

BOOKS: PURCHASING

Buying books online. By analyzing customers' buying habits to make further recommendations, online booksellers are among the most successful e-tailers. Among the pioneers of e-commerce on the Internet, online booksellers have also been instrumental in setting the blueprint for successful e-tailing. In particular, Amazon.com (*www.amazon.com* or *www.amazon.co.uk*) with features such as one-click ordering, has risen from the Web's version of a corner bookstore into a multinational retailer, selling a wide range of products. They cleverly let their customers do a lot of the work for them; such as getting users to review the books they have bought and using information on buying habits to make other recommendations.

)))▶ *Amazon, Barnes & Noble, Literature Web Sites*

BOOLEAN MODIFIER

An advanced search technique that can refine the results of keyword searches. They may sound like Transylvanian vampires, but boolean modifiers are actually

ABOVE: There is no need to visit the bookstore; online booksellers recommend their best-selling books

a useful way to search more accurately on the Web. While some search engines, such as AskJeeves, support natural-language searching, whereby a question can be typed in as a phrase, others, such as Excite, use keywords. This form of searching can yield many meaningless results. To increase the chances of finding the sites you want, you can introduce the boolean modifiers, such as AND, OR, NEAR or NOT, which will include or exclude certain words. For example, 'fish AND pop music NOT chips' brings up the pop star and excludes Britain's favourite takeaway meal.

)))▶ *Case Sensitivity, Keyword Search, Search Engine*

BOUNCED MAIL

Email that is returned to the sender; the wrong address is the most common reason for bounced emails. Email messages that cannot get through to their destination are bounced back to the sender. They may be

RIGHT: Mosaic browser view of Yahoo!
BELOW: Quicker than any speeding aircraft; you can send 33.6 Kbps of data information per second

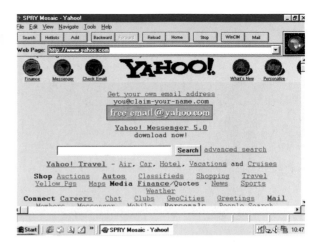

returned for a variety of reasons, but the most common are simply that the email address has been typed incorrectly or does not exist. When the receiving mail server gets the message that it cannot find a mailbox to match the name given, it uses the information sent with the message to return it to the sender, usually with some sort of explanation as to why it has been returned. Other reasons for bounced mail may be that the recipient's mailbox is full or the mail server is down.

))))➤ *Deleting Email, Email Address, Sending Email*

BPS

'Bits per second'; the speed of data transmission. The speed with which data is transmitted varies according to the type and quality of connection. The speed at which your computer sends information across a network, or through a modem to the Internet, is measured in bits per second. Currently, the fastest standard modems operate at 56K, which means that they can download (receive) information at up to 56,000 bits per second (56Kbps) and upload (send) at 33.6 Kbps. Typically, a broadband connection such as ADSL enables transfer speeds roughly 10 times that (560 Kbps) while leased-line connections are even faster. However, poor-quality phone connections and congestion on the Internet, particularly at peak times, mean maximum speeds are rarely possible.

))))➤ *Bit, Byte, Internet Connections, Modem V: Technical*

BROWSER

Software for surfing the Web. A browser is the software program you use to view pages on the World Wide Web. The two most popular browsers are Microsoft Internet Explorer and Netscape Navigator. Both of these browsers display web pages by decoding text files called HTML files, which contain the words, links to image files and instructions for laying them out in the browser window. The latest versions of Internet Explorer and Netscape Navigator are available to download free of charge. They can both support the newest web technologies such as streaming video and audio and Flash animations.

))))➤ *HTML, Internet Explorer, Netscape Navigator, Web Browser*

BROWSER WARS

The pioneer browser was Mosaic, the first Internet program with a graphical user interface (GUI). Its launch in 1993 helped to popularize the Web. Its author, Marc Andreesen, then developed the Netscape browser. Fuelled by a breakneck sequence of new releases, by mid-1995 Netscape had become the browser of choice for 80% of web surfers. In August 1995, Microsoft entered the fray with its own browser, Internet Explorer. It had one major advantage – it was free. Gradually Microsoft caught up with Netscape's technology, by version 4.0 it had drawn level, and has now overtaken Netscape in popularity. Netscape fans, meanwhile, had to wait three years for the launch of Netscape 6.0 in 2000.

))))➤ *Internet Explorer, Netscape Navigator, Web Browser*

BUFFER

A temporary storage area for holding information in a computer's memory. For example, a word processor uses a buffer to store files being worked on as it is quicker than continually reading data from the disk. When a file is saved, data from the buffer is updated to the disk. Similarly, when a document is printed, it is sent to a buffer from where the printer can draw the information at its own speed, leaving the computer free to work on other files. Multimedia files from the Web may also be buffered by a media player before being played.

)))) *Memory, Printers*

BULLETIN BOARD SERVICE

Electronic message centres, where users can post messages on a variety of subjects. As its name suggests a bulletin board service (or system) is really like an electronic message centre. Most bulletin boards are targeted to special interest groups, from fishing to politics, but many computer manufacturers also host bulletin boards as forums where their customers can download the latest patches and drivers and discuss with other users any issues they have. While some bulletin boards are reached via the Web, in the main they are accessed using a modem to dial in directly.

)))) *Discussion Groups, Newsgroups*

ABOVE: RealPlayer: Video Music Network - showing buffering

RIGHT: Burning-in a computer gives it a test drive to ensure there are no problems

BURN-IN TEST

If there is a problem with a computer's hardware it is likely to show itself within the first few days of use. Experienced users 'burn-in' their equipment by leaving it on and idle for several hours, or days, to make sure it is free of defects.

)))) *Crash, Hardware Needed to Connect to the Net*

BUSINESS WEB SITES

Business sites online. After recent dotcom history, any venture capitalists still around will be very determined. Find out, by going to sites such as *www.3i.com* and see what help there is to finance your business idea. Online magazines such as *www.entrepreneur .com* will take you through the pitfalls of starting your own business. There are also guides to the new (and old) economy, such as BusinessWeek (*www.businessweek.com*). If you need anything – a management consultant (*www.atkearney.com*), market research, a distributor (*www.fedex.com*) or any of the other ancillary services needed to run a company or expand it – they are all on the Internet.

)))) *Banking and Finance on the Net, Banking and Finance Web Sites*

BYTE

The basic measure of a computer's capacity. Short for binary term, a byte is the unit of storage on a computer that can hold a single character, such as a number, letter or symbol. It is created by combining eight bits together. Each bit can have one of just two values: 0 or 1. A computer's capacity, such as its memory and disk

space, is measured in bytes. For example, the base RAM is given in kilobytes (1,024 bytes), a floppy disk holds 1.44 megabytes (1.4 million characters), while a hard drive of 60 gigabytes contains some 1,073,741,824 bytes.

))))) *Bit*

CABLE MODEM CONNECTION

High-speed Internet connection; a connection that enables you to access the Internet via the TV cable. Computers using a cable modem can receive data at up to 1.5 million bits per second (1.5 Mbps). However, a number of homes share the same connection (node) so actual speeds will depend on how many try to access the Internet simultaneously.

))))) *Modem I: Introduction, Modem II: Choosing, Modem V: Technical*

CACHE

A special storage area to hold information, such as web pages, for speedy access. Pronounced 'cash' this is an easily accessed storage area where frequently used data is kept. Information is more quickly transferred from the cache than it is from other storage areas on the hard drive or memory. Web pages from the Internet are cached so that if you want to look at them again they can be loaded from your computer instead of having to be reloaded from the Web. However, the cached page might not be the latest version. To see whether it has changed you will occasionally need to click your browser's refresh button.

))))) *Memory*

CAD

'Computer-aided design'; once the preserve of super-computers, CAD systems are now run on ordinary PCs to create virtual models. The sheer processing power of today's computers has been an

advantage to designers of everything from bridges to furniture. Previously, computer-aided design software had to be run on specially constructed computers. Now designers, architects and engineers use it on ordinary PCs. With CAD programs they can draw precise blueprints on screen and model them as 2D or 3D images to see how the designs will appear, before anything is produced. Even so, it is not possible to allow for all eventualities with virtual models.

))))) *Design*

CALENDAR

A date and appointments application. The Microsoft Works suite contains a calendar program and various other calendar programs can be downloaded from the Internet, most having features for setting events and appointments.

))))) *Application, Download, Time-Related Web Sites*

ABOVE: Time was greatly important to the Aztec people (as illustrated in this calendar); nowadays we can simply download programs from the Internet to organize our lives

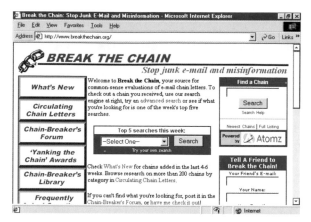

LEFT: Browser view of www.breakthechain.org

BELOW: Buying a CD over the Internet can be a good way to get a bargain

CARRIER (SIGNAL)

The frequency used to transmit information. The screeching and scratching sounds heard when a modem first connects to the Internet embody the carrier signal: the frequency, or sound tone, used by the modem to send data along a telephone line. Different characters are represented by changing the frequency of the carrier signal.

))))➤ *Modem V: Technical*

CALLBACK

A network security system. Callback is a complex security feature for people dialing in to a remote-access server on an office network. After they call in, the server immediately disconnects and phones them back on a pre-assigned number. In doing so, only authorized users from specific locations can access the network.

))))➤ *Dial-up Networking, Security I: Basic*

CAPTURE

A term meaning to save what is displayed on screen. To capture a screen is to save the information seen and store it in a file. In Windows, the current screen can be saved as an image by pressing the Print Screen key. The image can then be pasted into a document or graphics program. If you want to capture just the active window and not the whole desktop, press the Alt key and Print Screen. When video pictures are saved to the PC it is known as video capture.

))))➤ *Graphics File*

CARBON COPY

A copy of a message. Most email programs allow for two types of carbon copies (cc). With addresses in the cc box, a copy of the message is sent to the people listed. Addresses in the bcc (blind carbon copy) box mean that person will receive the message but their name will not appear, so anyone else getting the email will not know it has been sent to the blind-copied person.

))))➤ *Eudora, Forwarding Email, Outlook Express, Sending Email*

CASE SENSITIVITY

The accurate use of upper or lower case when typing web addresses or log ons. Be careful when setting up usernames and passwords to note which are lower-case and upper-case letters because some log-ons are case-sensitive. For example, Liberty with a capital L is seen as a different password to liberty with a lower-case l. Consequently, it is simpler, where possible, to use only lower-case letters.

))))➤ *Boolean Modifier, Keyword Search, Password, Search Engine*

CDNOW (www.cdnow.com)

Shopping web site. One of America's popular music purchasing sites, CDNOW sells videos and DVDs as well as CDs. Also featured is a CDNOW wireless radio service and news about the music stars.

)))))➤ *CDs and tapes, DVD, Video*

CDS AND TAPES

Music from the Internet; comparison shopping sites can help you find CDs at bargain prices. Having heard the song, there are lots of sites where you can buy a recorded CD or tape. Among the best known are the ubiquitous Amazon (*www.amazon.com* or *www.amazon.co.uk*) and the more specialist CDNOW (*www.cdnow.com*). Some sites offer sample tracks free of charge and you can even make up your own compilation CDs. Wanting to find the best bargain online? Try *www.dealtime.com*, which includes CDs among its comparison shopping services. Do a search for the CD you want and up comes a table of what is available, where and at what price.

)))))➤ *CDNOW, DVD, Video*

CENSORSHIP

The controlling of speech on the Internet. This controversial issue concerns the exclusion of violent, sexual and illegal material from the Internet. Government attempts at censorship are frequently opposed by anti-censorship groups. In Europe, there has been much debate over the accountability of ISPs for the content of third-party web pages. In the US, the Child Online Protection Act has been opposed by groups such as the American Civil Liberties Union (*www.aclu.org*). Parents can use the Ratings function in Internet Explorer to filter access to harmful sites, although the method is believed by many to be ineffective.

)))))➤ *Filtering, Freedom of Speech on the Internet*

CERN

The birthplace of the World Wide Web. Tim Berners-Lee invented the Web in 1989 while working at CERN, the European Organization for Nuclear Research in Geneva, Switzerland.

)))))➤ *Internet in the 1980s*

CHAIN LETTERS BY EMAIL

Nuisance emails; although they may seem trivial, email chain letters can be annoying. Email chain letters aim to coerce you into passing on hoax messages. Unlike typical hoaxes, the emails generally offer money or luck if you pass them on, playing on the fear of bad luck if the chain is broken. Sometimes the task they request may seem quite trivial making it difficult to identify a hoax. One way to make sure is to go to Break the Chain (*www.breakthechain.org*), where they have a list of 'letters' that have been added recently, together with an archive of previous hoax mailings.

)))))➤ *Hoaxes on the Internet, Sending Email, Spam*

CHANNEL

A multi-use term. A channel is basically a path for two-way communication and use of the word has spread widely. Within Internet Relay Chat (IRC), each specific discussion group, or chat room, is a channel. On the Web, sites that use push technology to send constantly updated information are sometimes known as channels. Subject sections within online services such as AOL are also referred to as channels, TV-style. Within the MIDI music standard there are several channels to which individual instruments can be assigned, while in graphics files a channel is one layer of an image that can be worked on separately.

)))))➤ *Graphics File, MIDI, Push Technology*

LEFT: A Carrier is the frequency used to transport information

CHANOP

A chat-channel moderator. In Internet Relay Chat (IRC), where each discussion group is known as a channel, the chanop, or channel operator, is the moderator. They are in charge of keeping things running smoothly in the chat room and they have the authority to throw out anyone unruly.

))))▶ *IRC*

CHAT

Online conversation. Chat has become one of the most popular activities on the Net. Entering a chat room is like walking into any social event. At first you don't know who is present or what is being discussed, but that is part of the fun. The rules of conduct in chat rooms are often enforced by monitors, who can eject chatters who misbehave. For example, it is rude to 'SHOUT' using capital letters, and vulgar or sexually explicit language is usually banned. Many chat sites require participants to use Internet Relay Chat (IRC) software.

))))▶ *Discussion Groups, IRC, Liszt*

CHECKBOX

A way of turning an option off or on. A checkbox is often used to select various options in a program. By clicking on the box, it is selected and either a tick or a cross appears to show it has been switched on. Usually, clicking

BELOW: Why chat on the phone; you can meet new people when you chat online
BOTTOM: The Internet is easy for children to use and can be educational

again will turn off the option. Checkboxes are fine when it is a simple choice of turning an option off or on, or where you can select several items together, such as choosing the newsletters to which you would like to subscribe. Where users can only choose one item from a list it is more usual to use a radio button.

))))▶ *Input, Radio Button*

CHILDREN AND THE NET I: INFANT AND PRIMARY

Online resources for young children. Kids find the Internet easy to use for fun, games, email, chat and instant messaging (IM). They constitute an enormous commercial market and thousands of web sites cater to them, offering games, animation, merchandise and 'edutainment' – entertainment activities with some educational value. In the UK, the BBC (*bbc.co.uk*) is a popular destination boasting a good range of resources, games and links. In the US, the 123 Sesame Street site (*aol.sesameworkshop.org/sesamestreet/*) is a well-regarded site that adopts many child-friendly guidelines. Roald Dahl (*www.roalddahl.com*) and Seussville (*www.randomhouse. com/seussville*) are two examples of story-based sites catering for primary-age children. Parents naturally want children's Web experiences to have educational value. A good starting point in the UK is the Parents Information

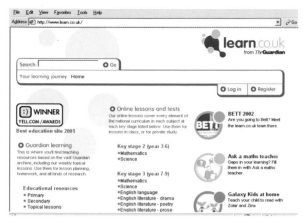

Network (*www.pin.org.uk*). Web sites geared to infant and primary level children in the UK range from subscription-based sites such as Spark Island (*www.sparkisland.com*) to 4Learning (*www.4learning.co.uk*), Channel 4's free site. There are some good American sites offering games or colouring pages for under-tens. Coloring 4 Kids (*www. coloringpage.org*) and PBS Kids (*http://pbskids.org*), for example.

))))▶ **Children and the Net II: Secondary, IM, Kid's Web Sites**

CHILDREN AND THE NET II: SECONDARY

Resources on the Net for teens. Secondary-level youngsters are spoilt for choice when it comes to web sites catering for them. For parents and teachers who want to offer guidance, good starting point sites include Cool Sites for Kids (*www.ala.org/alsc/children_links.html*), with links reviewed by the American Library Association, or The Kids on the Web (*www.zen.org/~brendan/kids. html*), an award-laden catalogue of web sites. It goes without saying that unsupervised teenagers will home in on the stuff that they want to look at, and parents might wish to try the Ratings function in Internet Explorer to limit the risk of exposure to undesirable material. Highly popular teen activities on the Web are chatting, instant messaging (IM) and, of course, exchanging music. The Napster system for swapping MP3 recordings caused a

ABOVE: Browser view of www.learn.co.uk
RIGHT: Chips have millions of electronic parts, which perform individual functions

teenage revolution in music consumption and spawned a rash of copycat services. Just two of the many fine UK educational sites are the *Guardian* newspaper's *www.learn.co.uk* and Facts of Life (*www.factsoflife.org.uk*), a health-education resource.

))))▶ **Children and the Net I: Infant and Primary, IM, Kid's, Privacy, Web Sites**

CHIP

An integrated circuit board. A chip is an electronic device made of a semi-conducting material such as silicon with an integrated circuit embedded in it. A typical chip contains millions of tiny electronic components that have been designed to carry out basic functions, such as adding and subtracting numbers (processor chip) or storing the results (memory chip).

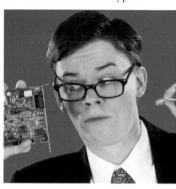

))))▶ **Memory**

CIX

'Commercial Internet eXchange'; a regulatory and information source on the Web. CIX is a leading provider of technical, business, policy and regulatory support and information to Internet Service Providers (ISPs), issuing white papers and press releases on Internet issues.

))))▶ **Internet in the 1990s, ISP**

CLIENT

A PC linked to a server; whether the PC itself, or a program, clients depend on the services of a host computer. Typically the client refers to both a local PC and the software that runs on it. It is linked, either through a physical network or over telephone lines, to a server, or host computer, that it relies on to carry out certain services. For example, an email program such as Outlook Express is a client program as it relies on the server to distribute and deliver the mail. So is the browser, which sends a request for a web page to a server, which in turn processes the request and returns the page.

))))▶ **Client/Server, Gopher, Server, Usenet**

CLIENT/SERVER

A network model where client PCs share the resources of a server. The Internet is a prime example of the client/server type of network. This is where the client computer, such as your PC, connects to a larger, more powerful computer, the server, from which it requests various services. It may be that it simply wants the server – also known as the host – to deliver the information that it has stored. Alternatively the client may ask for certain web pages to be delivered (from a web server) or email (from a mail server). The central server manages the resources that are shared by several client PCs.

))))➡ *Client, Server*

CLIP ART

Ready-made art software. Clip art is a collection of ready-made drawings, photographs, diagrams, buttons etc. that can be imported into various programs. For example, clip art is often used for the icons on web pages, such as an envelope illustrating an email address.

))))➡ *Graphics File*

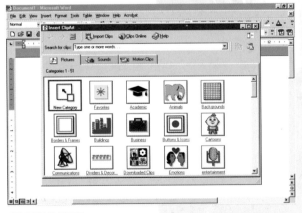

CLIPBOARD

Memory for copying. The clipboard is an area of memory that is used for temporarily storing data. For instance, if you copy a paragraph or a graphic, it is held in the clipboard ready for you to paste it elsewhere.

))))➡ *Cache, Memory*

TOP: People still prefer trying clothes on in a shop to buying them online
ABOVE: Microsoft Word's Insert Clip Art menu

CLOTHES: BUYING ONLINE

Technical wizardry has not yet been able to completely replace the benefits of trying on clothes before you buy and online clothes stores have been feeling the pinch. The disastrous story of boo.com showed that even if you could show an anorak from the back and sides it is not the same as being able to touch it and try it on. Because sizing is so variable, online versions of traditional high-street shops do better. So do those offering made-to-measure, such as the jeans manufacturers who will produce their clothes to the sizes requested online by the customer.

))))➡ *shopper.com, Shopping Online, Shopping Search*

COM

Domain name suffix. Every web site has a unique web address known as a domain name. In the US, domain names have two main parts, the top level and the second level, as shown: *http://www.secondlevel.toplevel*. The original top-level domains were intended to indicate the type of web site. These were:

.com	commercial sites
.net	network sites (e.g. ISPs, developers)
.org	organizations, mostly non-profit
.int	international organizations (restricted)
.gov	US government (restricted)
.mil	US military (restricted)
.edu	educational institutions (restricted)

Of these, the .com or 'dotcom' has become the best-known due to the dotcom boom and bust.

))))➤ *Address, Domain, Hostname, URL*

COM1

The name and number used to mark the first serial port in the back of a computer. It is used for attaching devices such as a modem, the mouse and even some printers (although they mostly attach to the USB or parallel port). COM is short for communications.

))))➤ *Port, Port Number*

COMEDY WEB SITES

Humour on the Internet. These are sites that are intended to be funny, rather than those that unwittingly are. The humour portal is *www.comedy.zone*,

with jokes, funny images and comedy videos. Comedy circus (*http://comedycircus.com*) also promotes tapes and videos of stand-up comedians, but along the way there are jokes of the day (be warned some are of an adult nature) and the chance to warp images of the famous, like Britney Spears. If you don't think there's anything funny about computers, then take a look at Tech Support Comedy (*www.techcomedy. com*), where IT guys get their revenge on the hapless users.

))))➤ *Entertainment Web Sites, Film and TV Web Sites*

ABOVE: There is enough comedy on the Net for everyone to find something amusing

COMMUNICATIONS SOFTWARE

Software program for electronic communications. A communications software program is one that works with the modem in order to transfer information to and from computers or online services. The bad news is that, of all of your computer's programs, this is probably the most difficult to understand. The good news is that, with a fair wind, you should only have to grapple with it when setting up your connection for the first time. Your ISP should provide you with a set-up CD that walks you through it. Otherwise, Windows users can use the Internet Connection Wizard.

))))➤ *Modem, Program, Software*

COMPANIES ONLINE (www.companiesonline.com)

Web site. This is a directory service run by Lycos, which provides information about thousands of companies in the US.

))))➤ *Business Web Sites, Online Directories*

COMPOSING EMAIL

How to compose an email message. Before creating an email message, you can choose how to compose it. If you use Microsoft Outlook Express, you can select Tools|Options|Compose and choose from various options that will determine how your emails are composed. The option that will make the biggest difference to the appearance of your emails, though, is the format of your messages. Select Tools|Options|Send. Your choices are either Plain Text or HTML. Plain text gives you just that,

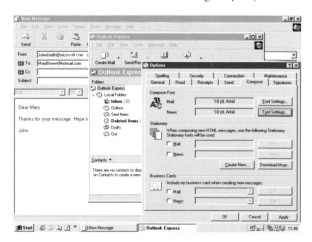

with no frills. With HTML you can format your emails to your heart's content. The email window will display a toolbar with buttons offering similar formatting controls to Microsoft Word.

Follow the steps below to compose a new email message in Outlook Express:

🖥 Click the Create Mail button

🖥 Type the email address of your recipient in the To: field

🖥 In the Subject box, type the subject of the message

🖥 In the message body area, type your message

🖥 Do one of the following: Click Send to send the message now. Click Send File|Send Later to send the message when you next go online

🖥 Click Save As to save the message until you are ready to send it.

))))➤ *Email, Email Address, Replying to Emails, Sending an Email*

COMPRESSION

A data file format; compression is a handy way to shorten download times from the Internet. Most programs or files downloaded from the Internet are in a compressed format – both to save storage space on the server and to shorten the download time. Compression works by removing repetitive information and spaces, but once the file is downloaded the information has to be restored to its original format. A lot of software comes as an .exe file, in which the uncompressing and installing is done automatically. Other compressed files, however, which usually have the .zip or .sit extension, have to be decompressed using utilities such as WinZip (for Windows) or StuffIt Expander (for the Mac).

))))➤ *Archive, StuffIt, WinZip*

COMPUSERVE (CIS) (*www.compuserve.com*)

Online Service Provider (OSP). Compuserve is an Online Service Provider that offers members a host of services and channels in addition to connecting them to the Internet. Founded in 1969, the company was one of the Web's pioneers of online services, most notably for being the first to offer email and technical support.

Now owned by America Online Inc, Compuserve focuses on adult and professional users, offering services such as Corporate Business Accounts. They provide resources for business users who use the system to conduct commercial research and keep up to date with the latest business developments. In addition to email and instant messaging (IM), subscribers can also make use of web centres that provide stock-market quotes and customized news feeds. Compuserve also now makes many of these services available to all internet users via its web site *www. compuserve.com*

A number of specialized services aimed at particular business sectors are offered. These include American Lawyer Media, a portal page tailored for lawyers; a custom service for the American International Group to cater for insurance brokers; and Airline Crew Services which provide online access and support to many airlines such as British Airways and Virgin Atlantic.

))))➤ *IM, Online Service Provider (OSP)*

COMPUTER

An electronic device for performing work and leisure tasks and for connecting to the Internet. Usually employing a keyboard, mouse and screen, the computer is run by an operating system and often has peripheral devices such as a printer and a modem.

))))➤ *Operating System, Peripherals, System*

THE SCREEN

COMPUTER NAMES

In a network, each computer has to have a unique name. It cannot be the same as any other computer on the same network. Double-clicking on My Network Places (or Network Neighbourhood on older PCs) brings up a list of the names of the other computers on the network.

)))► *Network, Network Neighbourhood*

COMPUTERS: PURCHASING ONLINE

Web-based PC sales. The Web has become a happy shopping ground for the PC bargain-hunters but, as with any online trade, there are precautions to take.

The growth of the Internet has enabled Dell, the pioneer of web-based computer sales, to develop from virtually a one-man band to a multibillion-dollar global company. Forget giant warehouses holding thousands of PCs in stock, or expensive high-street showrooms, the Web is the shop window. Place your order, choose the spec of the machine you want and it will be built to order.

It is a winning formula and has been copied by many others, including Gateway. A multitude of manufacturers are also using online shops as a direct route to the market, although they have to be careful it is not at the expense of their traditional retail channels.

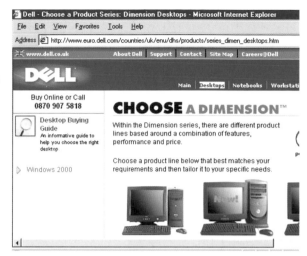

Many mail-order operations have also moved to the Web and this is probably the best way for the bargain hunter to source brand names at discounted prices. When buying computers online, as with any other product, you need to take precautions. In particular, as there is always the possibility of a breakdown with hardware, it is important to know what the returns policy is for damaged or faulty goods and what guarantees or warranties are offered.

)))► *Computer Web Sites, Software: Purchasing*

COMPUTING WEB SITES

From shareware to technical support, computing web sites can provide all the information you need. The Internet is geek's heaven. Once connected you can access a vast resource of knowledge and information. The problem comes if it's your Internet connection that you need help with. There are online troubleshooters for PC problems, from Microsoft's detailed but somewhat technical Knowledge base, to chat-enabled PC mechanics who will give you instant solutions (although normally for a price). Many of the reviews and technical articles from computing magazines are posted on the Web. The biggest collections are at *www.zdnet.com* (*www.zdnet.co.uk*) and *www.cnet.com*. They all have add-on services including loads of shareware and freeware that you can download.

)))► *Computers: purchasing online, Freeware, Shareware*

ABOVE: Browser view of http://www.euro.dell.com

CONNECTING TO THE INTERNET I: BASIC

You have probably already heard it from other people, but it is worth saying again just so that you know: getting connected to the Internet is the trickiest part of using the Web. The good news is that you should only have to do it once. Here are the recommended steps you should take, but bear in mind that because each service provider is a little different from the next, we cannot give the exact step-by-step directions for each one.

1. Choose the type of connection

The most appropriate type of connection for you will depend on the speed of connection you need, how much you are willing to pay and availability of the different types in your area. Your options should be one or more of the following:

Dial-up: this is the most common type and is widely available. It uses your telephone line and you will need a modem to connect your computer to it. This type of connection should enable you to choose from a wide range of ISPs.

Cable: if you have cable, then your best bet is to use the cable company for your connection. It will be happy to connect you and the connection will be faster than a dial-up.

ISDN (Integrated Services Digital Network): if available in your area, this type of connection is faster than a dial-up but is more costly to install and rent and is more suited for business use.

DSL (Digital Subscriber Line): this more expensive option is becoming more widely available and gives a higher bandwidth connection that is always on.

Satellite: this type of connection uses your satellite dish, if you have one.

2. Choose your service level

You need to decide whether you want to pay just for an ISP that gives you a bare-bones connection or an OSP that provides additional features as part of the service, such as instant messaging, chat, news and shopping.

3. Assess ease of set-up

For many people, this is the criterion that swings it! If you are getting online for the first time, you are much better off choosing a service provider that gives you a free CD that automatically installs the software you need and simplifies the configuration of the settings on your communications software. The alternative is to type in the set-up parameters yourself, following the ISP's instructions.

4. Assess the quality of technical support

Find out which ISPs have a good reputation for giving technical support, both online and by telephone. Forget any service provider that does not offer a free telephone support number. The time you are most likely to need technical support is when you are setting up the connection for the first time. Even with the best automatic connection CDs, there can be glitches to fix. Or you might want advice on the best dial-up telephone number to use. For many people, the quality of technical support is the one factor that can make them give up on one service provider and try another.

5. Assess the quality of service

You can only truly assess the speed and reliability of an ISP's connection by trying it out; some services such as AOL distribute free trial discs to allow you to do just this. You can also do some research by asking friends or consulting Internet magazines before making a commitment to an ISP.

6. Choose your ISP (Internet Service Provider)

Your ISP is the company that makes your connection to the Net. Also included here are the services sometimes referred to as OSPs (Online Service Providers) – these are services such as AOL and MSN that provide a lot more than just a basic connection. Make a careful comparison of the service providers.

7. Select a tariff

Each ISP will probably offer one or more tariffs to cater for subscribers with different requirements. Consider how long you will spend online each day, when you will surf, and select from the range of flat-rate, unmetered, off-peak or per-second payment types of tariff.

8. Set up your connection

Setting up your connection is much easier if your service provider supplies a set-up CD (or 3.5-inch floppy disk) that installs and makes the software configuration easy. All you have to do is follow the step-by-step instructions on the screen. The alternative is to type in the set-up details manually, usually by following printed instructions supplied by the ISP. And what a scary bunch of alphanumeric addresses, host names and ports they are! Be warned: it can be awfully tricky, and is best accomplished with a Net-savvy person sitting next to you! If you have chosen to set up your connection yourself and your computer is a PC with Microsoft Windows, you should use the Internet Connection Wizard. The icon for this will appear on your desktop. Double-click this icon and follow the on-screen instructions. If you have selected a type of connection other than a standard dial-up service, the setting up will probably be done by the service provider.

)))► *Bandwidth, Communications Software, Internet Connections, Modem I: Introduction*

CONNECTING TO THE INTERNET II: ADVANCED

 Under the advanced settings you can change the configuration for your dial-up connection to the Internet.

Once connected to the Internet you will seldom have to change any of the settings. But it may be that you change ISP and the connection is different. Or it may be you are set up on a network and have to connect to the Internet through a proxy server.

1. Change the connection settings

To change the connection settings in later versions of Windows go to the Control Panel, double click the Internet Options icon and then select the Connections tab.

2. Do a system security check

There is one interesting security feature here that you should check before changing other settings. There should

be a tick in the box by Perform System Security Check before Dialling. This way you will be given a warning to turn off sharing, if you have shared folders, before dialling up to the Net. In the box below Dial-up Settings you will see a

list of the connections you have installed. Highlight the one you want to change and click on settings.

3. Select the advanced settings

In the Connection To… box that opens, tick Use a Proxy Server and click on Advanced. In the box next to HTTP: type in the Address and Port Number (usually 8080) given to you by the ISP or network administrator. These settings only apply to this dial-up account, so if you use a different account, for example to access the Internet from home, it won't be affected. Click OK and you'll return to the Settings box. Under Dial-up Settings at the bottom, click on Advanced.

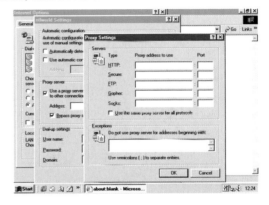

4. Choose connection time and frequency

Here you can set up the number of times the PC will attempt to redial the connection to your ISP and the time-delay between attempts. If the ISP is frequently busy you may want a high number of redial attempts. You can also select the time period (20 minutes is average) after which the dial-up connection is automatically disconnected if there has been no activity. This is handy if you have dialled up and then gone on to something else, forgetting that you are still connected.

5. Use the Firewall

With Windows XP you can also alter the configuration for Internet Connection Sharing and the optional firewall. Under Dial-up Settings select the Properties button. In the window that opens you can turn the Firewall protection on or off. You can also set how other computers access the Internet by sharing your connection.

)))► *Internet Connections, Internet Explorer, Modem II: Choosing, Modem III: Installing, Modem IV: Configuring, Modem V: Technical*

CONTROL PANEL

If you want to change the settings on your computer and it runs Windows, then the Control Panel is the place to go. To find it, follow these directions:

1. Click Start, and then point to Settings
2. Click Control Panel
3. Double-click the icon that represents the setting you want to change. These are just a few of the many settings you can change:

- Change the background of the desktop
- Add a new font
- Change the appearance of your mouse pointer
- Adjust the playback volume of your speakers
- Change printer settings

)))▶ *Properties, Recommended Settings, System, Windows OS*

COOKIE

A text file that helps identify users and customizes web pages. A cookie is a small text file sent by the server to your machine when you go to some web sites. The browser stores the message and sends it back each time it requests a page from that server. The cookie is helpful in identifying users. It can store log-on information so you do not have to re-enter passwords each time you visit the site. It also allows the server to personalize the information to you and to track the areas you visit. This has naturally aroused some concerns about privacy, but most browsers now give you the option to reject cookies.

)))▶ *Log On, Web Browser, Web Site*

COUNTRY CODE

Part of a web site address. At the end of a web site address it is common to see .biz or .info as a general guide to what the site is about. But for sites outside the US the address often ends with a two-letter abbreviation showing the country in which it is registered. So .au stands for Australia and .uk for the United Kingdom.

)))▶ *Address, Internet, URL, Zone*

CRASH

Computer failure where the PC stops working or a program halts unexpectedly. This is what happens when your computer goes wrong and freezes up. Often the first indication of death is simply a blue screen, or an inability to move the cursor. Sadly, any error messages with it are all too frequently totally incomprehensible. A crash can be caused by all sorts of problems with the software. Normally, it is because the PC has got itself into a terminal muddle, the software has bugs or there is some conflict with the hardware. Usually, the only resort is to try and escape a freeze by using the three finger salute (press Ctrl+Alt+Del at the same time) or restart.

)))▶ *Log On, Web Browser, Web Site*

CREDIT CARDS

Using credit cards on the Net. Many people are concerned about using their credit cards to make purchases on the Internet, although some experts say that it does not present a significantly greater risk of fraud than when you give your credit-card details over the telephone or you have your card taken out of your sight in a shop or restaurant.

To shop with maximum security, follow these guidelines:
Verify that the merchant uses the Secure Socket Layer (SSL) protocol; there are two ways to do this:

1. The address of the web page on which you submit your details should begin with https: instead of http:

ABOVE: Computers crashing can be very frustrating
RIGHT: www.cruel.com and one of the cruel sites of the day:
www.armory.com/~moke/mouse.html

2. A small 'locked padlock' icon should appear in the bottom right-hand corner of the browser window (Internet Explorer) or bottom left hand corner (Netscape Navigator 4.0 and later).

- 🖥 Print out and retain privacy policies, warranties, price guarantees etc.
- 🖥 Look for the Trust-e symbol or a Better Business Bureau online seal
- 🖥 Ensure that the merchant has a privacy policy
- 🖥 Keep close tabs on your cards and study your bills and statements carefully
- 🖥 Destroy or shred documents containing personal information
- 🖥 Be smart – don't shop online in Internet cafes

))))▶ *Credit-Card Safety, E-commerce*

CREDIT-CARD SAFETY

As a precaution, it is best to use just one credit card when shopping online. In the unlikely event of your card number being intercepted this would mean only one card is compromised. Some card companies offer an online trading guarantee and will refund any monies lost as a result of fraud.

))))▶ *Credit Cards, E-commerce*

CRUEL SITE OF THE DAY (*www.cruel.com*)

Not for the prudish, Cruel Site of the Day does what it says on the label: it presents a daily pointer to the tasteless, weird and wacky side of the Web.

))))▶ *Weird Web Sites*

CUTTING COSTS ON THE INTERNET

There are two main ways of cutting costs on the Internet :reducing the amount of time spent online and speeding up your performance once connected. The best way for you to cut costs will depend on what charges you incur. Typically,

this will be a mix of telephone charges and any subscription charge made by the ISP. There are many free ISPs, but first you should make sure these offer a local call rate. You should also add this number to any 'Friends and Family' type discount scheme offered by the telephone company. Inevitably, free services tend to be less reliable and slower at peak times than those that are paid for and this will mean a larger phone bill. By using either your browser or special software that accelerates the download, you can save web pages to your hard drive for browsing offline. Equally, you can reduce the time spent online by downloading emails and newsgroup messages to read and respond to offline. You should also use the most powerful modem possible. One other option to consider is that ISPs in most countries now offer all-inclusive packages. For a fixed amount each month you can access the Internet as often as you like, without incurring extra phone charges.

))))▶ *ISP, Phone Bills: Cutting Down On*

CYBER CAFÉ

Internet café. Cyber cafés have become increasingly popular venues in cities around the world for people who want to sip a coffee while surfing the Net, chatting online, reading the latest news or sending emails. They are also known as Internet cafés.

))))▶ *Surfing*

CYBERSPACE

Colloquial term for the Web. The idea of cyberspace was invented by William Gibson in his 1984 novel *Neuromancer*. This was an incredibly complex

3-D graphical representation made from the data on the world's computers. This visualization of a virtual reality has become hugely influential. Ten years later, it inspired two innovators, Mark Pesce and Tony Parisi, to propose a way of encoding graphical information so that a web browser could show a 3-D space that could be moved around in. It is called VRML (Virtual Reality Modelling Language).

))))▶ *Internet: Introduction, World Wide Web*

DATABASE

A collection of information organized to be easily searched; software that lets you enter information into one large, structured file so that it can be searched. Each separate entry is called a record and each individual part of a record is called a field. A file is a collection of records. For example, an address book is like a file, with a list of entries (records) that has several fields, such as name, address, telephone number etc. Much of the

ABOVE: Cyber cafés are popular in cities all over the world
LEFT: Cyberspace is a 3-D graphical representation of a 'computer world'

information on the Web is stored in searchable databases, such as the giant search engines and directories such as Yahoo and AltaVista.

)))))➤ *Application, Office Suite, Storing Files on the Net*

DEDICATED

Something that is devoted to, or reserved for, a specific use. For example, a dedicated line is a telephone line that provides a permanent connection to the Internet. It has no other purpose. A dedicated server only looks after the needs of a network or managing the printer resources.

)))))➤ *Printer, Scanner*

DEFAULT

The standard setting of an application. The default settings of a software program are the options it uses unless you specify otherwise. The default settings are also the factory settings that apply when you use software for the first time. The great thing about defaults is that you can change them to suit you. For example, if you like to read your email in the Verdana font, and you use Microsoft Outlook Express, you choose Tools|Options|Read, change all the font options to Verdana then click the OK button. You will now find that every time you read or print an email, Verdana will be the default font.

)))))➤ *Application, Properties, Recommended Settings*

DEJA.COM (*www.deja.com*)

Now taken over by Google and re-branded as Google groups, Deja is the web-based archive of all the Usenet group discussions. As such, it allows you to search the entire Usenet archive since 1995, containing more than 650 million postings. This is more than just an archive though – you can also add your own comments.

)))))➤ *Newsgroups, Usenet*

DELETING EMAIL

Removing unwanted email messages. Emails are often quick and topical communications and there is little need to keep them once they have been read. If you get unwanted messages such as junk mail or spam, you will want to delete these too. Deleting a message is simple. If you are using Microsoft Outlook Express, click

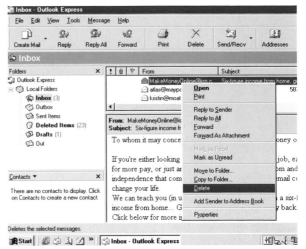

on the message you want to delete in the Message list and click Delete. Retrieving a deleted message is also easy. In Outlook Express, the message is put into the Deleted Items folder. To keep the message, drag it from the Deleted Items folder into the folder you want.

)))))➤ *Filtering, Junk Email, Receiving Email, Spam*

DELL COMPUTERS (*www.dell.com*)

Computer manufacturer. Dell Computers have become one of the most successful manufacturers of personal computers and were pioneers in selling computers via their own web site. The distinctive feature of their operation is that they assemble each computer to the buyer's requirements.

)))))➤ *Computers: Purchasing Online*

DEMO

Demonstration version of an application. A demo is a version of a software program that you can take for a 'test drive'. Demo software is widely available to download either from software vendors or from web sites that specialize in offering software of all kinds, for example Tucows (*www.tucows.com*). Many demos offer a limited set of features so that you can get a good idea of what they can do; others are time-limited and will cease to function after a set number of days. You can usually upgrade your demo to the full version by purchasing it online or by conventional payment methods.

)))))➤ *Application, Shareware, Tucows*

DES

'Data Encryption Standard'; the US government standard for encrypting data. DES is based on an encryption system in which a single key is used by both the sender and receiver. Simple to use, it is not as secure as public-key encryption, where one key that is readily available and one private key that is never transmitted are used for encryption/decryption.

)))))➤ *Encryption, Security II: Advanced*

DESIGN

'Before you put a really dark background on your web page, ask yourself this 'Why is it so much harder to drive at night than in the daytime?' This and other such thoughts to help you design your web pages come from the Art and Zen of web sites (*www.tlc-systems.com/webtips.shtml*). For other tips on designing a friendly user interface (UI) there is the well-respected Ask Tog (*www.asktog.com*). The difficulty with web design is that, as much as any visual appreciation, it also involves coding, so for help with HTML, JavaScript and the rest, check out Webmonkey (*http://hotwired.lycos.com/webmonkey*).

)))))➤ *CAD, Web Page: Creating II*

DETECTION

When installing new hardware that plugs into your computer, the system usually detects the new hardware and takes you step by step through the process of installing its supporting software. However, if the new hardware is not detected, you can install it by using the CD or floppy disk normally supplied with the hardware.

)))))➤ *Wizard*

DHTML

'Dynamic HTML'; a technique for creating dynamic web pages. DHTML takes the ordinary, static, web page and brings it to life. Using a combination of technologies, including HTML, JavaScript and CSS (cascading style sheets), it enables designers to control each element on the page. In this way images and text can be made to move, appear, disappear or change style as required.

)))))➤ *Animation, HTML*

DIAL-UP CONNECTION

The means of connecting to the Internet. The most typical connection to the Internet – over ordinary telephone lines – is being replaced by easier, 'always on' methods. The most common way of connecting to the Internet, particularly for home users, involves using a modem to dial up to a service provider. Because this is done over normal telephone lines it does not provide a very fast connection. The maximum speed for transferring information is 56,000 bps (bits per second) for downloading and 33,600 bps for uploading. However, with noisy lines and poor-quality telephone connections, the top speed is rarely achieved. The alternative to a dial-up connection is an 'always on' connection, such as ADSL, cable or a leased line.

)))))➤ *Connecting to the Internet I: Basic, Internet Connections*

DIAL-UP NETWORKING

A modem connection to a network. The process of setting up dial-up connections to the Internet has been simplified with the introduction of network connection wizards.

Originally introduced with Windows 95, dial-up networking (DUN) is a feature of Windows that enables users to connect to a network via a modem. Typically, DUN is set up to dial into the Point of Presence (POP) for your ISP (that is, your ISP's telephone number to ring for dial-up access to the Net). Some of the bigger ISPs will have several POPs in order to ensure local-rate access

DIAL-UP SCRIPTING TOOL

An automated dial-up. The tools to automate dial-up connections have been incorporated into Windows. Rather than having to manually enter log-on information, such as your user name and password to connect to a network or your ISP, it is much easier to automate the process. You can write your own script file to do this, using nothing more than a simple text editor. Since the early days of Windows, however, there has been a Dial-up Scripting Tool to help. Originally this was a separate program that enabled you to automate the dial-up and log-in process but now it has been incorporated into Dial-up Networking (DUN) and is accessed through the New Connection Wizard.

))))▶ *Dialer, Dial-Up Connection, Dial-Up Networking, Wizard*

DIALLER

A phone-dial utility. A dialer is part of a program that dials a telephone number for you using the modem. It is incorporated into dial-up networking for making the connection to the ISP or remote network. It is also a feature of fax or remote-access software.

))))▶ *Dial-Up Connection, Dial-Up Networking, Internet Connections, Phone Dialler*

DIGITAL

Technology that uses binary computing. The word 'digital' refers to the fact that the microprocessor or 'chip' at the heart of every computer and digital device processes data in digits. Digital data uses the binary system, which deploys only two values: 1 and 0. Digital technology is more accurate and can handle more information than analogue technology. For example, a digital DVD (Digital Versatile Disc) can hold more information than an analogue VHS video tape. Digital technology differs from analogue technology in that instead of processing a constant flow of data, it uses minute 'samples' of data taken at regular intervals.

))))▶ *Analogue, DVD*

wherever you are. DUN can be configured to log on automatically to the ISP but you will need to provide certain information, such as username and password. You can configure several different profiles (called connectoids) to store the connection details not only for online services, but also for any type of network accessed over the phones. To set up a new network connection in Windows XP simply launch the New Network Connection Wizard in the Network Connections folder (originally, DUN was accessed through the My Computer icon on the desktop). If you create a shortcut to any connection and save it to the desktop you can start up the connectoid just by double-clicking on it.

))))▶ *Internet Connections, ISP*

DIGITAL SIGNING

A message authentication scheme. Designed to bring trust to e-commerce, digital signatures are codes added to electronic messages that guarantee the identity of the sender. Like their paper counterparts, digital signatures are unique. To prevent them being forged they are also encrypted. Receiving a digitally signed message also shows that it has not been tampered with.

))))▶ *Encryption, Signature*

DIRECPC (www.direcpc.com)

An ISP. DirecPC provides high-speed access to the Internet via satellite for people with a clear view of the southern sky. This lower-cost service works in tandem with a dial-up connection that shares the communications load.

))))▶ *Dial-Up Connection, Satellite Connection*

DIRECT CABLE CONNECTION

A cheap and easy way to transfer files between two computers. If you only want to swap large files between two PCs occasionally, a direct cable connection is easier and cheaper than setting up a local area network (LAN). For a start, there is no need for network cards, although you will need

RIGHT: Instead of writing down all of your email addresses, LDAP organizes them for you

a cable physically to connect the PCs either via the serial or parallel ports. To access files on either computer you first need to run the DCC software, which is part of Windows, making one computer the host and the other a guest.

))))▶ *Network, Network Computer, Serial Port*

DIRECTORY

A folder in which files can be placed for organization. A directory can be thought of as a folder or cabinet that contains files and perhaps other folders. Computer manuals often describe directories and file structures in terms of an inverted tree. The files and directories at any level are contained in the directory above them. To find a file, you might need to specify the names of all the directories above it. This is called specifying a path. An example in Windows might look like this: C:\My_tax_files\Year_2000\Expenses_2000.doc.

In this example, the document 'Expenses_2000.doc' is inside 'Year_2000', which is a sub-directory within the root directory 'My_tax_files'.

))))▶ *Folder, Directory Service, Path*

DIRECTORY SERVICE

A set of rules for identifying and accessing network resources. This is, in essence, a way of identifying and accessing all the resources on a network and presenting them in a directory. The resources can be of all types – computers and printers or email addresses. Ideally, the directory service should organize the information in such a way that users can access the resources without knowing how or where they are connected to the network. One of the main directory service protocols is LDAP (Lightweight Directory Access Protocol), which is particularly useful for organizing databases of email addresses.

))))▶ *LDAP, Search Directory*

DISCUSSION GROUPS

Online conversation forums. In essence, discussion groups are similar to newsgroups, where people exchange their thoughts on a multitude of topics by posting messages and reading the replies. Practically anything can be covered in the groups and they follow interests as diverse as aromatherapy and snail breeding. Messages on a particular strand within a group are collected together into threads.

)))**▶** *Forum One, Newsgroups*

DISK TOOLS

Necessary for testing and maintaining your computer's hard drive, several tools come with Windows. Disk tools are a set of software programs that help you monitor the performance of your disk, maintain it, and ensure that it is storing data efficiently. Windows comes with several disk tools, which are stored in the Accessories folder. Disk Defragmenter will gather up data that is spread all over the surface of your disk and store it together, so programs run more efficiently. Disk Cleanup searches the disk for clutter that can be hampering performance, such as unused files or programs that are no longer needed.

)))**▶** *Maintenance, Program, Software*

DNS

'Domain Name System'; necessary because we find it easier to remember names, rather than numbers. The Domain Name System (or Service as it is sometimes called) is a network of servers that translate a site's domain name into the IP address needed to locate it. On the Internet, sites are found by their IP address – a block of four numbers separated by periods – rather than by name. The DNS servers do the translation. If one server does not know the number of a particular domain name it asks another and so on down the network until it finds the answer. For example, the domain name *www.google.com* is located by the IP address 216.239.39.100.

)))**▶** *Domain, Hostname, IP Address*

ABOVE: Online discussion groups cover a wide variety of topics

DIRECTX

DirectX enhances the playback of multimedia programs and games by enabling better access to the computer's hardware. This is the game-player's delight, a set of technologies that improves the playback of games, particularly those in 3D, and any other multimedia program. It works by providing a set of APIs (application program interfaces) that enables program writers to create programs that can directly access the hardware on a computer. They are able to do this even though they are not aware which hardware may be on the machine where the game is running. DirectX manages this by creating a special layer where general commands to the hardware are turned into specific instructions for the particular hardware on that machine.

)))**▶** *Application, Games on the Net, Multimedia*

DOMAIN

A group of computers that share the same resources and are administered together; these share the same domain and domain name, often the name of the company. On the Internet, domains are shown by the URL, or IP address. So, in *www.anycompany.com* the suffix .com is known as a top-level domain (TLD) and shows it is a commercial organization. Other TLDs are .edu for educational organizations, .mil for military and the newer .biz for business. 'Anycompany' is the part of the domain name that identifies the company or organization and is a more memorable version of the numeric address (IP address) that is actually used to locate the host computer.

⫸ *DNS, Hostname, IP Address*

DOTCOM BANKRUPTCIES (2000)

The failure of web-based companies. The wave of newly formed e-commerce companies that hoped to sell us everything from dinnerware to underwear all had the suffix '.com' and were dubbed 'dotcoms'. Very few of them were able to translate the heady optimism into anything like profit, and the trail of dotcom bankruptcies culminated in the crash in value of technology stocks on the Nasdaq market in March 2001. Many thousands of investors and employees kept hoping that the bubble would not burst right up until the last minute.

An early casualty was the now-legendary boo.com, which wasted £100 million trying to persuade people to buy chic sportswear from their poorly functioning web

site. The wave of dotcom bankruptcies was publicized on web sites such as Dotcomdoom (*www.dotcomdoom.com*) and spawned a new set of jargon phrases. 'Burn rate' was the speed at which dotcoms were spending investors' cash. 'Stickiness' was the idea that if surfers would only stick around a web site long enough they would buy something. 'Pink-slip parties' were gatherings in Silicon Valley and San Francisco where newly fired techies would drink and commiserate with one another.

⫸ *Internet in the 1990s: History*

DOWNLOAD

File transfer from a web site. Downloading means transferring a copy of a file or software program from a web site on to the hard drive of your computer.

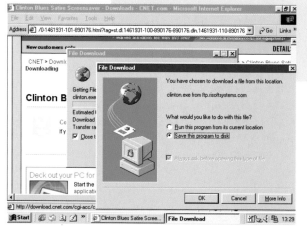

ABOVE: Afer the dot-com bankruptcies in March 2001 many businessmen had to re-think their strategies
ABOVE RIGHT: Drivers are able to control any device connected to the computer
LEFT: Internet Explorer\File Download (from cnet.com)

Any file transferred in this way is called a download. You can download files using a browser such as Internet Explorer or Netscape Navigator. These are some of the most popular types of file or software to download:

MP3 files: music files from sites such as MP3.com
Software: from sites such as Download.com (*www.download.com*) or from software companies, for example Adobe (*www.adobe.com*)
Web pages: you can download complete web pages to look at later
PDF files: Portable Document Files; you will need the free Adobe Acrobat program (*www.adobe.com/products/ acrobat/readstep.html*) to read these files

))))➤ *File Transfer, Freeware, Shareware*

DOWNLOAD.COM (*www.download.com*)

Software download web site. Download.com is a popular web site for Windows and Mac users who want to download software. The wide range on offer includes demo, shareware and freeware versions of business applications, Internet software and games.

))))➤ *Download, File transfer, Freeware, Shareware*

DRIVE LETTERS

How to identify PC drives. If your computer is a PC then the various drives it contains are identified by the following letters:

C: This is your hard drive, which stores all your files and software on an electro-magnetic disk
A: This is your floppy disk drive, which can read and write data up to 1.4 Mb in total. Floppy disks can still be useful for saving documents
D: This is your CD or DVD drive, if you have one installed

))))➤ *Mapping Drive/Printer, Network Drive*

DRIVER

Software that translates general Windows commands into specific instructions to control any devices attached to the PC. A special piece of software that sits between Windows and a particular device, such as a printer or keyboard. A lot of drivers are built into Windows, in support of its new plug-and-play approach, where new devices can be automatically recognized and configured accordingly. However, it does not always work and sometimes it is necessary to install updated drivers manually.

))))➤ *Software*

DSL

'Digital Subscriber Line'; a high-speed internet connection. New content services are developing to take advantage of the high-speed access to the Internet provided by xDSL technologies. xDSL groups together several technologies that provide broadband connections to the Internet over ordinary phone lines. xDSL works at a different frequency to voice traffic, so the phone line can still be used while being connected to the Internet. ADSL is the main variant of xDSL. It is asymmetric, as it downloads data faster than it can upload. This makes it better for broadcast-style services, such as radio or video on demand. With the newer symmetric DSL services (SDSL) the speed of data transfer is the same to and from the Internet. This is better for online gamers and video-conferencing.

))))➤ *ADSL, Bandwidth, BPS, High-Speed Connection*

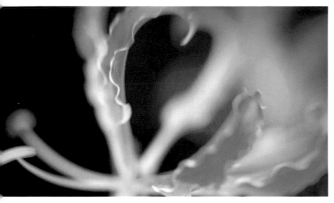

LEFT: *The DVD format combines excellent picture quality with superior sound*
RIGHT: *There is a wide range of educational material available on the Internet*
BELOW: *Browser view of www.eBay.com*

and books – yes; pet food and pizzas – no. There is growing public confidence in shopping on reputable web sites using credit cards. As with any business, e-commerce has its own jargon terms. For example: b2b means a business to business web site and b2c means a business to consumer web site.

))))➤ *Banking and Finance Web Sites, Credit Cards, Credit Card Safety*

DVD

'Digital Versatile Disc'; a new type of digital disc that can hold 4.7-17 GB (gigabytes) of data. The DVD-Video format can play a full-length movie complete with six-track Dolby digital audio and extras like out-takes and interviews. In the audio field, two rival formats are going head-to-head rather like a replay of the VHS vs Betamax battle. One consortium of companies is offering the DVD-Audio format, while Sony and Philips are pushing their Super Audio CD (SACD) format.

))))➤ *CDs and Tapes, Video*

EBAY (www.ebay.com)

Auction web site. eBay is the original Internet auction site and is one of the world's most successful e-commerce companies. It is one of the best web sites for simply browsing and marvelling at obscure, curious and strange objects that people buy, sell and collect with such a passion. eBay's various categories include coins, dolls and teddy bears, antiques and many more. eBay has sites around the world, so if you decide you want to buy or sell something, it is easy to do. You need to register your details first, then you can put something up for auction or bid.

))))➤ *Auctions Online, Yahoo Auctions*

E-COMMERCE

Doing business on the Web. E-commerce has become increasingly important since the late 1990s, despite the dotcom failures and the crash in value of technology stocks in March 2001. There is much more realism about what consumers want to buy online. CDs

EDI

'Electronic Data Interchange'; the standard for electronic document exchange. While EDI has been used for many years by companies exchanging documents electronically, it has not yet established itself as the backbone of e-commerce.

EDI is an international standard for the way companies transfer documents – such as invoices or dispatch documents – across a network. For additional security, the electronic messages between the two trading partners can be encrypted. Because each industry, sometimes even individual companies, have their own needs, there are also industry-specific guidelines known as EDI subsets. However, EDI has not been universally adopted and there are several rival methods for standardizing business-to-business e-commerce.

))))➤ *File Transfer, Network*

EDU

Top-level domain name. Part of a web address that shows it belongs to a university or other educational institution in the United States. In other countries the equivalent top-level domain name to .edu is .ac, short for academic, followed by the country code, such as .ac.uk for the United Kingdom or .ac.au for an Australian academic institution.

))) *Address, Education on the Internet, URL, Zone*

EDUCATION ON THE INTERNET

Using the Internet for learning. Education institutions were among the earliest users of the Internet and so it is appropriate that education is becoming one of the sectors that is reaping real benefits from the Net. A wealth of educational material for children of all ages is now available. Many countries are realizing that the Internet will be a vital factor in education in the future. In the UK, the government is investing heavily to provide broadband access to all schools and libraries, and is funding projects to develop new ways of providing education online.

))) *School and the Internet, Students and the Internet*

EMAIL

Electronic mail. Sending and receiving email is one of the most popular activities on the Internet. Millions of people – especially if they have access to the Internet at work – regularly check to see whether anyone has sent them an email. Email is very fast; it can reach the recipient in seconds. And it is cheap; you pay only for the cost of accessing your ISP even if your email is going halfway around the world. Email has generated its own informal language and customs. People use special abbreviations such as 'IMHO' (*In My Humble Opinion*) and 'emoticons', typographical symbols used to suggest emotions. For example ;-) means a smile and a wink. You can also attach other files such as a digital photograph to an email.

The commonly used applications for email are Eudora, Outlook Express and Netscape. Services such as AOL have their own easy-to-use email software as well. You can also send and receive emails via your browser by using an email site such as Hotmail (*www.hotmail.com*); this is ideal for people on holiday because they can access their email from an Internet café anywhere in the world.

))) *Attachment, Email Address, Composing Email, Sending*

EMAIL ADDRESS

 Everyone who uses email has an email address. When you send an email to someone you must type in their email address in the To: box. It is vital that you get it absolutely correct – there is no postman at the other end to compensate for a slight error. Any error in the email address will result in it being automatically bounced back by the addressee's server with a 'delivery failure' message attached. This problem is avoided when replying to an email because the sender's email is automatically inserted in the To: box so you do not need to type it.

Elements of an Email Address:

(**1**) tarquin (**2**) @ (**3**) foundry.co.uk

1. Username
Identifies the addressee
2. Separator
The @ separates the username from the domain name
3. Domain name
This is the name of addressee's web server
)))))▶ *Address, Internet, Composing Email, Email*

EMOTICONS

 See Smileys and Emoticons

EMPLOYMENT WEB SITES

Jobs' databases online. Searchable databases of jobs and job-seekers are changing the way people seek employment. Instead of devouring newspaper and magazine advertizements you can search a giant database such as the aptly named monster.com (*www.monster.com*, *www.monster.co.uk*). There are many others, whether it is a general employment site such as *www.totaljobs.com* or a specialist site such as *www.jobsfed.com* with its listing of jobs in the US Federal Government. On most sites you can post your CV so that employers can go looking for you. As their searches are based on keywords, online CVs have to be written in a way that maximizes the chances of them being picked out.
))))▶ *Companies Online*

ENCRYPTION

A way of securely sending information by translating it into a secret code that can only be unscrambled using the right key or password. By scrambling data into a secret code, encryption plays a fundamental part in ensuring that it is safe to send confidential information, such as credit-card numbers, over the Internet. Files are encrypted using a password and must be unscrambled (decrypted) using the same password

FURTHEST RIGHT: www.plinko.net
RIGHT: You could find your dream job using one of the many employment sites
FAR RIGHT: The Web covers many types of entertainment, from the mundane to the bizarre

(also known as a 'key'). In asymmetric encryption, more commonly called public-key encryption, there are two keys, one to encrypt the message and another to decrypt it. Encrypted files can be opened without a password but their contents will appear as a meaningless jumble of characters.

))))▶ *Encryption: History, Security II: Advanced*

ENCRYPTION: HISTORY

Encryption is the act of turning information into a code in order to send it to someone without a third party being able to read it. It has a long history going back at least to the Ancient Greeks. In the twentieth century, the US government controlled encryption until IBM developed their own system called Lucifer in the 1960s. Other companies soon followed suit and this led to the adoption of the Data Encryption Standard (DES) in 1973, followed by RSA, named after its creators. PGP ('Pretty Good Privacy'), a much more powerful encryption program, was introduced in 1986. There continues to be a fierce debate about the right of governments to break into the encrypted messages of their citizens.

))))▶ *Encryption, Security II: Advanced*

ENTERTAINMENT ON THE NET

Games were the earliest entertainment form on the Internet, taking off around 1997 with the advent of popular games such as Quake. Music became an

important part of the web landscape as artists such as Madonna performed online. With millions of MP3s being swapped via Napster by music fans, the record industry has been forced to offer online music or risk ruin. Streaming audio and video is becoming increasingly popular for those with broadband connections. It is predicted that TVs with hard-drives and games consoles like the Sony Playstation 2 will be increasingly used for entertainment.

))))▶ *Entertainment Web Sites, MP3*

ENTERTAINMENT WEB SITES

Entertainment on the Web. There are so many entertainment web sites, it is difficult to know where to start. If you are having a good day, send a virtual kissogram (*www.kissogram.com.au*) – not just animated lips but trembling butts and lickograms. Something more sedate? Head off to the World-Wide Collectors Digest and trade info about your latest collectible, whether baseball cards or sports memorabilia. Different type of collector? Trip along to the list of celebrity web sites (*www.celebsites.com*) or work out your future at Tarot Information (*www.facade.com/occult/tarot*) and try alternative forecasters such as Stichomancy, Biorhythm and I Ching.

))))▶ *Entertainment on the Web: History, Film and TV Web Sites*

ERROR CODES

Error messages when surfing the Internet. Error codes can bring your surfing to an abrupt halt. Below are the four most typical error messages and a brief suggestion of how you might tackle them. Sometimes, they can just arise through a glitch in the browser, so it is also worth simply refreshing (reloading) the page to see if that corrects it.

400 – Bad request – Incorrect URL: it then continues to list possible reasons that may have caused it, such as the page no longer existing. Try retyping the URL and check there are no typing errors.

401 – Unauthorized: Either you are not authorized to access the page or you have entered the wrong user name or password. Try re-entering the details.

403 – Forbidden: similar to 401, you need to be authorized to access the page. If you are authorized try re-entering the password.

404 – Not found – the host server is unable to locate…etc: By far the most common error message, it may simply be a link to the page is broken, the page is no longer there or there is a mistake in the URL you have typed.

))))▶ *Troubleshooting*

ESC KEY

The key in the top left-hand corner of the keyboard that is used to cancel an action. In Windows, pressing Esc has the same effect as selecting the Cancel button. You can press the Alt and Esc keys together (Alt+Esc) to move between active windows in an application.

))))➤ *Active Window, Application*

ETHERNET

LAN cabling standard. The heart of the office network, Ethernet is a cabling standard used for linking together computers and peripheral devices, such as printers. It is widely used for setting up the office LAN (Local Area Network) and can support data-transfer rates of 10 Mbps. A newer version, Fast Ethernet, supports speeds 10 times that (100 Mbps).

))))➤ *Network, Network Computer*

EUDORA

Eudora is a popular email client among those looking for a custom-built application to handle large amounts of mail. It is available for both the Windows and Macintosh platforms and comes in three

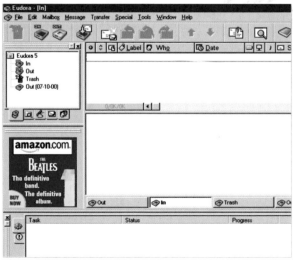

versions: an ad-sponsored free version; an ad-free paid-for version; or a free 'light' version that has no ads but comes with fewer features.

))))➤ *Email, Outlook Express*

EUNET

The European Unix network was one of the early networks that formed part of the expanding Internet during the 1980s.

))))➤ *Internet in the 1980s: History*

EXCITE (www.excite.com)

Web portal and search engine. Excite was launched in 1995 and is now one of the Web's prominent sites. It allows you to search through its web-page index or browse through its compiled directory of categories. It also functions as a portal, offering a range of services to persuade surfers to keep it as their home page. These include a web-based email feature similar to Hotmail, news and financial information, tools to customize the appearance of the home page, horoscopes and links to Yellow Pages, maps and recipes.

))))➤ *Home Page, Hotmail, Directory Service, Portal, Search Engine*

EXE FILE

A program file, unreadable to the human eye, that can be run directly by the computer. Short for executable, an exe file is a program that can be run directly by the computer's operating system. It is written in a form that only the computer can understand so, unlike source files where data is stored, it is unreadable to the human eye. The three-letter filename extension that indicates that it is a program is .exe. To run a file with an .exe extension all you need do is double click on it.

))))➤ *Application, Program*

EXPANSION CARD

Add-on hardware. Expansion cards live up to their name – they are plug-in cards, such as video adapters or internal modems, that extend a computer's abilities. Unlike some adapter cards, which are part of the main circuit board, these go in their own special slots and are also known as add-ons.

))))➤ *Adapter Card, Expansion Slot, Interface*

EXPANSION SLOT

Expansion slots are home to the expansion cards. These narrow slots let you plug in add-on cards to

increase the capabilities of the computer, such as adding extra memory. There are different types and sizes of socket and many new PCs now come with additional slots for special graphics cards.

))))➤ *Adapter Card, Expansion Card, Interface*

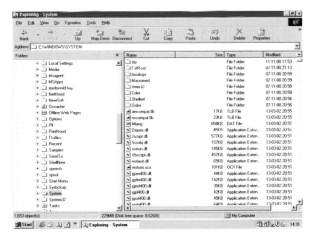

TOP: *Explorer provides all you need to make your first step into Web browsing*

ABOVE: *Windows' main navigation browser, Windows Explorer*

EXPLORER

This refers, *not* to Microsoft's web browser, Internet Explorer, but to Windows' main navigation browser, Windows Explorer. This does the same job as My Computer on the Windows Desktop – displaying the contents of all the directories and sub-directors (folders) on the various drives in your computer, viewing them by name, size, type and date. The main difference is that by default, Windows Explorer gives a 'two-pane' view, showing directories and sub-directories (folders) in the left-hand pane and the folders' contents (the files) in the right-hand pane; whereas My Computer, by default, shows files or folders in one window only.

))))➤ *Navigation*

EXPORT

File saving method. When you export a file from a software program, you convert it into a different format that can be read by another software program. You do this by choosing File|Save As in your application and selecting the appropriate type of format.

))))➤ *File Conversion*

EXTENDED WARRANTIES

Some PC vendors will offer extended warranties, but watch out for them. They are generally very expensive and better at boosting the retailer's income than protecting your investment.

)))⯈ *Computers: Purchasing Online, Shopping Online*

EXTENSION

Letters after the period (dot) in a file name. An extension is also sometimes called a suffix. It refers to the letters that are appended to the name of a file in order to identify it as being a particular type. In Windows, extensions always have three letters, but on the Web more letters are used. Here are some of the extensions you are likely to encounter:

.doc: a word processing document
.bmp: a bitmap file
.exe: an executable program file
.html: a HyperText Markup Language file
.gif: a Graphics Interface Format file, used for web graphics
.pdf: a document that can be read by Adobe Acrobat reader software

)))⯈ *Adobe Acrobat, File Extensions, Filename, HTML*

EXTERNAL MODEM

A device connecting a computer to a telephone line. If you want to use a dial-up connection to the Internet, you need to link a modem between your computer and your telephone socket. Follow the instructions that come with the modem to plug it into the serial, parallel or USB port at the back of your computer. Some modems require a power source or even batteries. In use, they usually display activity with lights at the front and make strange squawking sounds when hooking up to an ISP. There are two other types of modem: internal modems, which plug into a slot inside your computer; and credit-card sized PCMCIA modems, which plug into a slot on a laptop.

)))⯈ *Internal Modem, Modem I: Introduction, Modem II: Choosing, Modem III: Installing, Modem IV: Configuring, Modem V: Technical*

EXTRANET

A private site only accessible by authorized outsiders. Any intranet with something extra or the Internet with restrictions is known as the extranet. It uses Internet technology to enable business partners to link up and exchange information. It does so by allowing authorized outsiders to access part of the company intranet or web site and even to meet online within a type of virtual workplace.

)))⯈ *EDI, Intranet*

EZINES

Electronic magazines set up on the Web or sent via email. Ezine is short for electronic magazine and covers any web site that is presented in a magazine format. While some ezines are just web copies of their printed magazine counterparts, others have developed their own content and style. Probably the best example is Hotwired, where the online zine is completely different to the news-stand title. While most ezines are financially supported, magazine-style, by advertising, there is a

LEFT: A graphic on the Internet has a .gif extension
RIGHT: The Web includes sites on haute couture and fashion through the ages

growing movement to charge for content. Commonly, email newsletters are also called ezines.

))))➤ *Books: Electronic on the Net*

FAMILY AND THE INTERNET

Millions of homes now have access to the Internet and families around the world are finding that it has something to offer every member. Children of all ages love to surf the Net, play games, learn and chat to their friends. Teenagers love to visit web sites that feature their favourite music, television and sports stars. Swapping MP3 music files, chat rooms, instant messaging and email are all very popular with this age group. Parents find the Net useful for shopping, finding information and keeping in touch by email. Other members of a household might be interested in web sites for genealogy, hobbies and auctions. Parents who wish to shield their children from undesirable material can try using the Ratings function in Internet Explorer.

))))➤ *Genealogy, Home and the Internet, Kids' Web Sites*

FAQ

Frequently Asked Question. You will often see a link to FAQ or FAQs on a web site. This takes you to a page of questions and answers on topics related to the web site. They could, for example, provide explanations for some of the most often-asked queries about a product or service. A web site will usually encourage you to look for the answer to your question in their FAQs before

contacting someone in their customer-support department by email or telephone.

))))➤ *Help Menu*

FASHION WEB SITES

Haute couture on the Web, from runway videos to the latest fashion trends it can all be found on the Internet.

Take your place beside the catwalk with Virtual Runway (*www.virtualrunway.com*) to check out the latest Armani, Donna Karan or Vivienne Westwood. There are also plenty of style points for the *haute coutured* amongst us. More low budget, email-style consultant Mags at HeroineChic (*www.heroinechic.net*) will be your fashion coach. Alternatively, if you fancy those vintage style tap pants from the 1940s you can buy your period clothes from Enoki World (*www.enokiworld.com*) or find out the latest info on designers and models at *Hello!* (*www.hellomagazine.com/fashion*).

))))➤ *Entertainment Web Sites*

Frequently Asked Questions
about Microsoft
on comp.lang.java.advocacy newsgroup

Maintained by petilon@yahoo.com

Is Microsoft really innovative?

- ClearType not a Microsoft invention
- IntelliEye not a Microsoft invention
- "Microsoft's Real Problem: No Innovation" -- Dvorak
- Microsoft's claim that it's defending its right to innovate is a cruel joke -- Ralph Nader
  #### Operating System innovations
- Windows 98 is just bug fixes; don't pay for it

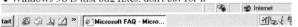

FAVORITES

 Method for saving web addresses. If you find a web page that you want to return to, there is no need to copy the web address: Internet Explorer has a function called Favorites that makes it easy to store addresses and use them again and again. In Netscape Navigator, this function is called Bookmarks. If you use Windows, click on the Favorites button on the menu bar in Windows Explorer or Internet Explorer to display the Favorites panel.

Here are the main things you can do with Favorites:

Add: to add a current web page to your collection of Favorites, click once on the Add button that appears at the top of the Favorites panel. A dialogue box appears, which gives you the option to alter the name of the web page if you wish.

Revisit: to revisit a web page, look for its name in the list contained in the Favorites panel. When the pointer turns into a hand, click on it once to be taken to that page.

Organize: you will find that your collection of Favorites grows rapidly so click on the Organize Favorites button at the top of the Favorites panel to organize them in separate folders.

Delete: to delete unwanted Favorites, click on the Organize Favorites button at the top of the Favorites panel, highlight the Favorite to be deleted and click on the Delete button.

))))➤ *Bookmark, Shortcuts*

FAX

Faxing from your PC. If you have a need to send or receive faxes you can do it using your computer. There are two ways:

1. Using software and modem

If you use Windows, you can use software such as WinFax Pro or Microsoft Fax. Fax software typically gives you a facility to type in the subject and cover-page message, a telephone book to store people's fax numbers, and a fax viewer to view incoming faxes. Using fax software on the PC does not have a very good reputation for ease of use or reliability.

2. Using a web-based fax service

This is regarded as a more reliable option for PCs. For example, Callwave (*www.callwave.com*) or eFax (*www.efax.com*).

))))➤ *Fax on Demand, Web-Based Faxing*

FAX MODEM

See Internal Modem

FAX ON DEMAND

Automatic fax retrieval. Information can be automatically faxed back on demand using a voice-supported modem and software. Such systems are often used by magazine publishers where readers want to order back copies of articles or obtain event information. Users choose the information they want from a printed list published in the magazine or from the spoken menu

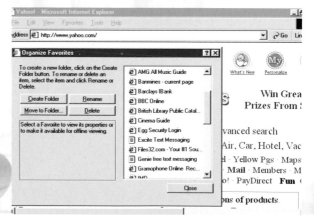

they hear when they ring up the fax on demand service. Then the documents they asked for will be automatically faxed back to them.

)))▶ *Fax, Voicemail, Web-Based Faxing*

FILE

Computer file. A file is a self-contained sequence of digital information that can be saved to a disk. Word-processing documents or spreadsheets are both examples of files. Files that can self-execute and perform functions are usually referred to by other names, such as applications, programs or utilities.

)))▶ *Application, File Conversion, File Extensions, File Size, File Transfer, Filename, Program*

FILE CONVERSION

Changing the format of a file without altering its content. For example, multimedia files need to be converted into plain text files to send across the Internet.

)))▶ *Export*

FILE EXTENSIONS

The end part of the filename, which indicates the type of information stored therein. File extensions are the letters at the end of a filename that show what type of file it is. This is a handy way of seeing what program is needed to open a file, without actually opening it. Among the common file types are:

.doc: Microsoft Word document

.bmp, .jpg, .gif: Image files that need a graphics program to open them

LEFT: Internet Explorer\Favorites\Organize Favorites

.exe: Program file automatically run by Windows

.html: Typically a web page, it can be viewed by a browser or other HTML-compatible program

.sea: Self-extracting archive on Apple Mac computers

.zip: Compressed file that needs to be unzipped (decompressed) before viewing

)))▶ *Extension, Filename*

FILENAME

The name given to a computer file. When you create a new file, you will need to save it on to your hard disk and give it a filename. It is worth getting into the habit of giving your files relevant and understandable filenames so that you can find them again easily. Otherwise, you'll soon discover how boring it is trying to find that very important letter in a directory full of files called document1, document2, document3 and so on. A filename can have letters appended after a period (dot); this is called a file extension and indicates the type of file. Many programs add an extension to your filename automatically. Word appends the extension .doc, for example.

)))▶ *Attachment, Extension, File, File Extensions*

FILE SIZE

The measure of disk space taken up by a file. The space a file takes up is measured in bytes and can be reduced by compression. A byte represents a single letter or character and typically file sizes will be shown in either kilobytes (kbyte) which is 1,024 bytes, or megabytes (MB), which is usually thought of as one million bytes (although it is, in fact, 1,048,576 bytes). As an indication of what this represents, the standard 1.44 MB floppy disk can hold 1.4 million characters, which is the equivalent of about 3,000 pages of information. To reduce the amount of space a file takes up it can be compressed using programs such as StuffIt.

)))▶ *Kilobyte, StuffIt*

FILE TRANSFER

Sending files between computers. There are numerous ways to transfer files between computers; the best one for you will depend on the type of connection

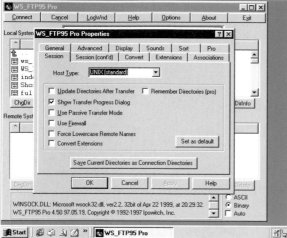

you have. It depends on whether you have a direct cable connection, whereby information passes through a modem or over a network. There are even wireless solutions and most modern computers support infrared, particularly to help synchronize files with PDAs. On the Internet the most commonly used standard for downloading or uploading files is the File Transfer Protocol (FTP), support which is built into many browsers. There are also stand-alone FTP client programs, such as WS_FTP for Windows or Fetch on the Macintosh.

)))➤ *FTP, FTP Search, FTP Server, WS_FTP*

FILM AND TV WEB SITES

Film and TV information. What is happening on the small screen and big is revealed in Cyberspace. Just about every major TV

BELOW: There are sites offering film and TV facts, gossip, reviews and listings
LEFT: File Transfer allows files to be sent between computers

channel now runs its own interactive site online, often with extras such as discussion boards, follow-up stories and background details to programmes. To find out what is on TV itself there are multi-channel listing services in most countries, such as Digiguide (*www.digiguide.com*) in the UK and Gist (*www.gist.com*) in the US. For film gossip and reviews there's the flamboyant *www.aintitcool.com*, while the insomniac's guide to all things about movies covering more than 280,000 films is the Internet Movie Database (*www.imdb.com*).

)))➤ **Entertainment Web Sites, Movies, Multimedia, Radio Online, WebTV**

FILTERING

Setting up rules to screen your emails and organize where they go. Filtering Spam sounds very messy but it is necessary if you do not want to drown in a sea of junk mail.

On average, most of us receive anything from 25 to 200 emails a day and that needs to be sorted into relevant folders. Most email client programs such as Eudora or Outlook Express do this filtering, by setting up rules. So, for example, you could create a rule whereby messages from a certain address, or person, or that includes a certain phrase, are automatically blocked or moved to a special folder.

))))➤ *Censorship, Junk Email, Receiving Email, Spam*

FINDING FILES ON THE NET

Search engines on software collections are now so comprehensive you get much more information than simply where to find it. It used to be quite difficult to track down software files when you only had a hazy recollection of the name. However, shareware software collections have become so comprehensive that today it is no problem. You can search for files by name, author or even type of program, as well as across several platforms. Sites such as *ZDnet.com* or *CNET.com* not only come up with possible downloads but also any related news stories and reviews and any comments about the files available from the message boards.

))))➤ **Download.com,** *Search Engine,* **shareware.com,** *Tucows*

FINDING PEOPLE ON THE NET

Because of the multiplicity of mail systems and the sheer vastness of the Internet, it is still quite difficult to track down someone's email address. There are email directories – the biggest of which are Bigfoot, WhoWhere and Yahoo. These pick up much of their data from newsgroup postings and the simple but effective trick of asking people to enter their own details. Consequently, they have massive databases but are still nowhere near being comprehensive. In particular the major online services with whom many people have their accounts, such as AOL and MSN, won't share details between them.

))))➤ *Bigfoot, Directory Service, Search Engine, WhoWhere*

BELOW: Email address databases help people to connect all over the world

FINGER

A useful, UNIX-based program that enables users to find out more information about other users, usually from an email address. You can establish whether they are currently logged on and on some systems you can get details of their name, address and phone number if they have been entered.

))))➤ *UNIX*

FIREWALL

Security gateway for networks. The hacker's greatest challenge, a firewall is designed as a gateway to stop unauthorized users from accessing a private network. It is often used to protect company intranets from snoopers. It can also screen messages going in and out for viruses and check them for any other security breaches specified by the company. There are several types of firewall and they can be hardware, software or a mixture of both. In one common method computers on the network are not linked directly to the Internet but go through a separate server (proxy server) that decides which messages or files it is safe to let through.

)))) *Network, Security II: Advanced*

FLAME

A flame is an angry or vicious message posted to a newsgroup. Often the writer is attacking some other user for his views but is doing so in a way that is particularly harsh or personal. If the attack is reciprocated a flame war has started.

)))) *Usenet*

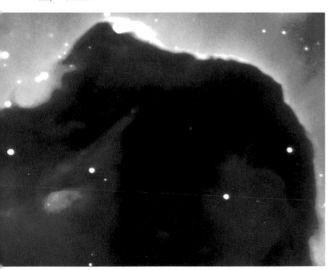

FLASH

Animation software program. Macromedia's Flash Player is a plug-in that plays animation in your browser window. It can be downloaded from *www. macromedia.com/software/flashplayer/*.

)))) *Browser, Plug-In*

FOLDER

Electronic container for files. A folder can be thought of as a container that holds files and perhaps other folders. A folder can also be traditionally called a 'directory' on Windows PCs. Computer manuals often describe folders and file structures in terms of an inverted tree. The files and folders at any level are contained in the folder above them. To find a file in Windows, you might need to specify the names of all the folders and sub-folders above it. This is called specifying a path. An example might look like this:

C:\My_tax_files\Year_2000\Expenses_2000.doc

In this example, the document 'Expenses_2000.doc' is inside the sub-folder 'Year_2000' which is inside the folder 'My_tax_files'.

)))) *Directory, Path*

FOOD AND DRINK WEB SITES

Food and Drink online; tips, recipes, advice, even the raw ingredients or the finished products are available via the Web.

Having made it into the dictionary as a name for simple cooking (doing a Delia), you can get more of the

ABOVE LEFT: Flame wars are vicious messages posted by angry users
ABOVE: You can download the Flash Player from Macromedia's web site quicker than lightning

wisdom of cookery writer Delia Smith at *www.deliaonline.com*. Whereas if you want to stir in advice from a wider range of great cooks, then Epicurious (*www.epicurious.com*) will satisfy your hunger. It also has a giant database of recipes for all culinary tastes. There are also many restaurant guides online, sites specializing in organic products, foods for vegetarians and even food-delivery services. For the wine buff there's Decanter (*www.decanter.com*) or for information about the finer points of whisky try (*www.scotch-whisky.org.uk*).

))))▶ **shopper.com,** *Shopping Online, Shopping Search*

TOP: Browser view of www.deliaonline.com

ABOVE: Food and drink site topics range from buying ingredients to wine tasting

RIGHT: In frag you must destroy your opponents

FORUMONE (*www.forumone.com*)

Discussion web site. ForumOne is a leading web site for finding web-based discussion groups from lists of thousands of topics.

))))▶ *Discussion Group*

FORUMS

Special interest discussion groups set up online for users to exchange views. These are essentially talking shops, like the meeting places of ancient Rome, after which they are named. The difference is, of course, that the exchange of views in the forums set up by online services, such as AOL and CompuServe and bulletin board services (BBSs), is done by posting open messages and reading the replies rather than chat. The forums cover a wide range of special interests. In the wider Usenet and Internet worlds, forums are more commonly called newsgroups or discussion groups.

))))▶ *Discussion Groups, Newsgroups*

FORWARDING EMAILS

Re-routing emails. Whether it is an individual message or all your mails to one account you can forward them elsewhere. Sometimes when you receive an email you may want to forward it to someone for their comments who has not been included on the original distribution list. It is quite simple to do. Usually the email client will have a forward button; click this, add your comments and send it. If you have several email accounts you can set up automatic email forwarding from your service provider's mail server, so any emails coming into one mailbox are automatically sent to another.

))))▶ *Replying to Emails, Sending Emails*

FRAG

First adopted by players of the online three-dimensional virtual-reality type action game DOOM, by id Software, frag has taken on a wider meaning among network gamers. As its name suggests, it means to fragment or destroy, or in gamers' terms, to blow the enemy to bits.

))))▶ *Games on the Net*

FRAMES

Frames enable several web pages to open within the same browser window. Love them or loathe them, frames provide a clever way to open several web pages within the same browser window. Because those pages may be from different sites, the effect can sometimes be garish. Although most browsers support frames, the early ones did not and many sites still offer the choice to view a frames or non-frames version. Frames are particularly useful for navigation. The left-hand frame (or, alternatively, the top frame) can be used as a static guide to other sections on the site. Click a link in it and the web page opens in another frame and can be scrolled independently.

))))➤ *Navigation, Web Page, Web Page II: Creating*

FREEDOM OF SPEECH ON THE INTERNET

Censorship on the Net. Particularly since the events of 11 September 2001, freedom of speech has come into sharp focus as a controversial issue. A fierce debate rages over the extent to which governments have a right to monitor and censor Netizens' speech to maintain public security. There is genuine concern about the dangers posed to children by violent, sexual and illegal material from the Internet. In 1995, the German government compelled Compuserve to exclude sexual newsgroups, also censoring gay and abortion discussions. In the US, the Child Online Protection Act has been opposed by groups such as the American Civil Liberties Union (*www.aclu.org*). Concerned parents can use the Ratings function in Internet Explorer to filter access to harmful sites, although the method is believed by many to be ineffective.

))))➤ *Censorship*

FREEDRIVE (*www.freedrive.com*)

File storage web site. If you need somewhere to store your files, you can put them on FreeDrive, which offers storage space on its server.

))))➤ *Storing Files on the Net*

LEFT: Browser view of http://easyweb.easynet.co.uk
BELOW: Freedom of speech on the Internet has recently come into sharp focus

FREE HOURS OFFERED BY ISPS

As an encouragement to sign on to their service, several ISPs, including AOL, offer new users up to 100 free hours online. It sounds good, but those free hours have to be taken within a certain time, usually a month, and the chances are you will never use them all. However, this does provide a good way of checking out an ISP before committing to it.

)))▶ *ISP, OSP, Server*

FREENET

A peer-to-peer network that extends the idea of the Web into a virtual information store. Freenet has taken the idea of the Web and tried to make it a totally free network. What makes it different is that it is a peer-to-peer network which means that information is shared between all the computers on the network; there is no central, powerful server that stores and delivers information to client PCs. Freenet uses the power of the member PCs around the world to create a virtual information store where anyone can put what they want as no one person controls the system. For more details see *http://freenet. sourceforge.net/*

)))▶ *Free Web Space, ISP, Server*

FREEPPP

Internet connection for Macs. Popular because it's free, FreePPP is a utility program for connecting Apple Macs to dial-up internet accounts. As its name suggests, it uses the Point-to-Point Protocol (PPP) to enable the computer to use the TCP/IP protocol that normally works over a network, through a phone connection.

)))▶ *Dialer, Dial-Up Connection, Macs: Connecting to the Internet*

FREEWARE

Free software. Freeware programs are really free; they have no strings attached other than the occasional copyright limitation. Some even include the source code. This is intended to encourage techy types to enhance the program or produce related software products. Software of this kind is called 'open source'. Many freeware programs, especially games, are written by enthusiasts in their spare time. They can act as a calling card, bringing their creators to the attention of potential employers or earning them kudos in the programmers' community. Look for freeware on popular download sites such as Download.com (*www.download.com*) or Tucows (*www.tucows.com*).

)))▶ *Download.com, Finding Files on the Net, Shareware, Tucows*

FREE WEB SPACE
(*www.freeweb-space.net*)

Web site offering free web space. This site acts as a guide to hosts offering free and paid space for your web pages on their servers. Free services often impose pop-up advertisements on every page.

)))▶ *Freenet, ISP, Server, Web Site*

FTP

'File Transfer Protocol'; provides an agreed way for data to be exchanged between computers, particularly over the Internet. Music, software, pictures, even books: the Internet is a veritable Aladdin's cave. But having found the treasures you want, how do you get them to your computer? The answer is the File Transfer Protocol (FTP), a standard way for moving files between computers that is particularly good for uploading and downloading files over the Internet. The protocol is an agreed format for transmitting data between computers that covers the type of error checking to be used, how the data is compressed and how the computers will indicate when they have finished sending or receiving the message. As the Web expands, it is getting easier to download files. Sometimes all that is needed is to click a link and the download starts, but in fact FTP will be working away behind the scenes.

There are other protocols for downloading files from the Web, such as HTTP, but these are not as efficient. FTP is still the most popular, but with files getting ever larger space on some FTP servers is at a premium. Large files also mean longer download times. Consequently, in order to speed it up and save space, most files will be compressed and the file will have to be uncompressed before being used.

)))))➤ *File Transfer, FTP Search, FTP Server, WS_FTP*

FTP SEARCH (www.ftpsearch.com)

Search web site. Visit this web site if you are looking for software programs to download by FTP. It has links to servers containing many kinds of software.

)))))➤ *File Transfer, FTP, FTP Server, WS_FTP*

FTP SERVER

An FTP server is the computer that enables you to upload or download files from the Internet. To start an FTP session the FTP client software on your computer connects to the server on the Internet. A program called the FTP daemon (pronounced demon) runs on the FTP server to control the log in. Once logged on a connection called a command, a link is established to enable the FTP server and PC to communicate with each other. Through this link it is possible to instruct the daemon to list what files are available, change directories and download them.

)))))➤ *FTP, FTP Search, WS_FTP*

FULL DUPLEX

Enables you to send data in two directions at the same time, as a modem does. A phone is also a full duplex device, as both parties can speak at once, whereas with a half-duplex device, such as a walkie-talkie, only one party can speak at a time.

)))))➤ *Sound Card, Sound Recorder*

GAMES DOMAIN (www.gamesdomain.com)

Games web site. An excellent site full of reviews, demos, downloads, chat, cheats and charts. What more could the games' fans want?

)))))➤ *Games on the Net*

GAMES ON THE NET

Online games. There are plenty of simple games online to choose from. These include chess, cards and backgammon, as well as puzzles for young children. However, the more complex and serious games are much bigger files to download, so be prepared for long download times, even for demo versions. To get the latest news about hot games, check out popular games sites such as Games Domain (*www.gamesdomain.com*).

If you are a really serious game-player you will want to play 3D games with multiple players. For this, you will need a fast connection, a fast processor, loads of RAM, and a 3D video acceleration card. You'll learn to grapple with problems such as 'latency', which causes delays in responses to your opponents' moves, or 'packet loss',

BELOW: Games can be played online or downloaded

which is when whole segments of data fail to arrive and have to be re-sent. Because data transfer speed is so critical to online game playing, it is helpful to find out which games servers are closest to you by downloading a program such as GameSpy (*www.gamespy.com*).

)))⯈ *Demo, DirectX, Games Domain, Sport on the Net*

GAP, THE (*www.gap.com*)

Online clothes store. The popular clothes outlet has its own stylish web site, offering areas such as GapKids, GapMaternity and GapBody. They offer

a Gap Giftfinder, with which you can search by price or type of gift and then buy it online.

)))⯈ *Clothes: Buying Online*

GATEWAY

A link between networks. Sometimes more like the guardhouse or watchtower, a gateway connects two different types of network. For example, it could be a link between different email systems, enabling users to exchange messages. Alternatively, it could be a connection to the Internet that may also be secured using a firewall.

)))⯈ *Firewall, Network, Network Protocol*

TOP LEFT: Browser view of www.gamesdomain.com
ABOVE: Clothes retail company Gap sell their goods over the Internet
LEFT: Just as the Arc de Triumphe links one part of Paris to another, so a gateway links various networks together

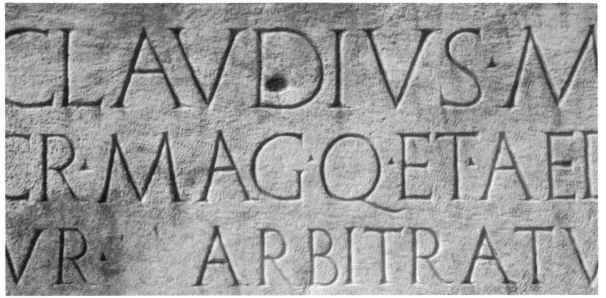

GENEALOGY

Tracing your ancestry online. The Web is a wonderful resource for those trying to trace their family history. They can share information with long-lost and previously unknown relatives across the world. Sadly, not all official archives are yet online. In the quest for information many families have set up discussion boards and web sites. Just do a search on somewhere like Google to see if there is one for your family name. There are sites that offer a professional ancestry-tracing service along with information, such as the Gathering of the Clans (*www.tartans.com/genealogy*), or links to millions of records, including censuses, such as *www.genealogy.com*.

))))▶ *Family and the Internet*

GIF

'Graphics Interchange Format'; the original graphics file format for the Web, GIFs are compressed for quick download time and can be used to create simple animation effects.

Pronounced with a hard G, the GIF was the first specifically designed graphics file format for use on the Internet. Created by CompuServe, it is still one of the most popular formats for images on the Web thanks, in part, to the fact that it is cross-platform and can be viewed on any computer. It also compresses files to save download time. The system it uses is 'lossless', which means that the quality of the image is not affected (unlike JPEGs, which use 'lossy' compression, where data is actually removed from the image to make the file smaller). Because of the way they are compressed GIFs are best used where there are solid blocks of colour, such as with logos, cartoons, or simple illustrations. The latest GIF standard (GIF89a) supports transparency. It is this which lets the background colour of a web page show through part of an image. Without it, many graphics on the Internet would appear inside a white box. GIFs also support interlacing, which means they appear layer by layer, so you can see what the graphic is like before it is fully downloaded. GIF images can also be combined together into a single file to create simple animation effects.

))))▶ *Animation, Graphics File, Picture Format, Web Page*

GO.COM (*infoseek.go.com*)

Portal. Now owned by Disney, this web site combines a search engine with links to Disney services, auctions, news stories, yellow pages and shopping.

))))▶ *Portal, Search Engine*

ABOVE: The Web can offer an insight into your family's history

GOOGLE (www.google.com)

Search engine. Google is widely regarded as the Net's best search engine, with its uncluttered interface and fast results, which are ranked according to the number of times people have linked to a page.

)))▶ *Search Engine*

GOPHER

Pre-web style archives used to store files on the Internet; they have now largely been replaced. Something of an anachronism, Gopher was the pre-Web way to store files on the Internet. It was developed at the University of Minnesota and named after their mascot, the short-tailed animal that conveniently embodies the idea of burrowing for information. Although it is now largely obsolete, some government bodies and universities still use Gopher sites to archive their material. It is searchable by two systems that have a global index of Gopher databases – Veronica and Jughead. However, most Gopher databases have been converted to web sites, more readily searchable from the Web. To access the original Gopher go to: *gopher://gopher.tc. umn.edu*

)))▶ *Internet in the 1980s: History*

GOV

A top-level domain name that reflects the fact that the owner of the domain is part of, or linked to, the government. While some TLDs, such as .net, are freely available to anyone that wants to register them .gov is more restricted.

)))▶ *Address, Domain, Government Online, Hostname, URL, Zone*

GOVERNMENT ONLINE

Digital services from the government. Governments are bringing their own services online in an effort to encourage their citizens to take advantage of the new digital age. There is plenty of material online, but its information value is variable. The interesting new developments are using the convenience of the Web for Government services – such as applying for driving licences, permits, passports or filling out tax forms. For a directory of what is available, try *ukonline.gov.uk/opengov/* in the UK or *www.fedworld.gov/* in the US.

)))▶ *Politics-Related Web Sites*

GO!ZILLA (www.gozilla.com)

Download software. Go!Zilla provides a free software program to improve your downloading. Its features include Automatic Error Recovery and Download Scheduling.

)))▶ *Download, File Transfer, Freeware, Shareware*

BELOW: Governments are now bringing their own services online

GRAPHICS CARD

Hardware circuit board. The electronic hardware circuit that produces the image on your computer's monitor. This can either be an integral circuit on your computer's motherboard or a separate board or 'card' that is plugged into an expansion socket. A graphics card is also known as a graphics adapter, graphics accelerator, video adapter and display adapter. If you upgrade to a monitor with a larger screen, it might be necessary to upgrade the graphics card inside the computer as well, in order to provide the required resolution and refresh rates on the screen.

)))⯈ *Adapter Card, Graphics File, Expansion Card*

GRAPHICS FILE

Picture-file formats. Graphics files are of two basic kinds – bitmapped or vector – and both appear on the Web. At its most basic, a graphics file contains data that describes an image, but that data can be of two very different types. Bitmapped, or raster, graphics are created by changing the colour of individual pixels (that is, bits of information are mapped to the pixels on the screen). Vector graphics are mathematically defined and thus are generally smoother and easier to resize.

Most of the graphics on the Web – usually GIF or JPEG files – are bitmapped, although they may have been drawn in a vector program such as Freehand or Illustrator first. One area where vector-based art is seen directly on the Web is in Flash animation.

)))⯈ *Flash, GIF, JPEG, Picture Formats*

GUI

'Graphical User Interface'; pronounced 'gooey'. The GUI is the user's friend. With a GUI front-end the program makes use of the computer's graphics to get things done. This is in contrast to a command-driven interface, such as DOS, where users have to type in instructions to control the program. Instead, you can use pointers, click on icons or select from menus to access files or programs. The GUI first became popular on the Apple Macintosh in the 1980s and it was subsequently adopted by Windows as a way of making it easier to use a PC.

)))⯈ *Graphics File, Icons, Interface, Menus, Windows*

HACKING

Breaking into computer systems. Originally 'hacking' meant messing around with computers and coding programs, but it is now used interchangeably with the word 'cracking' as a term for trying to break into computer systems illegally. However, hackers themselves do try and make a distinction. Whereas crackers are solely interested in breaking into a system, hackers do so more out of interest in testing their skills.

)))⯈ *Hacking: History of, Phreaker*

HACKING, HISTORY OF

Disrupting computer systems. Hacking is the act of breaking into, disrupting or abusing computer or communications systems. Here are some notable events in the history of hacking:

1960s   Students at MIT begin to fiddle with the college mainframe

1970s   Phone hacker ('phreak'), John Draper ('Cap'n Crunch'), uses a toy whistle and a home-made 'blue box' to make free long-distance calls

1980s   Electronic bulletin board systems (BBSs) for hackers spring up, offering tips, gossip and stolen passwords

1984   Hacker magazine *2600* begins regular publication

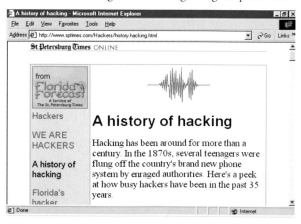

FAR LEFT: Hackers break the law by 'cracking' computer systems
LEFT: A hacker breaks into someone's personal code
BOTTOM LEFT: Browser view of www.sptimes.com

1986   The Computer Fraud and Abuse Act makes it a crime to break into computer systems in the US

1989   Hacker self-styled as 'The Mentor' published his 'Hacker's Manifesto'

1990   In Operation Sundevil, hackers are arrested in 14 US cities

1995   Hacker Kevin Mitnick is charged with stealing 20,000 credit card numbers

1997   AOHell is released, a freeware application that allows novice hackers to disrupt America Online for days

1999   A wave of hacks exploit security weaknesses in Window 98

2000   Hackers launch 'denial of service' attacks against eBay, Yahoo, Amazon and others

2001   Microsoft's web sites are targeted, preventing millions of users from accessing its web pages

))))▶ *Hacking, Phreaker*

HANDSHAKING

Initiating communications between devices. In effect, electronic greetings. Handshaking is the way two devices, such as modems, begin communicating. Handshaking starts when one device sends a message to the other saying it wants to

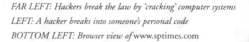

talk. Several messages are then sent back and forth between them to establish which protocol they should use to transfer data.

))))▶ *Modem V: Technical*

HARDWARE NEEDED TO CONNECT TO THE NET

There is a range of electronic devices you can use to connect to the Internet. Most people at present use a computer, either a PC or a Mac. This is the best option if you want to use the Net for business and leisure. Whatever type of computer you select, you will need a modem to connect it to an Internet Service Provider (ISP) via the telephone system. If your computer did not come with a modem built-in, your best bet is to fit an external modem and hook it up to the telephone socket. Other methods for connecting include satellite, cable and DSL, for which the service provider will install the hardware you need.

For people on the move, portable devices are becoming more popular for viewing web sites with specially designed pages. PDAs (Personal Digital Assistants), or palmtops, are hand-held devices with small screens. The next generation of 3G mobile phones will also offer improved web access. Many people are choosing to surf the Net on their TV by installing a set-top box that enables them to participate in services such as interactive TV games and shopping.

))))▶ *Connecting to the Internet I: Basic, Modem I: Introduction*

HAYES-COMPATIBILITY

A modem standard. Hayes was one of the original manufacturers of modems; the company may have disappeared but it has left its name to a standard set of commands that allow a PC to control a modem and send data over a telephone line. Any modem that uses the commands, also known as the AT command set, is deemed Hayes-compatible.

))))▶ *Modem V: Technical*

HEADER

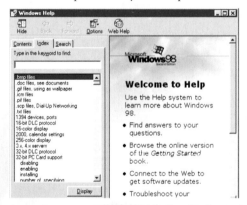

In email, the header is the part of the message above the body text. In newsgroups you can save download time by just viewing the headers, as they usually encapsulate the information that follows. In documents, headers are the area at the top of each page where you can put text, logos etc. When sending data each packet has its own header with information about it.

)))) *Application, Packet, Sending Email*

HEALTH AND MEDICINE WEB SITES

Whether it is for a diagnosis or for more information the Net offers a few healthy alternatives. Doctors are complaining that they have patients coming in requesting treatments for a problem they have self-diagnosed from information on the Web. If you want to try your medical skills there is an abundance of choice, such as Medline (*http://omni.ac.uk/medline*), the US National Library of Medicine's database. The main entries are free but some have to be paid for. For a more patient-friendly approach there are a number of online doctors, such as NetDoctor (*www.netdoctor.co.uk*) or HealthWorld (*www.healthy.net*), the health portal styled as a virtual village.

)))) *Education on the Internet*

HELP MENU

Onscreen guidance. If you have a problem or a question about using the Internet, or any aspect of your computer for that matter, your first port of call should be the Help menu. If your computer runs

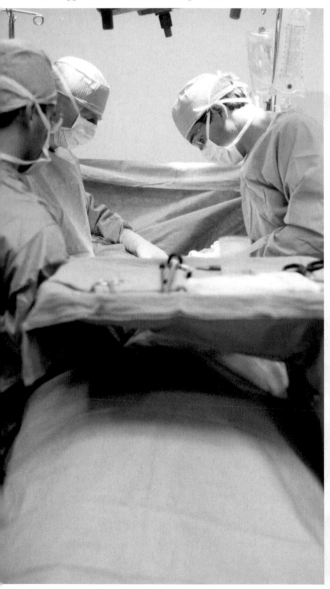

Windows, there is a very detailed body of information about every aspect of Windows. To find it, select Start|Help.

All the software programs you are most likely to come across for using the Net – Internet Explorer, Netscape Navigator, Outlook Express and Eudora, for example – have a Help menu to come to your aid when you are stuck. Internet Explorer offers guidance and tips on the

LEFT: You can now take your medical problems to an online doctor, but if you need urgent treatment you will still need to visit your own GP or hospital

RIGHT: High-speed connections are beginning to take over from the dial-up

most common topics such as Favorites, downloading, customizing and printing, as well as a glossary of useful terms and an index. If you do not find the information on Internet Explorer you need here, try the Microsoft Knowledge Base at *support.microsoft.com.* Another tactic when looking for answers to more general queries about applications or web sites is to seek out the FAQ (Frequently Asked Questions) page. Many web sites have them.

))))▶ *FAQ, Troubleshooting*

HIGH-SPEED CONNECTION

New high-speed connections to the Internet are emerging to replace the old-fashioned dial-up. The increasingly popular Digital Subscriber Line (xDSL) connections provide fast Internet access over existing phone lines. Alternatively, cable modems enable you to access the Net via the TV cable at speeds up to 100 times faster than a regular modem.

))))▶ *ADSL, Cable Modem Connection, DSL, ISDN, Modem*
V: Technical

HISTORY

Previously visited web pages. This is a feature of some Internet applications that maintains a log of the web pages you have visited. You can use it to look up and return to pages you visited earlier in the day or even weeks ago. If you use Internet Explorer, you can see the contents of the History list by clicking the History button, which then reveals the History panel on the left-hand side of the browser window. To return to a web page you find in the History list, simply click the page you want.

))))▶ *Bookmark, Internet Explorer, Internet Shortcuts*

HIT

Requests for a file from a server. This was originally the way to measure the popularity of a web site. Each time a file is requested from a web server it counts as one hit. As each page can contain many files (e.g. picture files) it will take several hits to download. Today, the number of individual visits is used as a more accurate measure of site activity.

))))▶ *Surfing, Web Page, Web Site*

HOAXES ON THE INTERNET

The story about the man who woke up with his kidneys stolen; the sympathy chain emails for a dying child; the messages to pass on with the secret recipe for Coca Cola and Kentucky Fried Chicken; are all Internet hoaxes.

If a story has been around long enough it can be raised to the status of urban legend. Just so you do not get caught out there is a newsgroup called alt.folklore.urban which gives you the lowdown on any stories doing the rounds. There is also a web site (*www.urbanlegends.com*) that archives some of the more interesting tales, while *www.scambusters.org* sheds light on what is true and what is false.

More difficult to spot, and ultimately more damaging, are those falsely warning about a new virus, such as the now infamous Good Times virus or Ghost. By passing on a hoax virus alert you may actually be creating problems rather than helping. If enough people within the same company pass on the alert it can grind the email system down to a halt. To check whether a warning is a hoax go to *www.europe.datafellows.com/news/hoax/index.html.*

))))▶ *Scambusters, Troll*

HOMES AND GARDEN WEB SITES

Expert advice and the tools to follow it with are all available through the Web. TV makeovers of everything from your kitchen to your decking have brought inspiration (and not a little perspiration) to the homeowner. DIY is fashionable and you can be your own interior decorator. For colour scheme guides, tips, tricks and discussions try *www.decoratorscrets.com*. If you want a more principled approach to harmonizing your home, try Geomancy Feng Shui (*www.geomancy.net*). If you want to make a water feature down in the vegetable patch, find help at *www.greenfingers.com* or for a comprehensive list of gardening links go to Gardening Launch Pad (*www. gardeninglaunchpad.com*).

)))➤ *Home and Internet, shopper.com, Shopping Online*

HOME AND THE INTERNET

Using the Net at home. For many homes, having an internet connection in the home is becoming as essential as having a telephone. The whole family enjoys using it. Children of all ages surf to help them with their

ABOVE: Gardening and DIY tips can be found on a number of sites
ABOVE RIGHT: Browser view of www.netscape.com

homework, to enjoy games, entertainment or chat. Parents find that the Internet is a great place for shopping, getting the latest news and for keeping in touch with friends and relatives by email. A word of warning, though: parents should keep a careful eye on the time spent online, unless they have an unmetered access account. They should also try to monitor the kinds of web site that their children are viewing.

Many home-owners find the Net convenient for finding local suppliers and builders. Most banks and insurance companies now have web sites and there are specialist sites that help you compare prices for insurance and mortgages. Fans of home decoration will find that many stores sell tools and materials online and offer DIY tips. Green-fingered gardeners will find a wealth of sites devoted to growing plants. Many are finding that it is feasible to telecommute, using their home computer to communicate with colleagues and customers.

)))⮞ *Family and the Internet, Home and Garden Web Sites, Telecommuting*

HOME PAGE

A browser's initial web page. The page that appears in your browser when you first connect to the Net. Web sites also usually refer to their 'front page' as their home page. When you use a browser application for the first time, the home page will default to the web site chosen by its maker: Internet Explorer (*www.msn.com*) or Netscape Navigator (*www.netscape.com*). You can change this if you wish. If you use Internet Explorer, for example, you should choose Tools|Options|General|Address. In the Address: box, type the address of the web page you would like as your new home page, and click OK. Some web sites offer a button that automatically makes it your browser's home page.

)))⮞ *Address, Browser, Default, Web Page, Web Site*

HOOVER'S (www.hoovers.com)

Business web site. Hoover's is one of the Net's leading sources for information about business in the US and also has sites catering for the UK and other economies.

)))⮞ *Business Web Sites, Companies Online, Online Directories*

HOST

Servers that enable other computers to link to them and use their resources. A host is essentially any computer that allows other computers to access it. The name is used interchangeably with a server. Just like any hospitality venue there are a range of hosts. Web servers will store and transfer the web pages requested, Usenet servers enable live chat, mail servers distribute and deliver emails, while FTP servers archive software for download. There are also web hosting providers who physically house (host) and maintain the web servers and communication lines, while others supply the content.

)))⮞ *ISP, OSP*

HOSTNAME

The server's domain name. More properly known as the domain name, the host name is the more memorable, named version of a server's IP address, such as *www.anycompany.com*. Each name has to be unique and is the address that locates the computer on the Internet. The domain name has to be translated into a numeric IP address by a DNS server.

)))⮞ *DNS, Domain, IP Address*

HOTBOT (www.hotbot.com)

Search engine. A favourite of many researcher's, Hotbot has advanced search filters – including date, languages and words to exclude – that help to refine your search.

)))⮞ *Search Engine, Directory*

HOTDOG

Web page editor. From the aptly named Sausage software, HotDog Professional is a fullyfledged web-page editor. As well as handling HTML, it can integrate cascading style sheets (CSS) and scripting technologies, such as ASP and JavaScript. For those wanting to create more simple web pages quickly and easily, there is a more basic version called Hotdog Express.

))))▶ *Web Authoring, Web Page: Creating I, Web Page: Creating II*

HOTMAIL (*www.hotmail.com*)

Email web site. Hotmail was the original web service to offer browser-based email. It is now owned by Microsoft and remains the premier browser-based email site. The beauty of the service is that you do not have to be sitting at your own computer to use email;

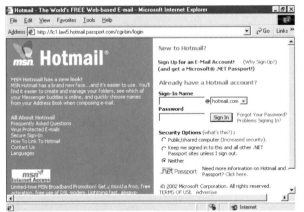

you can do it using a browser from anywhere in the world. It is ideal for people without their own computer or those on holiday. It is a simple matter to sign up and get an account, and then you can email to your heart's content from any Internet cafe in the world.

))))▶ *Browser, Cybercafé*

HOTSPOT

A link on an image map; one link among several on a graphic that takes you through to related pages or files. A hotspot is an area of an image that is linked to something, such as another web page or sound file. Normally, you can tell that there is a hotspot in a picture because the mouse pointer changes shape from an arrow to a hand. For example, a music shop web site might have a graphic with the different instruments it sells. Clicking on one of the hotspots could take you through to a linked page or play a demo sound file. Used well, hotspots can liven up a page.

))))▶ *Hover Links, Hyperlink, Hypertext*

HOVER LINKS

Under the Advanced Tab in Internet Options you can set Internet Explorer to display links on a web page only when you hover over them. This can be less distracting than always showing the links and more informative than never showing the links, which are the other options possible.

))))▶ *Hotspot, Hyperlink, Hypertext*

LEFT: HotDog, made by sausage software, is a web-page editor

HTML

'HyperText Markup Language'; a computer language. HTML is a standard set of codes that specify how words and images in a web page should appear in your browser's window. HTML codes control aspects of text formatting such as font, colour and size, and also enable the hypertext links between web pages. Every web page encoded in HTML can be displayed by browsers such as Internet Explorer and Netscape Navigator. The technically inclined surfer can see what the HTML version of a web page looks like by choosing View|Source from the Menu Bar. A complex document will appear in a separate window, containing all the HTML codes that make up that page.

))))➤ *Browser, DHTML, Hypertext, Web Page, Web Page Authoring*

HTTP

'HyperText Transfer Protocol'; Internet protocol. You will see it at the start of web addresses in the Address box on your browser, for example *http://www. msn.com.* It is the protocol that defines how hypertext information is delivered across the World Wide Web. It also determines what actions web servers and browsers should take in response to various commands. For example, when you enter an URL in your browser, this sends an HTTP command to a web server, directing it to transmit the requested web page.

))))➤ *Address, HTTPS, Hypertext, Internet, URL*

HTTPS

The protocol establishing that a secure connection is in place for transmitting confidential information over the Web. This is a secure version of HTTP, that allows private or confidential information to be sent over the Internet using SSL encryption. It is most commonly used at online stores when entering order information such as credit-card details. If the connection is secure then the URL in the Address box on your browser will start with https: instead of the more usual http:. There might also be a closed padlock showing in the status bar at the bottom of your browser window.

))))➤ *Address, HTTP, Internet, Secure Server, URL*

HYPERLINK

Method for linking web pages. To use a hyperlink on a web page, click on it once and the hyperlink takes you to another place in the same page or, perhaps, to a web page in another web site. If the hyperlink is a word or a phrase, it will probably be underlined and when your mouse pointer is over it, it will change into a hand, to let you know that it is 'hot'. A hyperlink can also be a photo or a graphic, and the part of the screen in which you click to activate it is called a 'hotspot'.

))))➤ *Hotspot, Hover Links, Hypertext, Link*

HYPERMEDIA

The terms hypermedia and hypertext are often used interchangeably. In fact, hypertext strictly refers to links to text, while hypermedia refers to links to multimedia, such as graphics, video and sound, as well as text. The notion at the heart of both is that rather than following information in a linear, sequential way we should be able to create our own route. Contrast a book where information – words, sentences, pages, chapters – is linearly structured, with hypermedia where it is not. There is no set order to access pages. Information can be expanded, reordered or explained, simply by the links the readers click.

))))➤ *DHTML, Hypertext, Web Page, Web Page Creating*

HYPERTEXT

Document system with linked elements. Hypertext was invented by Ted Nelson in the 1960s. Hypertext documents contain elements called hyperlinks. These are words and pictures that are linked to one another so that you can move around between them. When you click on a hyperlink, you are taken to where the link leads. It works in the same way if you are exploring within a single document, a web page or the entire World Wide Web. Although it is the most distinctive feature of the Web, hypertext can also occur elsewhere: in the pages of a CD-Rom encyclopedia, for example.

))))➤ *Hotspot, Hover Links, Hyperlink, Hypermedia*

IAP (INTERNET ACCESS PROVIDER)

See ISP

IBM (*www.ibm.com*)

Computer manufacturer. IBM (or 'Big Blue') once dominated the computer world with its pioneering mainframes. It famously invented the PC, and has now diversified into web technology and consultancy.

))))➤ *Computers*

ABOVE: IBM invented the PC and once dominated the computer world
RIGHT: Icons are small graphics that you can click to give the computer a command

ICANN

Technical management of the Internet. ICANN stands for the rather less catchy name Internet Corporation for Assigned Names and Numbers. It is a rather loose, non-profit coalition of business people, academics and user groups that have been brought together to take over responsibility for the technical management of the internet name and address system.

))))➤ *DNS, Domain, IP Address, Name Registration*

ICONS

Clickable graphics on a computer screen. Icons have been a vital part of using a computer ever since Apple introduced its pioneering Macintosh GUI (Graphical User Interface) and Microsoft belatedly brought in their imitation of it called 'Windows'. An icon is a small graphic on a computer screen that you place your mouse pointer over and click on to instruct the computer to carry out an action. It could be a double-click on a shortcut to open a file or start up a software program. Or, in a browser window, it could be a single click on an arrow icon that takes you to the top of the page, for example.

))))➤ *GUI, Shortcuts, Windows*

ICQ

An instant messaging program that lets users track friends online and communicate with them in real-time. Pronounced as 'I-Seek-You', ICQ is a popular

instant messaging system. Although it operates independently of AOL, it is owned by it and does have many similar features to AIM. Users can have real-time chats, play games, send messages or share files. Once you have installed the program you can create a list of friends

and contacts who also use ICQ so that you can be alerted when any of them come online. What's more, you can access your buddy lists from any web-enabled PC. However, ICQ does not yet support video chat as other IMs, such as Windows Messenger, do.

))))➤ *AOL, AIM, IM*

IM

'Instant Message'; real-time typed conversations. Although the chance to send an instant message to friends first took off in the home, it is quickly spreading to the workplace. A recent survey in the US found that office workers have doubled the time they spend swapping real-time messages to five billion minutes a year. What is not clear, however, is how much of that is work-related! Fortunately, not many employers insist their staff take advantage of the option available with some IMs to save a transcript of the conversation.

Yet business users spend only around a third of the time sending instant messages that home users do. Not surprisingly, given that they are both real-time typed conversations, many of the conventions used in public chat rooms are adopted in instant messages. So there is no shouting (writing everything in capital letters) but plenty of smileys (emoticons) to express how you feel. To make it easier, several IMs picture a range of emoticons you can click on to add to your message.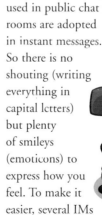
Others can be added by using special key combinations. To speed up the conversation you can also take advantage of the sort of abbreviated phrases and expressions used for texting to phones (e.g. C U for see you).

))))➤ *AIM, ICQ, MSN Messenger, Netscape Messenger*

iMAC

Stylish Apple computer. Introduced in May 1998, the iMac was Apple's computer for the new millennium. It was aimed at the first-time user and designed with the Internet in mind. Heralded as the most innovative new computer since the original Macintosh in 1984, it came with the screen and computer encased in a single stylish translucent plastic exterior. With a built-in 56 Kpbs modem and the promise of ease of connection to the Internet, it became very successful, selling two million in its first year. The iMac look, courtesy of Apple's Brit designer Jonathan Ive, has spawned a wave of colourful see-through computer products.

))))➤ *Apple Computer, Mac: Introduction, PC vs Mac*

BOTTOM: The colourful and stylish iMac has influenced computer products
BELOW: Image editors allow you to alter pictures and create stunning images

IMAGE EDITOR

Graphics software that enables you to alter images to create stunning effects. Image editing software has a variety of tools and filters that let you edit, change or create bitmapped images. Although the distinction with paint programs is blurred, image editors are generally used for modifying pictures, such as removing red-eye from photographs or touching up scanned images. Paint programs are more generally used to create the original artwork. However, you can create stunning special effects with image editors by superimposing and altering different layers of the image.

))))➤ *Graphics File, Picture Format*

IMAGE MAP

A picturesque way to navigate round a web site. With an image map, a picture or illustration is split into several zones usually showing what is available on the

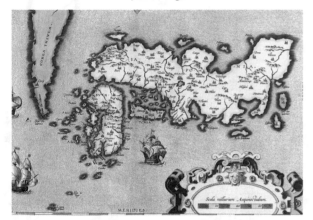

site. When a user clicks on any part of the image they are taken through to the corresponding web page.

))))▶ *Hotspot, Hyperlink, Hypermedia, Web Page*

IMAP

'Internet Message Access Protocol'; a superior way of retrieving email, compared with POP3. The IMAP gives you more features to manage your mail, while it is on the server. You can, for instance, search for keywords or download just the headers rather than the full text – an advantage if you are on a costly phone link.

))))▶ *Email, IP*

IMDB (*www.imdb.com*)

Movie web site. This content-rich web site has virtually everything the movie fan could want. There is a guide to films playing in the US that includes reviews, ratings and show times. All the latest releases on DVD and VHS are described and can be ordered by linking directly to Amazon.com. The movie and TV news sections will keep you up to date with the top stars and their projects. You can use its 'My Movies' feature to log your favourites and the database will let you know where and when they are playing. Games, competitions and message boards also add interest to the site.

))))▶ *Entertainment Web Sites, Film and TV Web Sites, Movies*

LEFT: Navigate your way around the web with Image Map
BOTTOM: Browser view of http://us.imdb.com

INBOX

Mail folder for incoming messages. In most email programs this is the mailbox, or folder, where incoming messages first arrive. Any unread messages in the Inbox are usually highlighted in bold. Most email clients also let you preview the message in a separate pane. As many of us can expect up to 250 mails a day the Inbox can soon get pretty crowded, so it is best to set up other folders where messages can be moved once read. You can also set up rules that automatically move messages containing certain keywords or addresses to a different folder.

))))▶ *Email, Outbox, Receiving Email*

INC. MAGAZINE (*www.inc.com*)

Business web site. Inc. Magazine is a resource centre aimed at small businesses in the US, with information on starting and developing your own enterprise, including financing, franchises and business plans.

))))▶ *Companies Online*

INPUT

To put information or instructions into a computer. For example, you can input text into a computer by typing it on the keyboard, you can input a photograph by putting it in a scanner, or draw a picture by moving your mouse pointer on the screen.

))))▶ *Output*

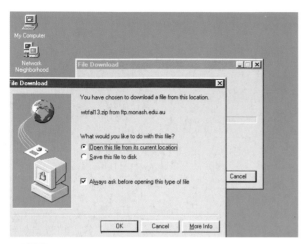

INSTALLING SOFTWARE OVER THE INTERNET

There are three basic stages to installing software over the Internet. First locate the program you want, and then follow the link to the download centre (having paid for the application, if necessary). From there you download the program's installer to your machine and double-click the icon for the downloaded file to install the program itself.

))))▶ *Download, Software Guides, Software: Purchasing*

INTERFACE

The visual link between computer and user. All modern computers have a graphical user interface (GUI), inspired by the pioneering Macintosh and copied in Windows. This interface is what you see on your monitor screen when you turn on your computer. These are the standard features of an interface:

Desktop: Screen area when all applications are closed down
Menu: Pull-down lists from which you can choose options
Icon: Small graphics that you double-click on to access drives, folders, files or applications
Toolbar: Vertical or horizontal rows of buttons that you can click on to select options
Window: Rectangles that enclose an open folder or document

))))▶ *Application, Folder, GUI, Icons, Macintosh, Windows*

INTERNAL MODEM

Device inside computer for connecting to the Net. If you choose a dial-up connection to the Internet, you will need a modem to connect your computer to the

telephone socket. The cheapest option – but not necessarily the easiest – is an internal modem. This is a circuit board or card that plugs into a slot inside your computer. If one is not already fitted, you need to remove the computer's casing in order to install it. Internal modems do eliminate some clutter from the back of your computer, but do not display the little lights indicating online activity that are featured on external modems. Some internal modems also offer fax facilities.

))))▶ *Connecting to the Internet I: Basic, External Modem*

INTERNET

Global computer network. The Internet – or Net, for short – is an international network of computers permanently joined together by high-speed cables and dedicated computers called servers. Everyone who uses the Internet has to connect via an Internet Service Provider (ISP) operating one of the servers. Once you are connected, you can communicate with every other computer on the Net, anywhere in the world. In addition to email, the World Wide Web has become the most important part of the Internet. The Net has created a new global space for commerce, publishing, news, the arts and education. Most of all, it is about people communicating with people in a way that has changed the world.

))))▶ *Internet: Introduction, ISP, World Wide Web*

INTERNET CONNECTIONS

Whether it is over the phone lines, wireless, by satellite or TV cables, there is an expanding number of ways to connect to the Internet. With fridges, toasters and trash cans being Internet-enabled there will soon not be an appliance that is not capable of connecting to the Net. What is more, those connections can be made across a variety of networks. The next generation of mobile phones are promising high-speed wireless access.

Digital Subscriber Line (DSL) technologies offer fast, always-on connections over existing phone lines. Satellite links connect those in more rural areas while cable modems bring the Internet in the home alongside the TV. Which suits you best will largely depend on the availability and cost of particular services in your neighbourhood.

))))▶ *Connecting to the Internet I: Basic, Connecting to the Internet II: Advanced*

ABOVE LEFT: Internet Explorer's File Download applet

LEFT: Diving into the world of the Internet can be an invigorating experience

INTERNET EXPLORER

Web browser software program. Internet Explorer is one of the most popular software programs for browsing the World Wide Web. It provides a host of features to make your browsing fun and productive. Introduced by Microsoft to rival the popular Netscape Navigator, it has versions for both Windows and Mac. The Windows version will be focused on here.

1. Launching and connecting

Launch Internet Explorer by either clicking on the Start menu, selecting Programs, then choosing Internet Explorer; or clicking on the Internet icon on your desktop. You need to be connected to the Internet to be able to browse web sites with Internet Explorer, so if Internet Explorer does not automatically start the dial-up procedure, you should manually connect to your ISP or OSP using the procedure they recommend.

2. The Internet Explorer window

The Internet Explorer main window has a range of features to help you browse the Web. The main elements are:

Title bar: This shows the title of the current web page

Toolbars: These allow you to navigate and control Internet Explorer

Standard buttons: These are for navigating around the Web

Main window: This is where the web pages appear

Go button: Click this after typing in a web site address to go to that site

Status bar: This bar at the foot of the window tells you what is going on

3. The toolbars

Explorer has four toolbars:

Menu bar: This displays Internet Explorer's main menu options

Standard tool bar: This bar contains the buttons you will use most often for browsing

Back: takes you to the previous page

Forward: displays the page on screen before you pressed the Back button

Stop: stops a web page downloading

Refresh: shows the latest version of the page

Home: displays the default home page

Search: opens the Search panel, giving access to search engines

Favorites: opens the Favorites panel for saving and revisiting favourite pages

History: opens the History panel, which logs previously visited pages

Mail: provides email options

Print: prints the current page

Edit: allows you to edit the code of the current web page

Address bar: Type the address of the web site you want to visit and click the Go button

Links bar: This has links to Microsoft-related web sites

4. Connecting to a Web Site

To connect manually to a web site, type in the address or URL of the site in the Address box and click the Go button. A web site address typically starts with 'http://www.' followed by the name of the web site. For example: '*http://www.bbc.co.uk*'. However, you often need only type the web site name as many web sites now

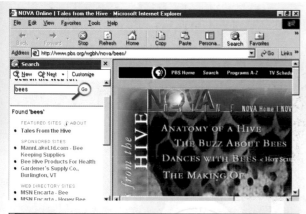

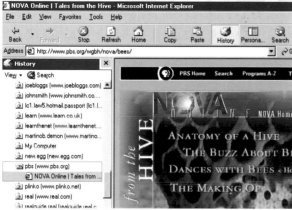

work fine without the 'http://' or the 'www.'. If you get an error message, the most likely causes are:

You mistyped the URL.
Solution: check your typing and click the Go button again

The link to the particular web page is not working.
Solution: try typing only the basic web address and finding the page on the site yourself

You have lost the connection to your ISP.
Solution: check your connection is working and try again

The server of your intended web site is busy.
Solution: try again in a couple of minutes

5. Navigation

The most useful and most exciting part of browsing the Web is clicking on hyperlinks and following them to new

destinations. Hyperlinks are words, buttons or images that, when clicked on once, take you to a different part of a page or perhaps to a different web site entirely. This is how you recognize and use these hyperlinks:

Words

This is the most common and easy to recognize type. The word or phrase is usually underlined and the mouse pointer changes to a hand when your mouse pointer is over it. Click on it once to follow the link.

Buttons

These can look like computer buttons, graphical icons or options in a menu. Your mouse pointer changes to a hand when you are over one of these links. Click on it once to follow the link.

Images

Explore around with your mouse to see if an image is a hyperlink. If the pointer changes into a hand, then it is. Click on it once to follow the link.

6. Favorites

This feature makes it easy to store web addresses and use them again and again. To use it, click on the Favorites button on the menu bar to display the Favorites panel. These are the main things you can do with Favorites:

Add: to add a current web page to your collection of Favorites, click once on Add to Favorites, which appears at the top of the Favorites panel
Revisit: to revisit a web page, click on its name in the Favorites panel
Organize: click on Organize Favorites at the top of the Favorites panel
Delete: to delete unwanted Favorites, click on organize Favorites, highlight the Favorite to be deleted and click delete.

⟫⟫ *Browser, Hyperlink, ISP, Macintosh, Netscape Navigator, OSP, URL, Web Browser*

TOP: Internet Explorer | Search toolbar | search for 'bees' and resulting web page
ABOVE: Internet Explorer | History toolbar | last page visited (www.pbs.org) appears
LEFT: Explorer can be launched by using the menu or icon on your desktop

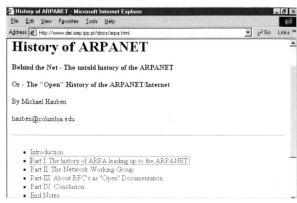

ARPA (The Advanced Research Projects Agency) was formed by the US Department of Defence, partly in reaction to the-then Soviet Union's launch of Sputnik in 1957. In 1969, the ARPAnet project was begun. It was intended to test the feasibility of linking together computers spread over a wide area to form a network. The theory was that if an atomic bomb put one computer out of action, the network could work round it and still function. It seems logical to us now, but at the time it was revolutionary. Many computer scientists could not see how it would develop; at that time computers were seen as arithmetic machines not as communication devices. The project was the beginning of the Internet.

))))▶ *ARPAnet, World Wide Web*

INTERNET IN THE 1970S: HISTORY

With the success of the ARPAnet, other research agencies and universities began to participate, widening the network of mainframe computers. Educational institutions in the US such as MIT, UCLA, Stanford and Harvard were joined after 1973 by European institutions, including University College, London and the Royal Radar Establishment in Norway. Other important elements of the Internet were developed during the 1970s: electronic mail (email), Telnet and FTP.

))))▶ *Email, FTP, Telnet, World Wide Web*

ABOVE LEFT: The clunky technology of the 1950s meant that the original computers were little more than gigantic arithmetical machines
ABOVE: Browser view of www.dei.isep.ipp.pt, *the untold history of ARPAnet*

INTERNET IN THE 1950S: PREHISTORY

 In the 1950s computing was in its infancy. Computers were gigantic machines affordable only by governments, research establishments and industrial corporations, and were regarded as powerful arithmetical and problem-solving devices. Inspired by the pioneering work of Alan Turing during and after World War II, the milestone EDVAC computer was introduced in 1949. The UNIVAC computer, launched in 1950, triggered the use of computers in business. The Soviet launch of Sputnik in 1957 galvanized the US into ramping up its technological progress by forming the Advanced Research Projects Agency (ARPA). This agency was later to come up with the novel idea of linking computers together to preserve data in the event of an atomic bomb attack. The result was ARPAnet.

))))▶ *ARPAnet, World Wide Web*

INTERNET IN THE 1960S: HISTORY

ARPAnet was the original computer network that became, 30 years later, the Internet we know today.

INTERNET IN THE 1980S: HISTORY

During the early 1980s further pieces of technology and protocol were added to the jigsaw. The TCP/IP protocol was introduced. This enabled multiple computers of differing types to exchange data. The Domain Name System (DNS), and the Network News Transfer Protocol (NNTP) were also developed at this time. In the mid 1980s, Internet Relay Chat (IRC) gained huge popularity. The most significant event occurred in 1989, when Tim Berners-Lee proposed a global hypertext project, to be known as the World Wide Web. It was designed to allow people to pool knowledge in a web of hypertext documents.

))))➤ *DNS, Hypertext, IRC, NNTP, TCP/IP, World Wide Web*

ABOVE: Every country in the world is connected through the Internet

INTERNET IN THE 1990S: HISTORY

The Net's communal spirit changed irrevocably in 1991 with the dropping of the 'Acceptable Use Policy', which had up to that time prohibited using the Net for profit. In 1991, Tim Berners-Lee released the first web server and web client. Further technical specifications such as URI, HTTP and HTML flowed from this innovator. The year 1993 saw the release of Marc

Andreesen's browser, Mosaic, the first Internet program with a graphical user interface (GUI). Its author went on to develop the hugely popular Netscape Navigator browser. In 1995, Microsoft entered the fray with its own browser, Internet Explorer. Microsoft gradually caught up with Netscape's technology, and, after version 4.0, Explorer began to overtake Navigator in popularity. With the Net's rise in popularity during the mid 1990s, thorny issues began to crop up. Censorship became – and remains – controversial, with governments and freedom-of-speech lobbies debating the rights to privacy versus the importance of public security and decency. Hacking almost became an industry in its own right, with groups around the world trying to steal secrets, credit-card details or merely make mischief. The late 1990s saw an astonishing rise in the Net's popularity as millions surfed, looking for information, entertainment and – it was believed – things to buy. The rush to cash in on the Net's commercial promise led to unprecedented investment in new technologies and a new kind of business dubbed 'dotcoms'. Millions of dollars were made by early investors, and millions more were lost as the bubble eventually burst with the crash of technology stocks on the Nasdaq index in March 2001.

))))➤ *Censorship, GUI, Hacking, HTTP, HTML, URI, World Wide Web*

INTERNET: INTRODUCTION

Overview of the Internet. So, what exactly is the Internet? The Internet, or 'Net' for short, is a global network of computers linked together so that they can exchange information. Anyone in the world can use, enjoy or learn from this information if they have access to an Internet connection. The Net can be accessed by many electronic devices: computers, specially equipped televisions, mobile phones or palm-top devices. But it is not just about technology. The real importance of the Net is what people are doing with it.

The Internet contains the World Wide Web, a collection of millions of web pages on every conceivable subject. It is changing the way children learn in schools, it allows people to shop online, enjoy entertainment and get the latest news. The Net also offers new ways for people to communicate with one another, allowing friends to keep in touch, and communities to interact. These

methods include electronic mail (email), a system by which people can quickly send and receive messages; Instant Relay Chat (IRC), which allows people to type messages to one another in real time; and newsgroups, where people can read and contribute to discussions on their favourite topics.

))))▶ *Connecting to the Internet I: Basic, Email, IRC, Network, Newsgroups, World Wide Web*

INTERNET SHORTCUTS

Web site links. With millions of web sites available, it is easy to forget the one that had the great recipe for tacos or the pictures of Marilyn Monroe. Fortunately, browsers come to the rescue with a bookmarking feature that keeps shortcuts to sites you want to revisit. In Netscape these links are called Bookmarks while in Internet Explorer they are referred to as Favorites. It is easy to organize them and group them together in subject folders, such as entertainment, legal, sports, etc. Most web sites also have a resources section with links to recommended sites.

))))▶ *Bookmarks, Browser, Favorites, Internet Explorer, Web Browser*

ABOVE: Anyone with access to the Internet can use and learn from its information
ABOVE RIGHT: Browser view of www.isoc.org

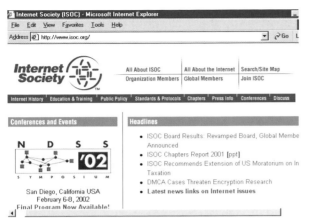

INTERNET SOCIETY (www.isoc.org)

Professional body. The Internet Society (ISOC) is a professional membership society, providing leadership in addressing issues that confront the future of the Internet.

)))) *Internet: Introduction*

INTERNET TELEPHONY

Using the Internet as a phone. Software programs enable you to use your internet connection to talk to someone else online. This is potentially a great saving on long-distance phone charges, as the cost is simply that of your internet access. However, sound quality is not yet as good as the traditional phone.

)))) *Communications Software, Phone Dialer*

INTRANET

A secure web-based information channel only available to people within a particular organization. The intranet is a web site, like any other, with useful information, discussion groups, even chat. Where an intranet differs is that it is only available to people inside a company or organization, or those who are authorized to use it. Access to others is prevented by a firewall. For companies spread over a large geographic area and across different time zones it is a much more cost-effective way to share information than setting up a private network. Where part of the intranet is open to authorized outsiders it is known as an extranet.

)))) *Extranet, Firewall, Network, Network Computer*

IP

'Internet Protocol'; the underlying part of the TCP/IP protocol, which is used by computers on the Internet to communicate with each other. The Internet Protocol (IP) element covers the way information must be packaged and addressed to make sure it reaches the right destination and can be properly understood.

)))) *IP Address, Packet, Protocol*

IP ADDRESS

The IP address, which can be static or dynamic, locates computers on the Internet. Just like any house number, an IP address marks the specific location of a particular computer on the Internet. For example 217.12.6.17 is the IP address for *www.yahoo.co.uk*. A DNS server translates the more easily remembered domain name into the numerical IP address. When you connect to the Internet your computer will also need an IP address. This will either be static – that is, it doesn't change each time you log on – or dynamic. With a dynamic IP address, you get a different one from the pool of addresses the ISP has for all its subscribers every time you connect.

)))) *DNS, ICANN, IP*

IRC

Internet Relay Chat is a chat system developed in Finland in the late 1980s, which enables people to connect from anywhere on the Internet and join in live discussions. It has established its credentials as a channel for eye-witness views with coverage of world events such as the Gulf War. To join an IRC discussion – called a channel – you need special client software and some knowledge of IRC commands to help you log on to the IRC servers that broadcast the discussions. As a result, some people find web-based chat rooms easier to use.

⟫⟫▶ *Chanop, Chat*

IRC COMMAND

Chat system command; commands enable you to control what happens during chat sessions. Some of the latest GUI-based client software for connecting to IRC discussions include buttons that cover most of the basic commands involved, but as IRC chat channels are so text-based, it is handy to know what the commands are. There are more than 100 of them, and the simplest way to get the list is from the command /HELP. When inputting commands it is important to add the forward slash at the beginning – otherwise it will be sent as a message to the group. Some basic commands include:

/JOIN<#channel>: Join this channel
/MSG<nickname><message>: Send private message to this nickname
/WHOIS<nickname>: Display nickname's identity

⟫⟫▶ *Chanop, Chat, IRC*

ISDN

'Integrated Services Digital Network'; the original high-speed connection to the Net. ISDN lines are being superseded by faster connections such as cable modems and the various flavours of Digital Subscriber Lines (DSL). Unlike the new generation of services ISDN does not offer the 'always-on'

connection to the Internet. Neither can it provide the speed. The capacity of a single ISDN lines is 64 Kbps, although most telephone companies double this number by supplying two lines. The line rental fee and telephone charges vary greatly according to the company and you will also need an ISDN modem and an Internet account with a service provider that offers ISDN access.

⟫⟫▶ *BPS, High-Speed Connection, Internet Connections*

ISP (INTERNET SERVICE PROVIDER)

'Internet Service Provider'; provider of connection to the Internet. The one thing you must have to access the Internet is a connection. For millions of people, this means via an ISP (Internet Service Provider), a company that operates one of the server computers that makes up the network and provides you with a means of connection. Every ISP will provide you with access to the Net and your own email address. There is another type of service called an OSP (Online Service Provider). They offer additional services such as a search engine, instant messaging, news and shopping. OSPs are highly popular and include AOL (*www.aol.com*) and MSN (*www.msn.com*).

1. Connection Methods

One or more of the following methods of connection might be on offer in your area:

Dial-up: The most common method, using your telephone line and a modem
Satellite: Requires a satellite dish
Cable: A good option if you have cable in your area
DSL: A faster 'always-on' service, but more expensive
ISDN: A faster service using a digital line

Many people are accessing the Net via their mobile phones and palm-top devices; they connect via an ISP suitable for their equipment.

2. Choosing an ISP

If you choose to connect via satellite, cable, DSL or ISDN, your ISP will probably be restricted to one or two companies that operate in your area. If, however, you choose a dial-up connection, you will likely have a much wider choice. Do some research before choosing an ISP: read Internet magazines, consult friends, consider your requirements. These are some suggested criteria:

Ease of connection
Ideally, choose an ISP that gives you a free CD that automatically installs the software you need and simplifies the set-up procedure on your computer.

Technical support
Assess an ISPs reputation for giving technical support, both online and by telephone, preferably by free -phone number.

Quality of service
You can only truly assess the speed and reliability of an ISP's connection by trying it out.

3. Opening an Account

You need to open an account with an ISP, just as you would with a utility company. Choose a tariff that suits the kind of usage you anticipate: heavy, occasional, evenings and weekends only, etc. You can apply for an account online, using someone else's computer, or by telephone. When you open an account, you can usually choose your username – this will become the first part of your email address; and you are usually issued with an initial password, which you can change to something more memorable when you get online for the first time.

> ⫸ *Account, DSL, Connecting to the Internet I: Basic, Cable Modem Connection, Dial-up Connection, Email, ISDN, OSP, Satellite Connection*

JANET

Joint Academic NETwork. A national network linking together universities, colleges and research institutes within the United Kingdom, started in the 1980s. Web sites with the suffix '.ac.uk' are connected to the Internet through JANET.

> ⫸ *Internet in the 1980s: History*

LEFT: Satellite is one of the media via which ISPs can connect users to the Internet
ABOVE: Browser view of www.msn.com

JAVA

High-level programming language. Many interactive applications that run from the Internet are created in Java, as it works across all computer platforms.

The Java emblem may be the coffee bean from which it takes its name, but in reality it is less refreshing. It is a high-level programming language developed by Sun Microsystems and is designed to work on any computer. This makes it useful for the Web as Java programs (applets) can be embedded on a page and will run in any Java-enabled browser (as most are). Through such applets you can add all sorts of features to a web site, such as news tickers, multimedia animations, database integration, or even interactive games.

))))▶ *Applet, Hypermedia, JavaScript, Multi-platform, Web Page*

JAVASCRIPT

Web scripting language. Despite the similarity in name, JavaScript is not related to Java. Originally developed for Netscape Navigator, it is a scripting language that is written directly within the HTML code on a web page. It allows designers to add interactive effects, such as mouse rollover effects, dynamically changing content and backgrounds.

))))▶ *Hypermedia, Java, Multi-platform, Web Page*

JPEG/JPG

'Joint Photographic Experts Group'; graphics file format. JPEG is a standard format for storing complex images, particularly photographs. It is widely used on the Web because it uses a technique called 'lossy compression', whereby redundant pieces of information are removed in order to reduce file size. The file extension is .jpg.

))))▶ *Graphics File, Picture Format, Web Page*

RIGHT: You can censor the Internet information available to your children
BELOW: Keyword Search - search for 'bees AND wasps'
BELOW RIGHT: Browser view of aol.sesameworkshop.org

JUNK EMAIL

Unsolicited email ads. Junk email is a nuisance. It is possible to set up filters to screen out the unwanted messages, but there is always the concern that

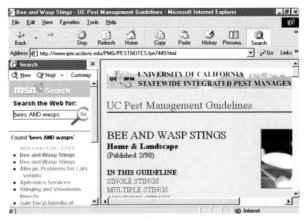

an important email might slip through. One way round this is to set up the filter to search the emails for keywords likely to be in junk mail and move any found to a special folder. Then you can occasionally scan the junk folder to check there is nothing important before you delete it.

))))▶ *Deleting Email, Filtering, Receiving Email, Spam*

K56FLEX

Information transfer standard for modems. Superseded by the new V.90 standard, K56flex was one of two rival technologies (the other was X2) offering fast downloads from the Internet at 56,000 bps using just the plain old telephone service (POTS). It does only work for download (upload is still 33.6 Kbps) and your Internet Service Provider must support V.90.

))))▶ *Modem V: Technical*

KEYWORD SEARCH

Search method. A word, or words, is entered in the search box rather than a complete phrase, as happens with natural text search engines. The combination of keywords can be altered using the

boolean modifiers (operators) AND, OR, NOT. Keywords are also inserted into the headers of web pages to be picked up by search engines for easy indexing.

))))➤ **Boolean Modifier, Case Sensitivity, Search Engine**

KID'S WEB SITES

Web sites for children. To direct your kids to the web sites you would prefer them to see, you could try being inconspicuously present while they surf, set up the Ratings function in Internet Explorer (if that is your browser), or you could direct them towards some of the child-friendly sites:

123 Sesame Street (*aol.sesameworkshop.org/sesamestreet/*)
BBC (*bbc.co.uk*)
Cool Sites for Kids (*www.ala.org/alsc/children_links.html*)
Great Sites page (*www.ala.org/parentspage/greatsites/*)
PBS Kids (*http://pbskids.org*)
Surfing the Net with Kids (*www.surfnetkids.com*)
The Kids on the Web (*www.zen.org/~brendan/kids.html*)
Yahooligans (*www.yahooligans.com*)

))))➤ **Children and the Net I: Infant and Primary, Children and the Net II: Secondary**

KILL FILE

Blocked news messages. This is a good way to cut down on spam. Some email clients and newsreaders enable you to set up rules that block messages from specific addresses or that contain certain keywords. The list of blocked addresses is known as a kill file or a bozo list.

))))➤ **Filtering, Newsreader**

KILOBYTE (Kb)

Used as a measure of memory and storage space, or file size. When describing storage a kilobyte is equal to 1,024 bytes, where a byte represents a single character. When measuring data-transfer rates it stands for 1,000 bytes. It is usually shown as Kb.

))))➤ **File Size**

LAN

 'Local Area Network'; a group of computers linked together in order to share resources. A LAN is just that, a local area network where several computers, all within a short distance of each other, such as in a group of buildings, are linked together. They can either be physically linked using Ethernet cabling or AppleTalk for Macintosh computers, or on a wireless LAN connected by radio waves. PCs on the network can exchange files or messages with other users connected to the LAN; they can also share facilities such as a printer or a single connection to the Internet. Each computer on the LAN is called a node.

)))➤ *File Transfer, Network*

LAND'S END (www.landsend.com)

Online clothing retailer. Fans of the out-of-doors Land's End look will enjoy shopping for leisure and sporting clothes on this web site.

)))➤ *Clothes: Buying Online, shopper.com, Shopping Online*

LAPTOP

See Notebook Computer

LATENCY

Linked to bandwidth, latency is the amount of time it takes a parcel of information to reach its destination. Its effect on the Internet is mainly felt by gamers, particularly in action games. If the latency is too high – that is, it takes too long for the information to arrive – it is practically impossible to play the game.

)))➤ *File Transfer*

LCD SCREEN

A notebook display screen. Notebook computers need a light display. Most use a liquid crystal display (LCD) screen. This works by passing a current through a liquid crystal solution that aligns the crystals so that they act like shutters, either allowing light through or blocking it. Such screens are expensive to manufacture, however.

)))➤ *Notebook computer*

LDAP

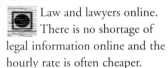 'Lightweight Directory Access Protocol'; protocol for accessing information directories. With millions of email addresses around it can be difficult to find an individual's address from just their name. Several 'white page' directories, such as WhoWhere (*www.whowhere.com*) offer this on the Web. They use a standard called LDAP, which contains rules for organizing directory databases.

)))➤ *Bigfoot, Directory Service, Search Engine, WhoWhere*

LEASED LINE

A dedicated phone connection. The most expensive solution for linking up to the Internet, leased lines are permanent phone connections. Also known as dedicated lines, they can also be used to connect offices or one computer to another. Unlike a dial-up link, the connection is always on and no-one else can use the line.

)))➤ *Dedicated, Internet Connections*

LEGAL SUBJECTS: WEB SITES

 Law and lawyers online. There is no shortage of legal information online and the hourly rate is often cheaper.

Married in haste, divorce online … the UK-based site (*www.divorce-online.co.uk*) offers self-help advice and access (for a small fee) from a telelawyer. It also covers DIY divorce kits in the US, and if all that works out, there is, somewhat incongruously, a dating service available. If you want to search the Web for just about any conceivable legal information try the Law Crawler (*www.lawcrawler.com*). Although US-focused, Law Crawler has international sections. If you prefer to prepare your own legal documents try *www.legaldocs.com* and if you need some advice or decide you want to find a lawyer check out FreeAdvice (*www. freeadvice.com*).

)))➤ *Government online, Politics-related Web sites*

LINK

 Movement between web pages. A link, or hyperlink, allows you to go directly to another part of a web page, or perhaps to a web site on the other side of the world. To follow a hyperlink, click on it once. If the hyperlink is a word or a phrase, it will probably be underlined and the mouse will change into a hand when you place your mouse pointer over it, to let you know that it is 'hot'. A hyperlink can also be a photograph or a graphic, and the part of the screen on which you click to activate it is called a 'hotspot'. When your mouse pointer is over one of these, it will change into a hand and you can click once to be taken to the destination web page. If the image has been 'mapped' (known as an 'image map'), various sections of the image are hyperlinked to different web pages or web sites.

)))▶ *Hotspot, Hyperlink, Hypertext, World Wide Web*

LINUX

A freely distributable open-source version of the UNIX operating system that runs on many platforms. Open source means that the source code used to write the program is made available to anyone that wants it, free of charge. As a result any programmer can alter or extend the program, which is then open to peer review and further refined to remove bugs and improve

ABOVE: Browser view of www.lawcrawler.com

ABOVE RIGHT: Whether you want a wedding or a divorce, online legal advice can help

the product. Linux itself was largely developed by the Norwegian Linus Torvalds and has the advantage of running on many platforms including PCs and Macs.

)))▶ *Operating System*

LISTPROC

A UNIX-based list-server program for handling the automatic management of mailing lists. ListProc, like LISTSERV and Majordomo, is a software program that automatically manages mailing lists and is designed to run on servers using the UNIX operating system. It was created by CREN, a non-profit organization for research and educational institutions. Like other list servers, ListProc handles the administrative chores of adding and removing members from the lists and distributing messages for tens of thousands of subscribers. It can manage large numbers of lists together, whether simple announcements, newsletters or fully fledged online discussion groups.

)))▶ *Email, List Server, LISTSERV, Mailing Lists*

LISTSERV

One of the first programs to manage mailing lists, LISTSERV now administers more than 48,000 public groups. It was first developed in the 1980s for BITNET, the Because It's Time Network, and was used extensively by universities, but has successfully transferred operations to the Internet. LISTSERV automates the administrative side of mailing lists and their distribution. Users send their request to be added to or removed from a list by email, and have the choice of thousands of communities, from dog news to classic games. For the full automatically updated catalogue of some 48,000-plus public lists, see *www.lsoft.com/lists/listref.html*.

)))▶ *Email, ListProc, List Server, Mailing Lists*

LIST SERVER

A mailing-list server. Mailing-list servers can manage mailings of everything from spam to real-time delivery of subscriber messages. A list server is quite literally a server that handles mailing lists, using programs such as LISTSERV and Majordomo. There are two basic types of list handled by the servers: one-way mailing lists, home of the dreaded spam, are used for advertising, promotions and newsletters; two-way mailing lists are for more traditional discussion lists, where those who have subscribed to the list interact with other subscribers. They either get real-time delivery, where messages from other subscribers are received as soon as they are sent, or digest delivery, where just a summary of messages received over a period of time is sent.

))))▶ *Email, ListProc, LISTSERV, Mailing Lists*

LISZT (*www.liszt.com*)

Discussion-group web site. One of the best web sites for linking to discussion groups, Liszt probably lists at least one discussion group on your favourite topic.

))))▶ *Discussion Groups*

LITERATURE WEB SITES

The works of Shakespeare, Lewis Carroll and Edgar Rice Burroughs are all featured in Project Gutenberg (*www.gutenberg.net*), which is making the text of out-of-copyright works of literature available for download. Elsewhere, poetry.com now features more than

3.1 million poets; while if you are a poet and stuck for a rhyme try the rhyming dictionary (*www.rhymezone.com*).

))))▶ *Books: Electronic on the Net, Books: Purchasing*

LEFT: Music, such as Franz Liszt's (1811–86), is among the many topics up for discussion on Liszt.com
RIGHT: You may find the work of PG Wodehouse on a literature web site
FAR LEFT: Browser view of www.izwa.co.za

LOCALTALK

Network cabling system. LocalTalk provides a quick and simple way to network Apple Mac computers (and others), but is relatively slow compared to other cable systems.

LocalTalk is the quickest and most inexpensive way to set up a network of Apple Macintosh computers and other peripheral devices such as printers. The LocalTalk cables support the AppleTalk network protocol, which is built into Mac computers and allows them to communicate with one another. It can even connect PCs if they have the special AppleTalk hardware and software needed. Setting up the network involves little more than physically cabling the computers together and it is easy to maintain. The main drawback is that LocalTalk networks are relatively slow, compared with other available cabling systems, such as Ethernet.

)))⮞ **Apple Computer, LAN, Macintosh: Introduction, PC vs Mac**

LOG ON

Term meaning to enter a system or web site. Each time you connect to the Internet, you will need to log on (sometimes called 'log in'). The appropriate dialogue box will appear, according to how your computer and connection is set up. If you are using Windows, with Internet Explorer as your browser, if you are not connected to the Internet when you click on to a remote site, Dial-Up Networking's Connect to dialog box will appear and will connect you automatically if you have saved your password in the Connect To box and have configured Internet Explorer either to 'Dial whenever a network connection is not present' or 'Always dial my default connection' (select Tools|Internet Options|Connections). Otherwise, you will need to call up the Connect To dialogue box manually. Some services, such as AOL, display their own dialogue box for logging on. Either way, you type in your username and password, click the Connect button and away you go. Some web sites require you to log on, if you are a registered user.

)))⮞ **Password**

LOOKUP

Directory enquiries for computers. Just like dialling 192 on a telephone, this is the computing equivalent of directory enquiries. In this case, one computer requests information from a directory held on another. It is most commonly found on large distributed networks and intranets, where directory services store the full network addresses of all the resources available. This central telephone directory can be used by any person on the network to find the address and location of anyone else or any resources they might want to use.

))))▶ *Network*

LURK

Expression meaning to hang around chat rooms; a chance to see what is going on in chat rooms and newsgroups before deciding whether to join or not. Lurking is common and it is possibly the best way to behave if you are new to a group.

Lurking also gives you time to discover whether the group is right for you and whether you want to contribute. However, in some of the more personal chat rooms lurking is discouraged.

))))▶ *Chat, Mailing Lists, Post*

LYCOS

Online destination; originally a search engine, then a portal, now an online destination. Where once portals were just an entry point and sign bearer for the Web, they are developing into stopping places in their own right. The Lycos network includes a shopping centre; a communication centre with chat, message boards and email; a download centre; a people finder (white pages); a business finder (yellow pages); as well as the underlying search engine. Lycos.com also has the usual rich content served by most portals covering everything from games to relationships.

))))▶ *Portal, Search Engine*

LYNX

The web without the pictures. Lynx is a free text-based web browser particularly favoured by UNIX users, originally created by the University of Kansas. Unlike more common browsers such as Netscape

Navigator and Internet Explorer it does not display graphics or manage JavaScript. As a result it is much faster, for those seeking information, particularly, say, on research networks. One side benefit for schools or office administrators is that they can check that unknown sites are appropriate to view without the embarrassment of being deluged with risqué pictures.

))))▶ *Browser, Web Browser*

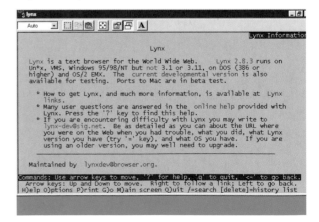

MACBINARY

File transfer protocol. The PC and the Mac differ in the way they store files. MacBinary is a file transfer protocol that saves the Mac-specific data with the file. As a result, the Macintosh file can be stored on a PC or UNIX machine or be sent over the Internet with its file information intact.

))))▶ *Apple Computer, Encryption, LAN, Mac: Introduction*

MAC: INTRODUCTION

A model of computer. Steve Wozniak and Steve Jobs started Apple Computers in 1976. Apple introduced the original Macintosh model to millions in 1984 in a TV ad based on Michael Radford's movie *1984*, depicting an Orwellian IBM world being destroyed by Apple's new computer. The Macintosh had a compact footprint, all-in-one casing and tiny 9-inch black-and-white screen; it cost $2,495. Incredibly, it had no hard disk so work had to be saved on to floppy disks. Its truly revolutionary feature, however, was a Graphical User Interface (GUI) and a mouse for pointing and clicking on the screen. The legacy of this design classic is such that all Apple computers are often fondly called 'Macs'.

))))▶ *Apple Computer, GUI, PC vs Mac*

MACROMEDIA FLASH

Flash creates animations with sound and interactivity. It uses vector graphics (in which shapes are mathematically designed rather than mapped to individual pixels) so images are smoother and file sizes lower. The movie files (with a .swf extension) are viewed through the Flash player, available free from the Macromedia site.

))))▶ *Animation, Hypermedia*

MACS: CONNECTING TO THE INTERNET

Connecting Apple Macs to the Internet. Mac owners wishing to connect to the Internet are advised to follow the guidelines given in Help|Topics|Connecting to the Internet. Here is an overview of the steps you should take to connect your Mac to the Internet using a dial-up connection:

1. Set up the modem

Many Macs have built-in modems. If not, connect an external modem. Set up the control panel called Modem following the vendor's instructions.

2. Set up PPP and TCP/IP

Your ISP should provide a disk that should make this procedure easier. Otherwise, follow the instructions provided by your ISP to manually configure the control panels, called PPP and TCP/IP.

3. Connect

With many services, such as AOL, you should simply double-click to start the service provider's software, enter your username and password and click the Connect button. If this software is not provided, you need to open the control panel called PPP and click the Connect button. Once you are connected, you can browse the Net using either the software program that is supplied by your service provider, or Internet Explorer or Netscape Navigator.

))))▶ *AOL, Apple Computer, Connecting to the Internet I: Basic, Internet Explorer, ISP, Modem I: Basic, Netscape Navigator, PPP*

ABOVE: Apple computers today are still known as Macs, after the original 1984 model
LEFT: Lynx browser
FAR LEFT: It is better to lurk before contributing in chat rooms, otherwise you may get too deeply involved

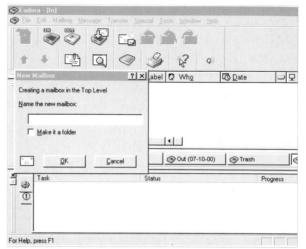

MACTCP

The method by which Apple Macs use TCP/IP to connect to the Internet, now largely replaced by the more efficient OpenTransport. As its name suggests, this is a driver that enables AppleMacs to use TCP/IP to connect to the Internet. It had the great advantage that it was largely user-transparent, i.e. if properly configured it could be accessed by any program without the user being involved. However, it has been superseded by Apple's OpenTransport communications architecture, which has brought in several enhancements in speed, performance and convenience.

)))▶ *Macs: connecting to the Net, TCP/IP*

MAILBOMBING

Attack by email. This brings the mail server to collapse by overloading it, usually by sending huge amounts of email or one giant mail. Virus writers create email worms that access users' address books and send the infected message to all their contacts, eventually crashing the server. Also referred to as denial of service (DoS) attacks.

)))▶ *Junk Email, Mailing Lists, Spam*

MAILBOT

Automated mail program. Your automated answering service, mailbots will respond to emails or carry out actions based on instructions in the message. One example is a mailing-list manager, which carries out a number of tasks without any human supervision.

It will accept messages sent in, send copies to the list members and handle requests to join or leave a mailing list. You can also set up your email client to reply automatically to any message sent or to forward it on to someone else.

)))▶ *Email, Program, Replying to Email, Sending Email*

MAILBOX

Container for email. A mailbox usually refers to a folder on the mail-server computer run by an ISP or OSP, that contains a person's email messages. If you use the popular AOL service, you will find that your email messages are contained in a mailbox.

It is divided into New Email – email sent to you that you have not yet read, Old Email – email that you have read and saved, Sent Email – copies of email that you have sent.

)))▶ *Email, ISP, Mail Server, OSP*

ABOVE: Eudora - New Mailbox
LEFT: A computer mailbox is a folder containing the user's email messages

MAILING LIST

Email-based discussion groups, where the administration can be handled automatically. A mailing list is a way of connecting people who share common interests. They are email-based discussion groups, which cover everything from growing palm trees to Chinese medicine. They may be open to anyone (open list) or subscribers may be vetted (closed list). Lists can also be moderated, where messages are screened by a list administrator, or unmoderated where all emails are automatically sent to everyone on the list. The distribution of messages and handling of subscriptions can be done automatically by a mailing list manager (MLM).

))))▶ *Discussion Groups, Email, List Server, ListProc, LISTSERV, Liszt*

MAIL SERVER

The central sorting office for your incoming and outgoing emails. Essentially the post office itself. It is here that incoming and outgoing mail is sorted and routed on. SMTP (Simple Mail Transfer Protocol) is the system used for sending messages between servers and also from your email client, such as Outlook Express, to the mail server. The server holds any messages received until you log on and retrieve them using either the POP3 protocol or IMAP. Once downloaded, the messages are usually deleted from the server, although copies can be kept.

))))▶ *Email, ISP, Server*

MAINTENANCE: COMPUTER

There are a number of tools for computer maintenance supplied with Windows. Disk Cleanup frees up your hard drive, Disk Defragmenter makes it run smoothly and Scandisk repairs it.

))))▶ *Disk Tools*

MAJORDOMO

A freeware mailing list manager, Majordomo doesn't handle mail delivery itself. Majordomo gets its name from the latin *major domus* ('master of the house'). It is free software for managing mailing lists that runs under the UNIX operating system. It does not handle the mail delivery itself, but controls the list for other programs to handle. When email is sent to the list by a subscriber it is automatically broadcast to everyone else on the list. Unlike

Internet-based newsgroups or forums the messages are only available via email and just go to members on the list.

))))▶ *Listserver, LISTSERV*

MAKING FRIENDS ON THE INTERNET

Friendship on the Net. One of the great things about the Internet is that it has opened up a host of new ways to meet people and make friends. Here are some of the best ways to make contact:

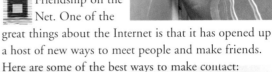

I. Chat
Many web sites have chat facilities where you can participate in online conversations on a variety of subjects. Chat rooms are often monitored by someone who ensures that people do not break the rules of chat. All good chat areas provide guidelines for conduct. Parents should take care that children only join reputable, secure chat services.

2. Discussion groups
These are organized by topic and are good forums for communicating with others who share your interests.

3. Email
Many people are finding that email provides a new way to keep in touch with friends. Email encourages quick and informal messages and has spawned its own language called emoticons. However, it does not convey extra clues such as your tone of voice when speaking, so be aware that you can be misunderstood when making a funny comment.

4. IM (Instant Messages)
This service, offered by popular OSPs such as AOL and others, is an even more immediate form of messaging than email. This system allows you to have a conversation in real-time with someone. It is ideal for gossip and chat.

))))▶ *Chat, Discussion Groups, Email, IM, IRC, OSP, Relationships: Advice on Smileys and Emoticons*

ABOVE: Windows provides maintenance tools, so there is no need to get a builder in

MAPPING DRIVES/PRINTERS

Sharing network resources. If you are connected to a local area network (LAN) you can use the disk drives on other PCs and share printers. To access the files stored on another computer's disk drive, or the printer, you have to map the route: that is, tell your PC the way to connect to it. In the process it will be given a different drive letter. In WindowsXP you can do this by clicking on the Map Drive button in My Network Places.

))))➤ *Network drive*

MEDIA

Media on the Web. On the Internet, 'media' (or 'multimedia') commonly refers to audio and visual elements on the Web. The following are the most common types of media you can enjoy:

Animation: Requires the Flash plug-in for your browser
Video: View in your browser as streaming media using RealPlayer, or Quick Time
Audio: Hear as streaming media using RealPlayer or Quick Time; online radio stations use this method; or download files (MP3s, for example) to play on your hard disk
Graphics: View in your browser; you can also download graphics to your hard drive

))))➤ *Flash, Hypermedia, MP3, RealPlayer, Streaming Audio/Video*

MEDIA PLAYERS

As the Internet becomes a true multimedia experience, your computer has to be able to handle everything from live music concerts to news bulletins and online film trailers. To do so it needs a media player. Among the best known are RealPlayer, QuickTime, Yahoo Player and Windows Media Player. Originally, players did little more than play back sound and video files. They still do this and by buffering the files they do so in near realtime, playing the song before the whole file is downloaded. In addition to this the top players can do everything from organizing your files into personal

TOP: Unlike the more traditional form of media: the newspaper, the web can display animation, video, audio and graphics
ABOVE: Windows Media Player

LEFT: *QuickTime Player*

BELOW: *Luckily, computers have better long-term memories than humans*

playlists, accessing streaming media, even recording (ripping) tracks from audio CDs and encoding them in a format that can be stored on your hard drive. Some players will burn tracks to your CD-RW or CD-R drive. But different players use different formats and will not always play files encoded in a rival format. As a result you will probably need to have several types of player on your PC. These can be downloaded from the manufacturer's web site or the site that hosts the material.

))))➡ *AVI, Media, MIDI, Movies, MP3, WMA*

MEMORY

Generally, any device that can store information, but the term is usually used to refer to data stored on chips. Every computer has some physical memory, also known as RAM (Random Access Memory), which stores data that can be accessed quickly. Electronic memory chips, like these, can only remember data for as long as the PC is switched on. By contrast, information stored on a disk remains even when the power is off, as it is stored magnetically.

))))➡ *Buffer, Cache, Chip, Clipboard*

MENUS

Onscreen lists of choices. Sets of options presented as lists in software programs. For example, Windows has its Start menu, which opens up to reveal all its other menus, and the Apple Mac desktop has a menu bar at the top of the screen.

))))➡ *GUI, Windows*

METACRAWLER (*www.metacrawler.com*)

Search engine. MetaCrawler is a metasearch program that searches the indexes of other search engines.

))))➡ *Metasearch Program, Search Engine*

METASEARCH PROGRAM

A multiple search engine; a metasearch program queries several search sites at once and then cleans up and merges the results. Every search engine has its particular strengths – areas where it may have the most comprehensive or recent information – but there is not the time to trawl through several sites to see which one would be best for a particular query. Metasearch engines have been developed to do just this. With programs such as Copernic Pro, the query is sent to several search engines and indexes simultaneously. When the results come back, the metasearch program goes through and removes any duplicates or dead links.

))))➡ *MetaCrawler, Search Engine*

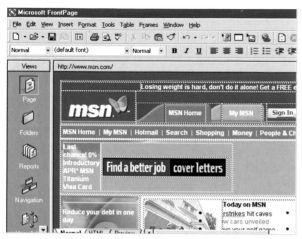

BELOW: MIME refers not to Marcel Marceau's profession, but to a file conversion format

http://support. microsoft.com and offers several ways to get help. There is the vast searchable database, dubbed the *Knowledge Base*, *FAQ lists* and *Newsgroups* where other users offer their experience.

)))) **FAQ, Help Menu, Troubleshooting**

MIDI

'Musical Instrument Digital Interface'; a standard for controlling musical instruments via your computer. A MIDI is a special interface that lets your computer control musical instruments, such as a synthesizer, keyboard or drum machine. To create a MIDI setup you need a MIDI interface for your PC – which is often part of a sound card – and a cable that runs to your musical instrument. The MIDI protocol also sets out how the musical messages are sent. The files themselves are small because they are like a musical score, where the notes and

MICROSOFT FRONTPAGE

Web authoring tool. For those who do not want to code their web page from scratch there are web authoring tools, one of the most popular of which, for Windows, is Microsoft's FrontPage. It is a good tool for beginners – or businesses wanting to get online quickly – as it offers a number of wizards to smooth the whole process. It also provides several themes and templates, complete with the art-work for backgrounds, icons and banners that can be easily customized to get you up and running. As well as an HTML editor FrontPage has its own site management tool. One drawback of FrontPage, as with most web authoring packages, is that it still produces 'bloated' code compared with the straight HTML-coding of professional web authors. That is, it takes more lines of code to achieve the same effect and it includes its own proprietary tags that may not be recognized by all browsers. There are also FrontPage extensions, scripts that run on the server and give you handy features for your site such as hit counter, user registration and surveys. However, to use these your web-hosting service provider needs to support FrontPage extensions.

)))) **Web Authoring, Web Page: Creating I, Web Page: Creating II**

MICROSOFT SUPPORT

Online product support. Perhaps it is not surprising given that most of the world's PCs run Microsoft operating systems, but Microsoft has a massive online support operation. It is accessible from

instruments are shown, the actual sound itself is not stored. MIDI files have the extension .mid.

))))➡ *Media Players, Music on the Internet*

MIL

Top-level domain name. If the end part of a web site's URL is .mil it indicates that the type of organization hosting the computer is linked to the military. In fact, .mil is one of the predefined suffixes, such as .gov and .edu that are known as top-level domains.

))))➡ *Address, Domain, Hostname, URL, Zone*

MIME

'Multipurpose Internet Mail Extensions'; file conversion format. MIME is taking over from uuencode as the preferred way of sending email attachments across the Internet. Any binary file attachment, such as a picture, spreadsheet or program, needs to be converted into plain ASCII text to be sent over the Internet and then reassembled, i.e. decoded at the receiving end. Many email clients now support MIME as the best way to do this. The same MIME standard can also be used by web browsers and servers to show files that are not in the normal HTML format.

))))➡ *Sending Email*

MIRROR

A duplicate web site or FTP server that is set up to reduce the load on the original server. It is an exact copy and has the advantage that it makes access to sites or files faster. Normally mirror sites are set up in different geographic regions. So, for example, the shareware site Tuscows has several mirror sites dotted around the world. If you select the one nearest to you it is likely that you can download files faster than if you were trying to access a central server in the US.

))))➡ *File Transfer, FTP*

BELOW: Mirror sites are set up to reduce traffic on the original server
FAR LEFT: www.msn.com home page in Microsoft FrontPage

MLM

'Mailing List Manager'; list server program. MLM programs will automate the handling of subscription requests and the distribution of postings to those on the lists. It does not do anything that could not be done manually, but it automates the whole process and is scalable, so it can handle lists sent to a few subscribers or to tens of thousands. MLM programs will respond to any email requests sent to them and primarily handle requests to join or leave mailing lists. They also manage the broadcast of messages to those on the list, although they do not always handle the delivery directly.

))))➡ *Email, ListProc, List Server, LISTSERV, Mailing List*

MODEM I: INTRODUCTION

Device connecting computer to telephone line. Modem is an acronym for MOdulator-DEModulator. It is a device that enables a computer to transmit data over telephone lines. It does this by converting the computer's digital data into analogue sound waves for transmission (modulating), and converting incoming analogue sound waves back into digital data (demodulating).

You need a modem in order to connect your computer to the Internet via a dial-up connection. There are two types for a desktop computer: internal and external.

Internal modems: these come as standard with many computers. They are circuit boards plugged into an expansion slot inside the computer. A cable between the computer and the telephone socket is required.

External modems: these are separate plastic boxes that come with at least two cables. One connects to the appropriate socket at the rear of your computer; the other goes into the telephone socket. Many also have their own power cord.

Many modems also function as fax machines and answering machines, and you might find these features important to you. The most important consideration, though, is likely to be how fast a modem can transmit and receive data. The latest models transfer data at up to 56 Kbps and older types work at 33 Kbps and 28.8 Kbps.

))))➤ *Connecting to the Internet: Basic, External Modem, Internal Modem*

MODEM II: CHOOSING

Choosing a modem. If you do not have an internal modem already built in to your computer and you want to connect to the Internet via a dial-up connection, you need to get yourself a modem. Here are the main things you should consider when choosing one:

1. Internal vs External

Internal modems are more fiddly to install but are neater. External modems are easier to install but add a little clutter.

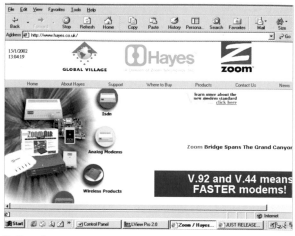

2. Speed

This is how fast the modem can transmit and receive data and is measured in bps (bits per seconds). The latest models can transfer data at 56 Kbps and older types work at 33 Kbps and 28.8 Kbps. Bear in mind, though, that the data transfer speed is limited by your telephone line, which could be slower than your modem!

3. Voice/Data

Many modems can switch between voice and data modes. In data mode, the modem acts like a regular modem. In voice mode, the modem acts like a regular telephone.

4. Auto-answer An auto-answer modem enables your computer to receive calls in your absence.

5. Data Compression Data compression enables modems to send data at faster rates.

6. Flash Memory Modems equipped with flash memory can be updated if necessary.

7. Fax Most modern modems are fax modems, which means that they can send and receive faxes.

))))➤ *Connecting to the Internet: Basic, External Modem, Internal Modem*

MODEM III: INSTALLING

Installing an external modem is a fairly simple process, thanks to the modern PC's plug and play capabilities. However, they do have their individual quirks so before you start it is advisable to read the manufacturer's instructions for any special requirements. The first step is to connect the modem physically. It needs an external power supply, so connect it to the mains supply using the cable or power adapter provided. While the PC is off, attach one end of the serial cable to the modem and the other to the PC. This will usually be to the COM 1 port, but you may have a mouse installed there, in which case use COM 2. Plug one end of the telephone cable into the modem and the other into the telephone socket, switch on the modem and power up the PC. With plug-and-play the operating system will usually detect the new hardware automatically as well as its make and model and then install all the drivers needed to make it work correctly. Some external modems attach to the USB port. The process is fairly similar, although the modem software may need to be installed first, before the device is physically connected to the PC.

))))➤ *External Modem, Internal Modem*

MODEM IV: CONFIGURING

Not all modems are automatically detected when connected to the PC and sometimes help is needed to configure them. The process is fairly similar for any Windows-based PC and involves launching the Install New Modem Wizard. With WindowsXP this is done from the Phone and Modem Options control panel. To get there go Start|Settings|Control panel|Phone and Modems Options. On the Modems tab click Add. Windows will automatically try and detect the modem, to prevent this tick the box by:

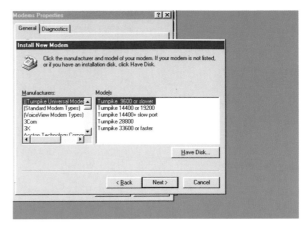

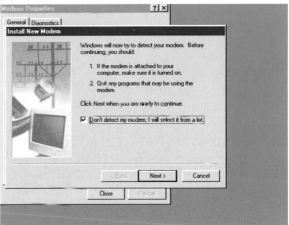

Do not detect my modem; I will select it from a list and click next. From the list select the appropriate manufacturer and model for your modem. Alternatively, if the manufacturer has supplied a disk with the drivers on it, select Have Disk… and browse to where the file is located on the CD-Rom or floppy disk. Click next. Having installed the drivers you then need to tell the operating system which port is being used. Select the right one from the list that appears, it will usually be COM 1 unless you already have something installed there, and then click Finish. Your modem should now be ready to connect you to the Internet.

))))➤ *External Modem, Internal Modem*

LEFT: Browser view of www.hayes.co.uk

ABOVE: Follow the instructions: installing your modem should be simple

etc. When you dial up to the Internet, via your service provider, you are connecting to a modem attached to their server. When the basic connection between the modems is established they exchange information in a process known as handshaking. Through the handshake the modems establish what protocols they both support and decide which transmission speeds and error-checking method to use. Although the fastest modems run at 56 Kbps download (33.6 Kbps upload) noise on the line frequently forces modems to connect at lower speeds.

))))➤ *External Modem, Handshaking, Internal Modem*

MODERATED MAILING LIST

Mailing list administration. Censorship or sensible? With moderated mailing lists, messages are sent to the list administrator before being distributed to other subscribers. This way the messages can be screened by the administrator (moderator) to make sure they are relevant to the list and that they are not duplicated. This is a good way to cut down on spam. In some cases the moderator will also check that the mailings do not contain any inflammatory, offensive, or abusive, statements. With unmoderated lists all messages are automatically sent to everyone listed.

))))➤ *Email, ListProc, List server, LISTSERV, Mailing List, Moderator*

MODERATOR

Mailing list administrator. A moderator is part censor and part administrator. With moderated mailing lists, messages are sent to an administrator before

MODEM V: TECHNICAL

Whereas the computer works on digital signals, binary bits of information that are either on or off, the telephone works with analogue information, a continuous stream that varies in frequency and strength. The modem enables the computer to send data over the phone lines by converting digital signals to analogue to send (modulating) and then back again to receive (demodulating). It is from this MOdulating/DEModulating that the modem gets its name. The modem is controlled by software on the PC using the AT command set (it is also known as Hayes after the modem manufacturer of that name). This tells the modem what to do, such as open the line, dial a number, transmit data

RIGHT: Movies on the Net are used mainly for trailers and webcasts

being sent on to the other subscribers. This way the moderator can make sure the messages are linked to the list's theme and cut out any spam. Moderators will also check that mailings do not contain anything that might cause offence. Similarly with newsgroups a moderator has the authority to block any messages that they believe are inappropriate.

)))➤ *Email, ListProc, List Server, LISTSERV, Moderated Mailing List, Spam*

MOSAIC

The first web browser. Mosaic, the original web browser, was invented by Marc Andreesen. It had a graphical user interface (GUI), and its launch in 1993 helped to popularize the Web. Its author went on to develop Netscape Navigator.

)))➤ *Browser, GUI, Internet in the 1990s: History, Netscape Navigator, Web Browser*

MOVIES

Currently, most movies seen on the PC screen are trailers. Depending on the speed of your connection, they are somewhat jerkily played back in a small screen window by your media player. However, as broadband connections such as ADSL become more popular, the Internet is seen as a great delivery mechanism for movies on demand. Services are likely to spring up over the Internet, not just for the Hollywood blockbusters but for video webcasts of concerts and conferences as well.

)))➤ *AVI, Film and TV Web Sites, IMDB, Media Players, Video*

MPEG/MPG

'Moving (Motion) Picture Experts Group'; a standard format for video files that uses lossy compression techniques. It is an industry body that develops the standard for video file compression. Many video clips on the Internet are saved as MPEG files and will need a plug-in to play them back. MPEG (pronounced m-peg) uses a type of lossy compression to get the file size as low as possible. It does this by storing only the changes from one frame to the next rather than the entire frame. The file extension is .mpg.

)))➤ *AVI, Media, Media Players, Movies, Video*

MP3

Audio compression format; a sound file format that is leading to controversy in the music industry over illegal trading. MP3 is the file extension for MPEG audio layer 3, a standard for audio compression. It can shrink a sound track by 12:1 without affecting the sound quality. However, special software is needed to rip the tracks from a CD and for playback. Because MP3 files are small they are easily transferred across the Internet and the music industry is worried that it makes it easy for copyrighted songs to be traded illegally.

)))➤ *Compression, Hypermedia, Media, Sound File*

TOP: *Browser view of* www.mp3.com
ABOVE: *With this shower MP3 player you can scan tracks and sing as you wash*

MSN (*www.msn.com*)

Online Service Provider and portal. Microsoft's MSN web site is one of the most popular web sites and a main rival to the AOL service. It functions both as an OSP and a portal. Subscribers in the US can connect to the Internet using MSN as an OSP, with a choice of dial-up or faster DSL connections. MSN is also a portal for all users of the Internet that offers a host of features and content including MSN Messenger, Hotmail, search, shopping, chat and news.

⟫⟫▶ *AOL, OSP, Portal*

MSN MESSENGER

Demand for the convenience of instant messaging (IM) has grown so dramatically that Microsoft now includes an IM program in its new operating system, Windows XP. Dubbed Windows Messenger it provides real-time voice, video and text communications, not to mention multi-player games, file downloads etc. It is a more advanced program than MSN Messenger, which is Microsoft's IM program for anyone running any other

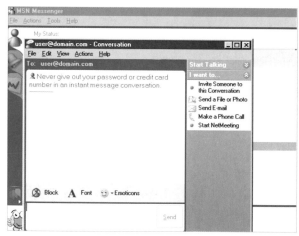

type of Windows or using the Macintosh operating system. Currently, it does not handle video, but it deals with the back-and-forth messaging much as any other IM

TOP: The method of message delivery has come a long way since the nineteenth century
ABOVE: MSN Messenger | Instant Message

client does. Like the other programs, contact details are stored on the server as well as the local machine so you can access your list of friends from any Messenger-enabled computer (although not from the Web). However, you can use Messenger for PC-to-PC phone calls and for PC-to-phone calls. It also provides access to Microsoft's new web-based service .NET Alerts, which lets you know instantly of everything from sports scores to the latest software updates. Useful as they may be those alerts won't be picked up by non-Microsoft IM clients as rival IM systems still cannot communicate with each other. This means that to talk to all of your friends and contacts you will need several IM clients.

))))▶ *AIM, ICQ, IM, Netscape Messenger*

MUD

'Multi-User Dungeon'; role-playing games and chat. MUD has spread from its beginnings as a multi-user role-playing game to real-time chat using fantasy characters.

Its exact meaning is as murky as its name suggests. MUD can stand for Multi-User Dungeon, or Domain, or Dimension. It reflects the way MUD has spread across the Net. Essentially, MUDs are fictional worlds where many users can join in a role-playing game, at the same time, and interact with each other. But it has also evolved to cover real-time chat, set in 3D worlds, where users take on imaginary identities (avatars) to represent them in this virtual world, or cyberspace. MUDs are also called 3-D worlds and chat worlds.

))))▶ *Games on the Net, Usenet*

MULTIMEDIA

Audio and visual media on the Web. Any combination of text, graphics, video, animation or audio within a web page or an application. Faster modems and broadband access are making it possible to enjoy various forms of multimedia on the Web. The following are the most common types of multimedia:

Animation: Requires the Flash plug-in for your browser
Video: View in your browser as streaming media using RealPlayer, or Quick Time
Audio: Hear as streaming media using RealPlayer, or Quick Time; online radio stations use this method; or download files (MP3s, for example) to play on your hard disk
Graphics: View in your browser; you can also download graphics to your hard drive.

))))▶ *Flash, Hypermedia, Media, MP3, Streaming Audio/Video*

MULTI-PLATFORM

Also referred to as cross-platform, multi-platform is where software or hardware devices work across a number of different platforms. For example, the LINUX operating system can be run on Intel-based PCs as well as Motorola-based Apple Macintosh computers, while Java is a high-level programming language that will work on any computer platform.

))))▶ *Apple Computer, Java, Linux, Mac: Introduction, Windows Operating System*

MULTI-TASKING

Operating systems can appear to run several programs at once by allowing them all processor time and switching quickly between them. Multi-tasking is when an operating system runs several tasks (programs) at the same time. In reality, as it has a single processor, the computer is switching very rapidly between the tasks to give the impression that they are running in parallel. The most common type of multi-tasking, used in the latest versions of Windows and UNIX, is pre-emptive multi-tasking where the operating system gives each program a slice of processor time. Generally, the active program, the one in the foreground, gets most of the processing time while those in the background get less.

))))▶ *Application, Multithreaded, Program, Windows*

MULTITHREADED

In complex programs multithreading enables several processes to run simultaneously. Whereas multi-tasking is running several programs at once, multi-threading is running several processes within a single program. The program switches rapidly between the different processes, called threads. For example, a multi-threaded application such as Word can print in the background; or a browser, such as Internet Explorer, will download several images at once in order to speed up performance. With computers that have several processors it is possible to create multithreaded programs that work in parallel running different threads on different processors. But care has to be taken to make sure the threads do not interfere with each other.

▶ *Application, Multitasking, Program, Windows*

MUSEUM WEB SITES

History in digital form. If you are stuck for where to start The National Virtual Museum is a gateway to museum attractions and galleries around the UK, or for further afield try the directory of online museums at *www.icom.org/vlmp/*. Virtual galleries can be as inspiring as the real thing, like New York's Museum of Modern Art (*www.moma.org*) or London's National Gallery (*www.nationalgallery.org.uk*). Often described as one of the great wonders of the Internet is the Library of Congress site (*http://memory.loc.gov*), with its multimedia history of America that features more than seven-million digital items from more than 100 museums.

▶ *Art Web Sites, Education on the Internet*

MUSIC ON THE INTERNET

Music is one of the key selling points of the Internet, whether it is to listen to, to buy, to share Napster-style, to talk about or to perform. It is thanks in part to the development of the MP3 format, which enables sound files to be compressed, making them quicker to download, while keeping near FM-radio quality. Coupled with the increasing sophistication of the

media players, such as Winamp and RealPlayer, streaming audio is the new force on the Web. That means you can listen to a piece of music as soon as it starts to download, as it transfers quickly enough to keep up with the

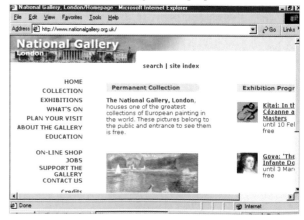

ABOVE RIGHT: Some museums can now be viewed virtually on the Web
RIGHT: Browser view of www.nationalgallery.org.uk

playback. Because MP3 files are small while maintaining quality, they are easily sent across the Internet. File-sharing services such as Napster arose that enabled users to find and exchange MP3 files directly with each other. The music industry became worried that copyrighted songs were being traded illegally. After a series of court battles that involved the suspension of file-sharing and the introduction of a membership service, new measures have been introduced to protect copyright material further.

)))) **CDs and Tapes, DVD, Media Players, MIDI, MP3, WMA**

NAME REGISTRATION

Like any company name, a domain name needs to be registered. It is the domain name that uniquely identifies and locates your system on the Internet. There are many commercial registrars who sell domain names and nearly all provide a search facility so you can check whether your chosen domain name is still available.

)))) **DNS, Domain, Network Solutions**

ABOVE: Music can be heard, bought, downloaded, discussed and performed online
RIGHT: You can now appreciate nature from the comfort of your armchair

NAME SERVER

Maps domain names to IP addresses to enable computers to communicate with one another; more typically known as a DNS server. The name server maps the name of a web site to its numerical IP address so that other computers can communicate with it. In effect, it is a giant database distributed to name servers all around the world. When an URL is typed into the browser, it asks the closest name server to translate this into an IP address. If the name server has come across this address recently it will return the information from its cache and reply. If not, it will work its way through other name servers until the answer is found.

)))) **DNS, Domain, Host, IP Address**

NATURE WEB SITES

Nature on the Internet; virtual world guides to the environment and life in our real world. London's Natural History Museum (*www.nhm.ac.uk*) is also a portal to the pick of internet resources on natural history through its link with the Resource Discovery Network. This search engine has sites reviewed by academic experts and can be a little dry in style. The

less modest Environmental Organization Web Directory (*www.webdirectory.com*) claims to be the Earth's biggest environment search engine. If you prefer to view nature from your armchair then discover the habits of the Great White Bear or listen to dolphins talking on PBS (*www.pbs.org/neighbourhoods/nature/*).

)))) **Education on the Internet, Science Web Sites, Weather Online**

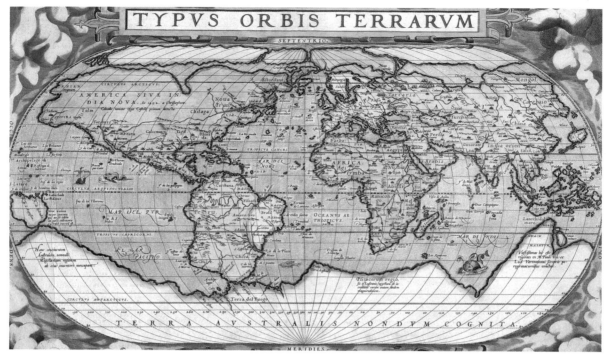

NAVIGATION

Finding your way around the Web. The beauty of the Web is that – with the help of a browser such as Internet Explorer or Netscape Navigator – you can go anywhere you like simply by pointing your mouse and clicking. Here are a few ways to navigate the Web:

1. If you know the address of the web site you want to visit, type its address in the Address box of your browser and click the Go button.
2. Use the Back and Forward buttons to go to the previous and next pages.
3. Click the Home button to go to your home page.
4. Click on hyperlinks – whenever your mouse pointer turns into a hand, you can click on the word or image and be taken to wherever the link leads.

➤ *Browser, Explorer, Internet Explorer, Hyperlink, Netscape Navigator, Web Browser*

NET

Top-level domain name; originally for companies involved with networking, .net is now generally used, just like the new TLDs, to help satisfy demand for domain names. Like most of the predefined top-level domain names, such as .org, demand for web addresses is such that old distinctions have disappeared. Any company can register their domain with the final .net tag. To help satisfy the growing demand the number of top-level domains has been widened. Among the new ones introduced are .biz and .info.

➤ *Address, Domain, Hostname, URL, Zone*

NETIQUETTE

Etiquette on the Net. A contraction from internet etiquette, this covers the basic rules of how to behave when surfing the Net. Every area of the Net has its own particular netiquette, such as not sending flames to people in newsgroups, although some still do overstep the mark. For example, whether you are sending an email or chatting it is rude to shout (that is write everything in CAPITAL letters). To a certain extent, the rules of netiquette are policed by other users. They will speedily object if they think you are crossing the borders of polite behaviour.

➤ *Discussion Groups, Flame, Internet, Mailing Lists, Newsgroups*

LEFT: You can travel anywhere you like – on the web of course – just by clicking your mouse

RIGHT: Netscape Composer with a page from www.netscape.com

NETSCAPE COMPOSER

HTML editor. Composer is a WYSIWYG (What You See Is What You Get) HTML editor that is packaged with the browser Netscape Navigator. It is a more basic product than full web-authoring suites such as Microsoft's FrontPage, but its benefit is that it allows the creation of simple web pages and it can be used by people who have no knowledge of HTML. It lets a user insert links, images and tables, format the text, check spelling and then publish – upload the files – to your web server.

)))⯈ *Web Authoring, Web Page: Creating I, Web Page: Creating II*

NETSCAPE MESSENGER

Email client. As the email client of Netscape's suite of internet tools, Messenger enables you to send, receive and organize email messages. As with Microsoft's messaging program, Outlook Express, Messenger handles newsgroup messages as well as normal emails. On setting it up you will need to enter details of your service provider's incoming mail server (POP3 or IMAP) and outgoing mail server (SMTP). Messenger lets you set up filter rules to organize mail that comes in automatically, such as deleting the message (handy for junk mail), or moving it to a different folder.

)))⯈ *AIM, ICQ, IM, MSN Messenger*

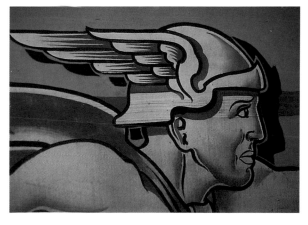

NETSCAPE NAVIGATOR

Web browser software program. The Netscape Navigator browser was launched by Netscape in 1994. Its author was Marc Andreesen, the inventor of the pioneering Mosaic browser. Netscape offered a wave of new releases with improved features, and by mid-1995 it had become the browser of choice for 80 per cent of web surfers. Since then, Microsoft's rival browser, Internet Explorer, has overtaken Navigator in popularity. The Netscape company was sold to AOL Time Warner. Netscape 6.2, the latest browser suite from the company, includes integrated email accounts, instant messaging, address book, search and other tools and plug-ins.

)))⯈ *Browser, Browser Wars, Internet Explorer, Mosaic, Web Browser*

NETSCAPE SUPPORT

Online support from Netscape comes at different levels depending on the degree of technical knowledge you have. Access to Netscape's online support is from their web site at *http://help.netscape.com/*. There is a quick help section that deals with user queries on the browsers or Netscape's services, such as its download centre, its Instant Messenger program or its personalized portal, My Netscape. With the browsers it goes through common problems and installation or upgrade issues. It also has links to a reference section and the developers' section where much more detailed technical information and discussion groups are available.

)))⯈ *FAQ, Help Menu, Netscape Navigator, Troubleshooting*

NETWORK

Computers linked together. A network is a group of computers connected together so that they can exchange data. Computers on a network are sometimes called nodes. Computers and devices that allocate resources for a network are called servers. The first network of computers was the American ARPAnet. It was built in 1969 to test the theory that a network could withstand an atomic bomb attack better than any other configuration. This was the ancestor of the Internet. We now find it difficult to see the point of computers without networks. Networks are identified by different names according to their size and function.

1. Internet

This is, of course, the best-known and largest of them all. It is a global network of servers to which millions of people are linked. The Internet itself comprises many networks. At their core are the backbone networks, which are large optical cable systems linking centres in major cities around the world.

2. Intranet

A privately operated network that employs Internet technology and applications to enable people within an organization to browse web pages, use email and messaging.

3. Extranet

A network operated by an organization that connects to another organization's network using secure Internet technologies, usually for business purposes.

4. Local-area network (LAN)

A network of computers geographically close together, usually in the same building or complex. Local-area networks typically allow people in an organization to share printers, share internal information on web pages and communicate by email or conferencing systems. A single LAN can be connected to other LANs to form a wide-area network.

5. Wide-area network (WAN)

A network of computers that are typically spread over a wide geographical area. They can combine any number of local-area networks. The world's largest WAN is the Internet.

Networks can be linked together by different means. These can range from cables or wireless systems to telephone lines, leased lines or satellite links. Networks have other features that distinguish them. A network's topology is the geometric arrangement of a computer system, such as bus, star, or ring. The protocol of a network defines the rules and signals that computers on the network use to communicate. There are two main types of network architecture: client/server, in which multiple client computers are connected to a single server; peer-to-peer, in which multiple computers communicate without needing a server.

))))▶ *Internet, Network Computer, Network Drive, Network Neighbourhood, Network Protocol, Network Server*

NETWORK COMPUTER

A minimal spec computer that relies for its power and storage space on the network server. The network computer is a slimline version of a full PC; accordingly, it is sometimes referred to as a thin client. In essence, it is a slimmed down computer that relies for its storage space and much of its processing power on the network server. The idea is that most people do not need the power of a typical PC, so the thin client will have minimal memory and processor power. Often it will have no hard drive at all and will instead use the server to store data. Network computers that are specifically designed to connect to the Internet are also known as NetPCs.

))))▶ *Network, Network Drive, Network Neighbourhood, Network Protocol, Network Server*

NETWORK DRIVE

Disk drives on other computers on the network that can be accessed and used. On a peer-to-peer network (where there is no server and each PC has roughly the same capabilities and role) it is quite simple to set up sharing. For each computer to see the other they need to be

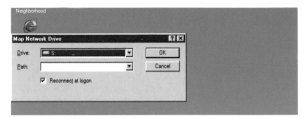

using the same protocol and to be assigned to the same workgroup with sharing enabled. On a client/server architecture the sharing of resources is typically controlled by the network server.

))))▶ *Network, Network Computer, Network Neighbourhood, Network protocol, Network Server*

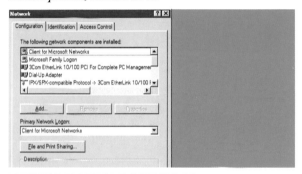

NETWORK NEIGHBOURHOOD

Despite its new name of My Network Places, the Network Neighbourhood (NN) remains an access point to all shared resources on local networks and the Internet. The Network Neighbourhood has gone through something of a rebrand with the latest flavours of the Windows Operating System and has been renamed My Network Places. It serves essentially the same function, however, as a window accessed from its desktop icon to all the shared connections available to your computer. It has been extended under WindowsXP to cover Internet-based connections, including access to online storage spaces and shortcuts to favourite web sites. Using the Map Drive button you can launch a Wizard to assign drive letters to remote drives and folders and make them accessible locally.

))))▶ *Network, Network Computer, Network Drive, Network Protocol, Network Server*

ABOVE: To see which network components have been installed on your computer click on the Network Neighborhood desktop icon and select Configuration

NETWORK PROTOCOL

A network communication standard; computers sharing a network need to use the same protocol in order to communicate successfully. If one computer uses a different protocol from the others, they will not be able to understand one another. On LANs, where computers are typically within the same building, the most popular network protocol is Ethernet, which can transfer data at speeds up to 10 Mbps. The newer version, Gigabit Ethernet, transfers data at a supersonic 1 gigabit (1,000 Mb) per second.

))))▶ *LAN, Network, Network Computer, Network Drive, Network Neighbourhood, Network server*

NETWORK SERVER

Machine that controls activity on the network. It is usually a dedicated computer (meaning it does nothing other than its server tasks), which runs the network operating system and controls what happens on the network. In order to control the traffic over the network all the workstations (PCs) on the LAN need to connect to it. The network operating system, such as Windows 2000, determines who is authorized to access the network. It also manages users' access to shared resources on the network, such as storage drives and printers.

))))▶ *Network, Network Computer, Network Drive, Network Neighbourhood, Network Protocol*

NETWORK SOLUTIONS

Internet registration services. Now owned by VeriSign Inc., this site offers domain name, digital certificate and also payment services.

))))▶ *DNS, Domain, Name Registration*

ABOVE: Newsgroups are global discussion forums that can stimulate discussion on a variety of subjects

NEWSGROUPS

Global discussion forums. Most newsgroups are part of Usenet, the worldwide bulletin board. Using a newsgroup reader, people can post messages or reply to existing ones from other users. Discussions on particular topics, within the general subject area, are grouped together into threads. The newsgroups may be moderated, whereby each message is first screened by an administrator to make sure it is appropriate before being posted. Some newgroups, however, are unmoderated; in unmoderated newsgroups all messages are automatically posted. If you subscribe to a newsgroup, new messages to that group will be delivered to you whenever you check the news server.

))))▶ *Newsreader, News Server, Usenet*

NEWBIE

A newcomer to the Internet. New users have to get their experience somehow and among the newsgroups and chat rooms the best way is to lurk. With the projected global growth of the Net there are millions of newbies yet to come online. While it is fairly easy – and anonymous – to surf the Web for the first time, chat rooms and newsgroups are more challenging for the newcomer. This is why it's a good idea to lurk – observe what's going on – until you feel ready to take part.

))))▶ *Discussion Groups, Internet, Lurk,*
Mailing Lists, Newsgroups

RIGHT: Surfing the web for the first time can be something of a revelation
ABOVE: There is something for everyone on the Internet, whether it is reading
the New York Times *or catching up on the latest tennis news*

NEWSGROUPS: A SELECTIVE DIRECTORY OF GROUPS

Newsgroups cover every imaginable subject, from aliens to TV gossip. The newsgroups themselves are divided into hierarchies. The top-level categories include 'rec' (recreation), 'alt' (alternative) and 'comp' (computing). These are then subdivided into further categories, such as alt.fan and can then be further subdivided, e.g. alt.fan.james-bond. There are also a number of newsgroups on adult themes and on some of the murkier habits of hacking and cracking. Just because you can find it on the Internet, though, does not mean it is legal. Below is a highly selective guide to illustrate the enormous variety of groups available.

Art
alt.ascii-art How to make the most of your smileys
alt.binaries.pictures.utilities Graphics software

Books
alt.usage.english Grammatically correct
biz.books.technical As it says on the cover
alt.books.pratchett For fans of author Terry Pratchett

ABOVE: Air 'your' views on alt.politics.usa.msc
RIGHT: You can keep up with the latest headlines with News Online

Business and finance
alt.business.import-export The ins and outs of business
Misc.invest.stocks Tips for the brave

Comedy
rec.arts.comics.marketplace Trade those old comics
alt. fan.dr-pepper Goes with a fizz
alt.fan.monty-python The original comic home of spam
alt. flame When you need to get nasty, insults and abuse

Games
alt.binaries.games.quake Time to Quake
comp.sys.ibm.pc.games.flight-sim Flight simulator games

Computers
comp.protocols.tcp-ip If you really want to know more
comp.security.firewalls Protect from hack attack
comp.sys.mac.apps Software for Apple Macs

Food and drink
alt.coffee A strong brew
alt.food.chocolate Not as addictive as the real thing
rec.food.recipes Grandma's apple pie
rec.food.veg.cooking Vegetarian surprise

Hobbies
rec.crafts.winemaking Chateau du plonk
rec.gardens.orchids Fine blooms
alt.collecting.autographs Trainspotters to the stars
soc.genealogy.misc Tracing the family line

Health

alt.folklore.herbs Do they work?

alt.yoga Find the best positions

Folklore

alt.folklore.ghost-stories Tales of the unexpected

alt.folklore.urban Urban myths

Law

alt.censorship Say what you want

misc.legal.moderated Legal debate that is moderated

Music

alt.music.kylie-minogue You should be so lucky…

rec.music.classical Classical vibes

rec.music.reggae Bob Marley and co.

Newsgroups

news.announce.newgroups Latest additions

news.announce.newusers New user guide

Paranormal

alt.dreams What does it all mean?

alt.hypnosis That sleepy feeling

alt.paranormal More tales of the unexpected

Pets

alt.pets.ferrets One to keep down the trousers

rec.pets.alligators Should you keep any in the bath

rec.pets.cats Feline fun

Politics

alt.politics.elections About those ballot papers

alt.politics.usa.misc On your soapbox

Space and Aliens

alt.alien.research UFOs et al

sci.space.news The more official line…

Sport

alt.fishing Tales from the river bank

alt.sports.soccer.european.uk Football to the Brits

rec.climbing For gentle relaxation

rec.skiing.snowboarding Icy adventures

TV and movies

alt.movies.silent Pre-Teletubbies

alt.showbiz.gossip All the latest talk

alt.tv.simpsons Cult TV

alt.tv.teletubbies Even greater cult TV

rec.arts.movies.review Your chance to be the critic

rec.arts.tv.soaps.misc Get in a lather

))⧫ *Newsgroups, Newsreader, News Server, Usenet*

NEWS ONLINE

News services on the Internet. The 11 September 2001 terrorist atrocities in America were probably the sternest test of online news services. While information was being constantly updated, traffic to the sites was so heavy that many people could not access the pages or they downloaded very slowly. Despite the technical difficulties this event illustrates how the Internet has become part of the fabric of our daily lives and a vital source of news on rapidly changing events. Almost all the major newspapers in the world, from the *New York Times* (*www.nyt.com*) to *The Guardian* (*www.guardianunlimited. com*) in London have an associated web site with daily online content. This is also the case with the major television news organizations such as the BBC (*www.bbc. co.uk*) and CNN (*www.cnn.com*). Stories from press agencies such as Reuters and AP are delivered by news feeds to the main portal sites around the world. There are also thousands of local and regional newspapers that publish online, so if you are in Dubai and want to know what is going on back home you can find out with a click of the mouse.

))⧫ *News Search Services, Politics-Related Web Sites, Weather Online*

LEFT: Discuss your favourite pet at a newsgroup for pets
ABOVE: You'll find lots of sport newsgroups on the Net

NEWSREADER

Reader for newsgroup messages. The newsreader is the special software that enables you to send and read newsgroup postings. The postings are essentially like email messages although they use a different protocol, the Network News Transport Protocol (NNTP). As a result it is often the email client, such as Outlook Express or Netscape Messenger, which acts as the newsreader. There are also stand alone newsreaders available, such as Agent for the PC and NewsWatcher for the Mac. Most readers carry out similar functions. As well as handling the posting of messages they have options for how long to keep messages, how much to download, etc.

)))))➤ *Newsgroups, News Server, Usenet*

ABOVE: Newsreaders facilitate the sending and reading of newsgroup messages

NEWS SEARCH SERVICES

Finding news. If you're looking for news, this is the page for you: *searchenginewatch.com/links/ News_ Search_Engines/.*

NEWS SERVER

A newsgroup message distribution server. Messages sent (posted) to a newsgroup are basically like email messages. A database of them is kept on a news server. Usually, your nearest server will be run by your ISP. Each server is regularly updated with nearby servers, but the frequency of this will vary. Some servers update instantly, others only daily. So, while your message will appear instantly to you it might not show up elsewhere for a few hours. Similarly, not all servers take all the newsfeed, or newsgroups. Because of the vast volume of messages, sites only keep postings for a few days before they 'expire' them to make way for new ones.

)))))➤ *Newsgroups, Newsreader, Usenet*

NICKNAME

Pseudonym for the chat rooms. In chat rooms it is usual to give yourself a nickname to identify yourself, rather than use your own name. This is also the case for some online bulletin boards and discussion groups. Hence you can find yourself having a conversation with doudec4 and chaganougat, or picking up investment tips from professor pricealwaysdrops. Nicknames are also referred to as 'screen names' or 'handles'. With larger service providers such as AOL, it is likely your own name is already registered so many use a nickname as their screen name.

)))))➤ *Chat, IRC*

NNTP

'Network News Transfer Protocol'; message transfer protocol. NNTP is the protocol within the TCP/IP suite that covers the transfer of messages between newsgroups and newsreader software, such as Outlook Express. In particular, the protocol covers the rules for posting, distributing and retrieving 'reading' messages from Usenet, the bulletin-board system that can be accessed through the Internet as well as other online services.

)))))➤ *Newsgroups, Newsreader, News Server, Usenet, Network Protocol*

NODE

A connection point on a network where there is a device, such as a computer or printer, that is capable of communicating with the other devices on the network. Each node is given its own unique address, specified by its Data Link Control Identifier (DLCI), so it can be easily identified in communications.

)))))➤ *Network, Network Neighbourhood, Network Protocol, Network Server*

NORTHERN LIGHT (*www.northernlight.com*)

Search engine. A favourite search engine among researchers, Northern Light features a large index of the Web and organizes pages into topics. It also offers 'special collection' sets of documents from newswires, magazines and databases. Searching these documents is free, but there is a charge to view them.

))))➤ *Search Directory, Search Engine*

NORTON ANTIVIRUS

Anti-virus software. Norton AntiVirus, like similar programs, isolates and removes any viruses found on your system. It is available as a standalone product or as part of a suite of computer-maintenance utilities. The program can monitor your PC in the background for any suspicious activity suggesting virus attacks, and regular updates can be downloaded automatically from the Web.

))))➤ *Anti-virus Software, Virus Checker*

NOTEBOOK COMPUTER

Light portable computer. A notebook is the smallest form of portable computer, that has a keyboard that can support conventional two-handed typing. It has a hinged lid that opens to reveal the screen. It has a compact keyboard, and a touch-sensitive pad instead of a mouse. According to the model, a host of features can be built in, including DVD drives and internal modems. You can connect a notebook to external devices such as printers and networks as you would a desktop computer. It is also possible to connect other devices to a notebook, such as a conventional keyboard, monitor and mouse.

))))➤ *Portable Computer*

BELOW: Like their namesakes, notebook computers are light and portable

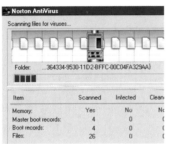

NSFNET

Early network. NSFnet was established in 1986 by the US National Science Foundation by linking together super computers in five universities. It was one of the founding networks of the Internet and has since been expanded to include many countries around the world.

))))➤ *Internet in the 1980s: History*

NULL MODEM CABLE

A serial cable to link PCs. A null modem cable is especially designed to connect two computers together, directly via their serial ports. This is particularly useful if you want to hook your laptop up to a desktop PC to swap files and it can provide a faster link than, for example, an infrared connection.

))))➤ *Port*

OCR

'Optical Character Recognition'; a program to turn scanned documents into editable text. OCR is a software program that can take text stored in an image file format – such as from a fax or a document that has been scanned into a PC – and convert it into characters that can be edited with a word processor. For text recognition to work well, the document has to be as free as possible of any marks, creases and shaded backgrounds. Even if it is, the reliability of the text recognition varies enormously. OCR programs are improving all the time, however, and they remain a better option to use than having to re-type the original document.

))))➤ *Scanner*

OFFICE SUITE

A suite of programs in a box that enable you to handle everything from organizing your time to writing documents and mastering presentations. Office suites are designed to provide you with the right combination of programs to fit your needs. The collection of programs is sold at a lower price than if you bought each of the applications separately. Most suites are aimed at office or school environments and include personal organizers, word processing, presentation, spreadsheet and database programs. Among the best-known suites are Microsoft's Office, Lotus' SmartSuite and Corel's WordPerfect Office.

))))➤ *Application, Calendar, Database, Spreadsheet, Word Processor*

OFFLINE

To accomplish tasks on a computer while not being connected to the Internet. For example, you can type and read emails offline, and go online to send and receive them.

))))➤ *Online*

OFFLINE BROWSING

Viewing web pages offline using special software to download web pages and save them on your hard drive, enabling a user to browse through them without running up the costs of being connected to the Internet. In Internet Explorer when you save pages as Favorites you have the option to make them available for offline viewing. Also when you use a browser's History function you can view the pages offline that you have visited recently on the Net, provided the cache where they are stored hasn't been cleared.

))))➤ *Browser, Internet Explorer, Netscape Navigator, Online, Web Browser*

OFFLINE READER (OLR)

A way to minimize online costs by enabling newsgroup messages to be read and answered offline. Offline readers (OLR) can save you money, by minimizing the time you are online. Whether it is your newsreader software, such as Outlook Express, or a commercial conference system, such as CompuServe, the principle is the same. The offline reader enables you to connect to the system, download the messages and then disconnect. You can then read through the postings and reply, at your leisure, to those that interest you. When you are ready you can go online again and the OLR will post your messages and update any discussion groups before disconnecting.

))))➤ *Database, Newsgroups, Newsreader*

OLE

'Object linking and embedding'; the foundation for sharing information between documents. OLE enables you to take an item (an object) from one program and paste it into another, keeping the format the same as the original. You can either paste the object itself (embed it) or just add a link to it.

))))➤ *Application, GUI*

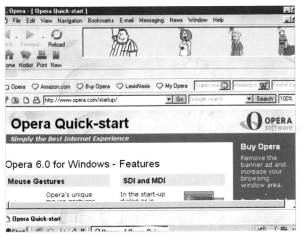

LEFT: www.opera.com (Opera's home page) viewed in Opera v. 6 browser
BELOW: Opera has a vocal group of supporters

The Open Directory (*dmoz.org*) Uses volunteer editors to compile links on their specialist subjects; Netscape, Google and Lycos are among the services that use their information

Yahoo (*www.yahoo.com*) The Web's most popular online directory uses a team of around 150 editors and lists over one million web sites

))))➤ *Directory, Directory Service, Search Directory, White Pages*

ONLINE

Connected to the Internet. The expression 'going online' means connecting to the Internet. You need to be online in order to browse the Web or use other Internet services such as email or chat. A modem is online when it has successfully established two-way communication with your service provider's modem. Many external modems have a light to indicate this. A printer can also be online when it is connected to your computer, powered up, and is ready to print.

))))➤ *Connecting to the Internet I: Basic, Internet, Internet Connections, Offline*

ONLINE DIRECTORIES

Collections of links to web sites. An online directory is a web site that provides links to a large number of web sites, organized into categories according to subject. In contrast to a pure search engine site, the links in a directory are evaluated by humans for relevance. Here are some of the most useful online directories:

LookSmart A human-compiled directory that provides results to MSN Search, Excite and others

Lycos Main listings come from the Open Directory project with secondary results from the FAST Search engine

Northern Light (*www.northern-light.com*) Offers 'special collection' sets of documents from newswires, magazines and databases. Searching these documents is free, but there is a charge to view them

OPERA

Although not as widely used as Internet Explorer or Netscape Navigator, Opera has a steady and vocal group of supporters as an alternative web browser. Its main benefits are its speed and size. Known as the 'browser on a

diet' it still has most of the features of its bigger brothers. It's handy for people who do not have the powerful machines demanded by other browsers and is finding a market on non-PC Internet devices. The free version is ad-supported; to turn off the ads you have to pay for it.

))))➤ *Browser, Web browser*

OPERATING SYSTEM

Software program that runs a computer. Every personal computer has an operating system. It is the software program that is launched automatically when you turn the computer on. It controls how the computer works and provides the environment in which all the other applications (Word or Internet Explorer, for example) operate. It provides the graphical user interface (GUI) that you see on the screen, and the basic menus and functions that apply throughout the computer. The operating system is the main distinguishing feature between the two principal types of personal computers. IBM-compatible PCs come supplied with the Windows operating system, and Apple computers run the Apple OS operating system.

))))▶ *Apple Computer, Linux, PC vs Mac, Windows Operating System*

ORG

Top-level domain name. Short for organizations, if a company has .org as its top-level domain name it usually signifies that it is some sort of charitable or non-profit group. However, there is nothing to stop any type of company registering as a .org and there are distinct advantages. Research suggests that people trust sites with addresses that end in .org rather more than commercial sites which have .com as their TLD. Consequently, some commercial sites are adopting the .org tag to improve their business.

))))▶ *Address, Domain, Hostname, URL, Zone*

OSP

'Online Service Provider'; commercial supplier of online services. The distinction between Online Service Providers (OSPs) and Internet Service Providers (ISPs) is becoming increasingly blurred. Traditionally, the difference has been one of scale. OSPs, such as AOL and CompuServe, were large operations offering their subscribers a number of services including messaging, discussion forums, information channels and access to exclusive content from a range of third-party providers. Now many of the ISPs, such as Freeserve and MSN, offer the same and they all offer Internet access.

))))▶ *ISP (Internet Service Provider), Server*

OUTBOX

The folder where email messages are stored until sent. The Outbox is the folder where email clients, such as Outlook and Outlook Express, store messages that are ready

LEFT: It may be that you are not in a position to visit friends, in which case you may wish to email them instead

to be sent. Messages are held in the Outbox until the next time the program connects to the mail server or the send/receive button is pressed. If you open a message in the Outbox and change it, it will not be sent. You need to press the Send button again. Messages waiting to be sent are shown in italic. You can also set an option to send messages immediately when they are received in the Outbox.

▶ *Email, Forwarding Email, Inbox, Sending Email*

OUTLOOK EXPRESS

Email software program. Outlook Express is an electronic mail (email) application that comes with Microsoft's Internet Explorer. It gives you a range of features that help you to send, receive and organize your email messages. These include an easy-to-use interface for email, an address book for email addresses, a newsgroups facility, as well as tools for customizing the way Outlook Express works. If you use Windows, you can start Outlook Express in two ways: click Start, select Programs, then click on Outlook Express; double-click on the Outlook Express icon on your desktop.

Here is a quick summary of what you can do with Outlook Express.

1. Email
With Outlook Express you can compose, send, receive and reply to emails. An email can contain text, images and hyperlinks.

2. Attachments
You can attach a document such as a Word file to an email. Providing you have the appropriate application, you can also read attachments that are sent to you.

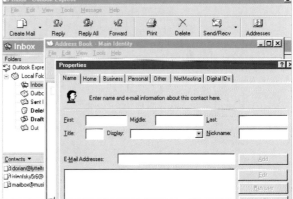

3. Address Book
You can compile your own database of contacts. For each contact you can store their email address, telephone numbers, postal address and other details.

4. Newsgroups
This is a useful feature to help you participate in newsgroup discussions.

5. Work Offline
To save on phone bills, you can compose and read emails offline (while you are not connected to the Internet). You can then go online (connected to the Internet) when you want to send and receive messages. Use your usual Connect To dialog box methods to go online and offline.

TOP: Email from Musicmatch in Outlook Express containing text, images and hyperlinks
ABOVE: New Contact window in Outlook Express' address Book

The most useful features of the Outlook Express Window are listed below. You can customize the window so that it displays only the features you find useful by selecting View|Layout.

Menu bar: contains general options that appear in other applications, such as File and Edit

Toolbar: contains buttons to activate Outlook's main features

Outlook bar: gives you shortcuts to your most used folders

Views bar: lets you show or hide emails of different types

Contacts bar: lists all the contacts in the Address Book

Folders bar: click on one of the folders inside this panel to make it the active folder

Message list: displays the emails contained in the active folder (how these are viewed can be configured by selecting View|Current)

Preview panel: when you click on an email in a message list, you can preview it here

Status bar: shows the current activity and the status of your Internet connection

))))➤ *Email, Email Address, Composing Email, Eudora, Folder, Newsgroups, Offline, Online*

OUTPUT

Information from a computer. Output is data taken from a computer for a purpose. It can take many forms, for example, the visual display on a monitor screen, printing words and images on paper or sending data down a telephone line via a modem.

))))➤ *Input*

PACKET

Any information sent over the Internet, whether web page or email, is split into small packets of data to be reassembled at the other end. As with any mail package, these packets have to be addressed to make sure they go to the right place. This is done through the TCP/IP protocol.

))))➤ *Internet, Packet Loss*

RIGHT: Like any regular mail package, packets have to be addressed to make sure they go to the right place

PACKET LOSS

As with any delivery service, not every packet will make it to its destination, leaving the message incomplete. Under the TCP/IP protocol there are methods for checking packets have arrived intact and for re-sending them if they have not. If a high percentage of packets are lost in transit there is a problem with the connection.

))))➤ *Internet, Packet*

PAGE

Documents on the Web that together make up a web site. Each page is viewed through a browser and it has its own unique address, or URL, which enables it to be located. The page itself can be made up of many elements, including text and graphics. Increasingly, it is

Cap.ᵗ Bedlow carrying letters to Forraigne Parts.

sending and wireless internet features. A pioneering palmtop was Apple Computer's Newton MessagePad, released in 1993, which used a stylus rather than a keyboard for input. With improved handwriting recognition technology, palmtops have become hugely popular. Leading manufacturers in this field include Palm, Handspring and Compaq.

))))▶ *Notebook, Portable Computers*

also likely to have some animation, play sounds or even video clips. As the page is often bigger than the browser window (or screen) that views it there are scroll bars, which can be used to move around the page.

))))▶ *Web Page, Web Page: Creating I, Web Page: Creating II*

PALMTOP COMPUTER

Hand-held computer; Personal Digital Assistant (PDA). A tiny computer that can be held in one hand – hence the name. A typical palmtop offers personal organizer functions such as address book, calendar and calculator, while many models have mobile phone, fax

PARALLEL PORT

The socket at the back of your PC that connects it to a printer or other peripheral. The parallel port sends data over several wires simultaneously, so it is generally faster than a serial port where one bit is sent at a time. The first specification, often called the Centronics interface after the company that designed it, has been superseded by newer ports. The EPP (Enhanced Parallel Port) and ECP (Extended Capabilities Port) both support two-way communication and are 10 times faster. Macintosh computers use a special kind of parallel port, the SCSI port.

))))▶ *Interface, Port, Serial Port*

ABOVE: *Palmtops offer personal-organizer facilities among other functions*
LEFT: *Browser view of palmtops at* www.compaq.com

PASSWORD

Secret access code. Once so reminiscent of spies and the cold war, passwords are now mostly just an inconvenience. The little row of asterisks that mark the secret series of characters in a password are popping up everywhere. You need a password to access your computer, the Internet, email, even some files and folders. Then each and every web site where you register or subscribe will want a username and password. Such passwords are meant to ensure unauthorized people cannot access either your computer or a site, but in practice it is only effective against the casual intruder. A determined hacker will have no trouble getting hold of the information. They are helped by the fact that users avoid the confusion of passwords by adopting a single, easily memorable one, such as their name. In fact, the most difficult passwords to crack involve both letters and numbers and should be at least six characters long. Windows also gives you the option to save passwords so you do not have to fill them in each time you log on or visit a site. However, more secure sites won't let you and some encrypt the connection.

))))➤ *Case Sensitivity, Log On*

PATCH

Programs are in effect like recipes: there a list of ingredients called variables and a list of instructions called statements, which tell the computer what to do with them. Like any recipe the chances are they won't turn out perfect every time. Sometimes it is down to a mistake in the recipe, an error in the code. If the mistake is sufficiently serious, such as a security problem in an email client, the software publishers will release a patch. This is a small section of new code to replace the faulty code. Rather than replace the whole program only the faulty bit is patched (fixed).

))))➤ *Application, Program Errors*

PATH

The route from one PC on a network to another, or to a particular file stored on a disk. It's usually shown by a pathname. For example, the pathname to the folder on your hard drive where you store your files might be: C:\My Documents\. Information sent over the Internet can take a very convoluted path to its destination. There are tracker programs, such as McAfee's Visual Trace, which map the route your communications are taking.

))))➤ *Directory, Navigation*

PC VS MAC

The big computer battle. If you are planning to buy a computer, the first question you will have to ask is: Do I buy a PC or a Mac? A PC is any IBM-compatible Personal Computer running Windows (there is another free operating system called Linux but it's mostly for techies). A Mac is the popular name for all personal computers made by Apple. Your second question might well be: What's the big deal, both types of computer do pretty much the same thing, don't they? Yes they do – but this issue arouses such strong opinions that you are unlikely to get a totally unbiased opinion, particularly from a Mac owner. So here's a quick comparison chart.

Quick Comparison
Popularity: Probably 95 per cent of all personal computers are PCs, but Mac fans have unswerving loyalty to their Apples

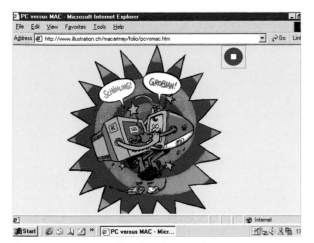

Cost: PCs are generally a bit cheaper than Macs

Design: Macs are more stylish and colourful, PCs tend to look boring or clunky

Internet: Both PC and Mac run the popular applications such as Internet Explorer, Netscape, Outlook Express and Eudora

Interface: The Mac is easier and more intuitive to use than a PC

Software: The PC has a much wider choice of games, multimedia, education and business software

Hardware: There is a much wider choice of printers, scanners, modems etc. for the PC

))))▶ *Apple Computer, Mac: Introduction, PCs: Introduction; Windows Operating System*

PCI

A fast route to the processor for parts of the computer that need to move large chunks of information around. An acronym for Peripheral Component Interconnect, this is a local bus or high-speed connection that can access the PC's processor. It is most often used in computers for network or graphics adapters where they need to exchange large chunks of information fast in order to boost performance. Most modern computers have a PCI bus as well as the more general ISA expansion bus, which enables expansion boards to access the processor and memory. However, it is believed that PCI will eventually replace ISA altogether. The PCI bus is also used on some of the newer Macintosh computers.

))))▶ *High-speed Connection*

PCMCIA MODEM

Credit-card sized devices that slip into the Personal Computer Memory Card International Association (PCMCIA) slots in a notebook computer. The advantage is that they are hot-swappable, i.e. they can be plugged in and will be recognized by the computer without having to restart. PCMCIA cards, commonly called PC cards, can be used to provide a number of add-on features. They can work as storage drives, network adapter cards or as connections to external disk drives.

))))▶ *Modem I: basic, Modem II: Choosing, Modem III: Installing, Modem IV: Configuring, Notebook Computer*

ABOVE: Macs tend to be used more than PCs for design purposes
ABOVE LEFT: Cartoon by Alex Macartney of battle between PC & Mac at www.illustration.ch/macartney/folio/pcvsmac.html

PCs: CONNECTING TO THE INTERNET

Getting online with your PC. If you are using a PC running Windows, you should consult the Windows Help for detailed information about connecting to the Internet. You can connect to the Internet by various means, although the cheapest and most common method is via a dial-up connection. This method requires a telephone line and a modem to connect your PC to the telephone socket. Here is an overview of the steps you should take to connect using a dial-up connection.

1. Unless your PC was supplied with an internal modem, you need to buy a modem and install it, following the manufacturer's instructions. You then set up your Internet connection by following either 2 or 3.

2. Set up your connection using an Internet Service Provider's (ISP's) software. Most ISPs will supply you with a CD that makes it easy to set up a connection using their own software.

RIGHT: The manuals for many programs can often be viewed in PDF format, such as this one - the manual for the email application, Eudora

3. Set up your connection manually. If your ISP does not supply a CD, they will provide printed instructions for setting up your connection manually. Use the Internet Connection Wizard that comes with Windows to make this process as painless as possible.

))))▶ *Connecting to the Internet: Introduction, Internet: Introduction, Internet Connections, PCs: Introduction, Windows Operation System*

PCS: INTRODUCTION

IBM-compatible personal computers. A PC is an IBM-compatible personal computer (IBM made the original PC). All new PCs come with the Windows operating system pre-installed and this is what most folks use. Probably over 95 per cent of personal computers are PCs, so it is likely that this is the kind you have. A typical modern PC comes as a set of components: a desktop or tower computer with an internal modem, a 3.5-inch floppy drive, a hard drive, a DVD or CD-ROM drive, a monitor, a keyboard, a mouse and a pair of speakers. There are many brands of PC available with an enormous range of specifications and deals to choose from.

))))▶ *PCs: Connecting to the Internet, PC vs Mac, Windows Operating System*

PDF FILE

Document format system. Most e-books, instruction manuals and other documents that you can view or download from the Web are saved as PDF files (they have the extension .pdf). PDF stands for

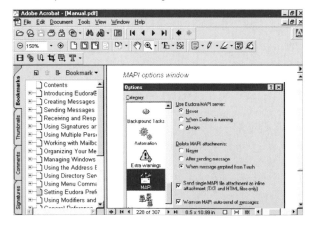

Portable Document Format, which is a system devised by Adobe that enables documents to be viewed as they were originally formatted. Because the documents look the same regardless of which computer or platform they are viewed on, the technology is particularly popular for companies wanting to present a consistent corporate brand. In order to view a PDF file in your browser, the special Adobe Acrobat reader is needed.

))))➤ *Adobe Acrobat, Multi-Platform, Viewer*

PERIPHERALS

Secondary hardware devices. Peripherals are the extra pieces of hardware you connect to your computer for input, output or storage. They include printers, scanners and modems.

))))➤ *Input, Modem I: Introduction, Output, Printers, Scanners*

PGP

'Pretty Good Privacy'; a system using public key cryptography to send emails securely, devised by Philip Zimmerman. PGP uses the public key encryption method to enable emails to be sent securely. This works by having two keys, one public one private. The public key is freely sent to any contacts that you want. When they want to send you a secure email they encrypt the message using the public key. As you are the only one with the private key that unlocks it, only you can open the message. It can also be used for digitally signing messages.

))))➤ *Encryption, Privacy, Security I: Basic, Security II: Advanced*

PHONE BILLS: CUTTING DOWN ON

Reducing telephone bills. Choose the tariff from your telephone company or service providers that best suits your intended usage. Consider an unmetered flat-rate tariff if you use the Internet a lot during the day. If you have a tariff that offers cheap or free calls in the evenings and weekends, restrict your surfing to those times. If you use Windows, you can set the software

to disconnect if the connection is idle after a set time limit (in Internet Explorer, select Tools|Internet|Options| Connections|Settings|Advanced).

Tip 1 Adults: Work Offline As Much As Possible! Browse offline – that means saving web pages onto your hard disk to read offline at your leisure. Read and write emails while you are offline, and only go online to send and receive them.

Tip 2 Kids: Don't leave them surfing on the Net while you go shopping!

))))➤ *Connecting to the Internet I: Basic, Cutting costs on the Internet, Offline browsing*

PHONE DIALER

Dial-up connection utility. In some versions of Windows it is a stand-alone utility to dial telephone numbers from your computer using the modem attached to a phone line. It is accessed from the Accessories menu and includes its own speed-dial list. Many fax or remote access programs also include dialers.

))))➤ *Dialer*

ABOVE: If you have a dial-up connection, your telephone bill will increase.

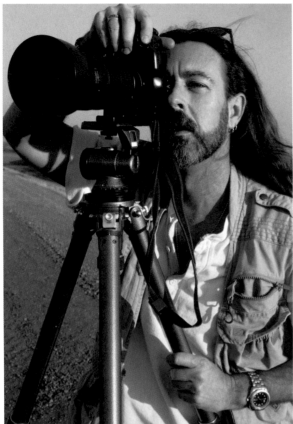

account. As with the hacker, the intention may be simply a battle of wits to see what can be done with the system, but at a more malicious level it can also block telephone services and wreck equipment.

)))⏵ *Hacking, Hacking: History of*

PICS

'Platform for Internet Content Selection.' Part of the move to safer surfing, the PICS protocol enables web pages with inappropriate or offensive material to be blocked. In effect, PICS-compliant sites label web pages with information about the content on that particular page, which can be picked up by a user's browser. Depending on the rules you have set down the page will be displayed or blocked. In Internet Explorer preset PICSRules can be imported using the Advanced tab on the Content Advisor accessed by going to Tools|Internet Options.

)))⏵ *Censorship, Filtering*

PHOTOGRAPHY WEB SITES

There's no better way to learn than from the experts, which is the clear philosophy behind Masters of Photography (*www.masters-of-photgraphy. com*), which hosts galleries of images from some of photography's greatest talents. For a more current hall of fame view the British Journal of Photography's (*www.bjphoto.co.uk*) top sites, which visitors can also rate online.

)))⏵ *Art Web Sites, Pictures: Sources for*

PHREAKER

The phreaker is a close cousin of the hacker. While the hacker uses the phone system to try and break into secure systems illegally, the phreaker is more concerned with tricking the phone system itself. Phreaking is typically used to cheat the system in order to get free calls or have calls charged to somebody else's

PICTURES: SOURCES FOR

While the biggest source of photos is in the expensive stock libraries there are cheaper options. Most of the big photo libraries have sites online (for a listing see *www.photographiclibraries.com*), where you can search for the images you want and download low resolution copies. These can be expensive but some, like Gettyworks.com (*www.gettyworks.com*), offer low-price collections or individually priced photos for web use. While most royalty free images come in clipart collections there are some stock photos available free online, such as at the aptly named *freeimages.co.uk*.

))))➤ *Art Web Sites*

PINE

A popular email client for people using character-based UNIX systems. Pine, which was developed at the University of Washington, also has its own techie joke. The name PINE can stand quite ordinarily for Program for Internet News and Email. But it is also an acronym for Pine Is Not Elm. Elm (itself short for electronic mail) is another program for reading and composing email messages on UNIX systems that has largely been replaced by the more fully featured Pine.

))))➤ *Email, UNIX*

PING

Internet connection troubleshooter. A good way to troubleshoot your Internet connections. By pinging another site you can see whether the problems are at your end or on the network. Despite its catchy name, it actually stands for Packet Internet Groper. It works by sending a small packet of information to a specific IP address and waiting for a reply.

))))➤ *Internet Connections*

PICTURE FORMAT

The three basic formats for pictures on the web all have different qualities, which affect when they should be used. In the early days of the Web there was just one format for images: the GIF. It is still popular, particularly for images that have only a few, mainly solid colours. For more complicated graphics, such as photographs, it is better to save the file as a JPEG. A third picture format called PNG is emerging, which combines the qualities of the other two. Like JPEG it supports millions of colours (against the 256 supported by GIF) but still compresses files smaller than the GIF. The only drawback is that it is only supported by the more recent browsers, so is not yet widely used.

))))➤ *BMP, GIF, Graphics File, JPEG/JPG, TIFF*

PIRATED SOFTWARE

Illegally used software. Software may be pirated by borrowing a friend's copy of a program and installing it on your PC, or by making an unauthorized copy. There are also online archives of warez or appz, pirated software, usually but not entirely games, made available for anyone to download.

))))➤ *Software, Warez*

TOP: Browser view of www.gettyworks.com
ABOVE: Browser view of www.freeimages,com

PIXEL

A pixel makes up the smallest single point on a display that can be turned on or off to create an image. On a monitor, pictures are displayed by dividing the screen into thousands or millions of pixels. Each pixel represents a single point in the picture. How many colours can be seen depends on the number of bits used to represent each pixel. With modern monitors it is millions of colours. Although each pixel is a distinct colour they are so close that they appear to blend together.

))))➤ *Graphics File, Picture Formats*

PLATFORM

The software or hardware that is at the base of your computer, such as the PC or Macintosh. Normally the platform will be a combination of both the microprocessor (the hardware) and the operating system (the software). PCs are often described as being part of the Wintel platform (Windows operating systems with Intel processors). Some applications can be cross-platform, meaning that they run across several platforms. For example, the operating system Linux is an open-source version of UNIX that works on both a PC and Macintosh hardware platform.

))))➤ *Operating System*

PLAYING

 See Games on the Net

PLUG AND PLAY

Attaching a new printer or modem to your computer is a lot easier now. With most modern PCs you can 'plug' in your new device and 'play' it, without having to configure the system or physically change the switches as used to be the case. This is also described as hot swappable, because you can plug devices in and take them out without restarting the PC. The operating system is set to recognize a much wider range of plug-and-play devices but it does not always work and sometimes you will have to add them manually.

))))➤ *Adapter Card, Windows Operating Systems*

PLUG-IN

An add-on that brings extra features to bigger programs, such as web browsers. Most commonly associated with browsers, plug-ins are mini-programs that plug-in to bigger ones to give them some added function. For example, Flash is a plug-in that runs the Flash-created animations used on some web pages. Similarly, the Adobe Acrobat plug in lets you read PDF files from within your browser, rather than having to download them and then launch a separate program to view them. If a plug-in is needed to view a file there is usually a link to a web page where it can be downloaded.

))))➤ *Browser, Program, Web Browser*

ABOVE: Pixels are tiny points on a screen that when viewed together are not visible to the human eye

RIGHT: Browser view of www.conspire.com

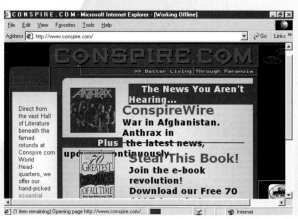

POLITICS-RELATED WEB SITES

Political parties accept the Net is a fast track to potential voters as those who observe politics, whether commentators or conspiracy theorists. To varying degrees the political parties in most countries have realized that the Internet is a separate channel of communication in its own right. In the UK the three main political parties have their sites (*www.labour.org.uk*, *www.conservative-party.org.uk*, *www.libdems.org.uk*), as do the two main political forces in the US (*www.democratic-party.org*, *www. townhall.com*). But probably as revealing are the sites offering political commentary (*www.time. com*) and those of the pressure groups, such as Friends of the Earth (*www.foe.co.uk*). There's even a site for those who think it's all a conspiracy (*www.conspire.com*).

)))➡ *Government Online*

BELOW: Many web sites poll their visitors on a variety of subjects

POLLING

A system for enabling your fax modem to make regular, automatic checks of other fax machines to see whether they have a fax to send you. It works by a kind of master/slave scenario. The modem polls the other machine; that is, it queries each 'slave' device to see whether they have any data to transmit. If the slave says it has data the fax is sent, if not the master moves on and polls the next machine. As persistently, many web sites are polling their visitors to get their views on everything from the site itself to the price of suntan oil.

)))➡ *Fax*

POP

'Point of Presence'; essentially, your entry point to the Internet. Each Internet Service Provider (ISP) provides a telephone number to ring for dial-up access to the Net. Some of the bigger ISPs will have several numbers, or POPs, distributed around the country so that users only have to pay local rates to connect to the Internet. Although thousands of users may call the same POP they are in fact dialling into huge banks of modems. Even so, at peak times of the day you might get the busy tone from your ISP's point of presence if too many people are trying to connect simultaneously.

)))➡ *Internet Connection, ISP*

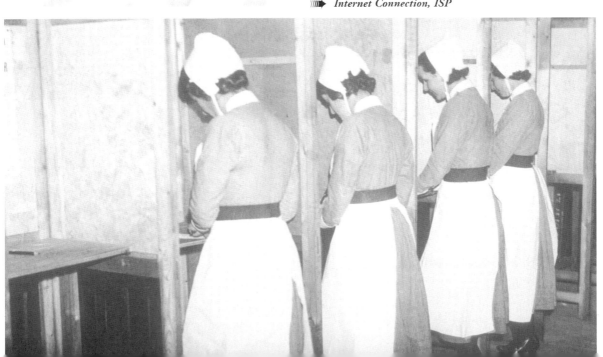

POP3

'Post Office Protocol'; a flexible method for retrieving messages from a mail server. Most Internet mail accounts use this protocol to get messages from the mail server. In effect, the server is like a post office (hence the name) that holds the mail until you go online to collect it. Once downloaded from your account, the messages are usually deleted from the server, although there is an option to keep them. One advantage of POP3 is that armed with the incoming mail server address, user name and password you can collect your mail on another computer or set up your email client to check for mail at several accounts over the one connection.

))))▶ *Email, Protocol, SMTP*

PORN ON THE NET: FILTERING

Blocking sexually explicit sites. The Internet has many X-rated areas. Even if you don't go looking for them, they will try and find you. Many seemingly innocent URLs are linked through to adult sites. There is

software available such as Net Nanny, Cybersitter and Cyber Patrol that attempts to screen out any unsuitable sites. Such censorware screens not only sexually explicit material but also sites promoting drugs, crime or hatred and intolerance. The major browsers also include content advisors, which use a ratings system to enable users to set the level of bad language, sexual content and violence they are willing to accept.

))))▶ *Censorship, Filtering*

PORN ON THE NET: HISTORY

Internet porn. Pornography has been around a lot longer than the Internet and it should come as no surprise that the Internet porn industry is a thriving one. Interested adults will have no difficulty in finding such services, but it presents a very worrying problem for parents because typing the most innocuous words into a search engine can bring up unwanted links to porn sites. Notable attempts to restrict porn include the German authorities banning certain newsgroups on Compuserve in 1995, and the Communications Decency Act in the US, later overturned.

))))▶ *Censorship, Filtering, Internet in the 1990s: History*

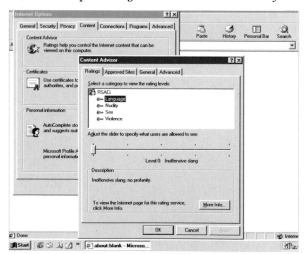

PORT

A connection for linking a computer to a peripheral device. Most computers will have several types of port, including a serial port usually used for connecting a modem and a parallel port traditionally used for connecting a printer. However, the newer USB ports are likely to take over from both of these as the preferred way to connect external devices. Not only do they support plug and play, but devices are also hot-swappable, i.e. they can be added or removed without restarting the machine.

)))⯈ *COM1, Parallel Port, Serial Port*

PORTABLE COMPUTER

Small computers. The term 'portable computer' generally refers to the type of computer that can be readily carried around and has a keyboard that can be

ABOVE: Portable computers are diminutive machines that run on batteries
FAR LEFT: Browser view of www.netnanny.com
LEFT: Click on Internet Explorer | Options | Content | Content Advisor to set the levels of suitable content that you are willing to accept

used in a conventional two-handed way. Notebooks fall into this category and are the thinnest of this type. All have a hinged lid that opens to reveal the screen, and can run on internal batteries or using a power adapter. Many have features such as CD-ROM drives and internal modems. The newer and much smaller palmtops can be considered as portable computers. Non-portable personal computers are usually called desktop computers.

)))⯈ *Notebook Computer, Palmtop Computer*

PORTAL

Gateway to the Internet. Portals are your gateway to the Internet, but before you start your travels they have a range of services on their site that they hope will keep you there. The first web portals were the online services, such as AOL, that provided a massive amount of exclusive content as well as messaging services and forums. Now most of the traditional search engines, such as Yahoo and AltaVista have transformed themselves into information gateways, with email, chat and discussion groups alongside more traditional content and the search engine.

)))⯈ *Directory, Web Site*

PORTFOLIO TRACKING

Tracking your share prices. There is a glut of investment information on the Web, much of it free. There are analysts' reports, news stories, company announcements and investment strategies. As importantly, there are portfolio services available to chart when your dotcom share becomes a dot goner.

Portfolio trackers are provided by financial news services such as the *Financial Times* (*www.ft.com*) or *www.thestreet.com*, investment advice sites such as *www.motleyfool.com*, or stockbrokers like Charles Schwab (*www.schwab-worldwide.com*).

The information provided within the portfolio is variable, but at its most basic it should include the sell (Bid) and buy (Ask) price and the close price for the previous day. Based on the number of units of a particular share you hold and the price you paid for them it should automatically calculate what the value of the holding is and what profit (or loss) that amounts to. It should do the same for the portfolio as a whole. Most prices are delayed by 15–20 minutes during the trading hours of the stock market in question, although some sites offer portfolio listings with real-time prices, usually for a fee. Many will support the portfolio with share charts that can be used by those with the knowledge of technical analysis for signs of when to buy or sell.

))))➤ *Banking and Finance on the Net, Banking and Finance Web Sites, Stockbrokers Online*

PORT NUMBER

An identifying number is assigned to each program using TCP/IP to connect to the Internet. These virtual ports mean that IP packets relating to a specific task go to the right place. For example, there are well-known port numbers that are permanently assigned, such as email messages sent under SMTP go to port number 25. Other programs, such as Telnet, are only assigned temporary port numbers that lapse once they have finished. Not that there's a shortage of numbers, there are 65,535 port numbers available under TCP.

))))➤ *Chat, Internet, Program*

POST

When you send a message to a newsgroup, whether it is the start of a new thread or a reply to an existing one, you are posting it. This is just like sending email and is handled by your newsreader, which is often your email client as well. When you post, the name of the newsgroup you are reading is normally

LEFT: Posting a message to a newsgroup is similar to sending an email

entered automatically. You need to type in the subject, as this identifies the thread and most newsreaders will not send a message with an empty subject line.

))))⏵ *Newsgroup, Usenet*

PPP

 'Point-to-Point Protocol'; a set of commands that allow a computer to use the TCP/IP protocol that normally works over a network, through a phone

connection. The transmission control protocol/Internet protocol (TCP/IP) is the way in which PCs talk to each other over the Internet. You need to use the PPP system if you want to connect to the Internet using a modem. It is more reliable than the older SLIP protocol that it replaces, as it double checks to make sure that the Internet packets arrive intact and re-sends any that don't.

))))⏵ *Internet Connections, Protocol, TCP/IP*

PRICELINE (*www.priceline.com*)

Shopping web site. One of the leading 'name-your-price' web sites, Priceline claims it can save you up to 40 per cent on bargain airline tickets, hotel rooms or car rentals.

))))⏵ *Shopper.com, Shopping Online, Shopping Search*

PRICESCAN (*www.pricescan.com*)

Shopping web site. Pricescan is a shopping guide giving price comparisons on a wide range of goods such as books, computers and sports equipment. You can enter the specification of the product you want to buy and their system displays the search results ranked by price.

))))⏵ *Shopper.com, Shopping online, Shopping Search*

PRINTERS

Devices for printing computer output. A printer is essential for printing letters to send by snail mail (postal service), or printing emails and web pages to read or keep for future reference. Here is a quick comparison of two types of printer for home use.

Inkjet

These are generally reasonably priced and are available in black and white or colour. Expect to pay more for better resolution and quicker printing.

Laserjet

The black-and-white models are more expensive than inkjet printers and colour versions much more so. They usually print faster than inkjets and are worth considering if you run a business from home.

))))⏵ *Buffers, Peripherals, Scanners*

ABOVE: Web sites such as Priceline can save you money on flights, hotels and cars
LEFT: Browser view of www.pricescan.com

PRIVACY

As a member of the Internet community, you have every right to be concerned about preserving your privacy while you are online. This issue is a controversial and compelling one that embraces freedom of speech and national security; pornography and the safety of children; security, cybercrime and hacking; online shopping and commercial ethics.

Freedom of Speech and National Security

The extent to which governments have a right to invade privacy in order to maintain national security and public safety is a hotly debated one. In the US, lobby groups are urging the government to stay within the terms of the Constitution in its efforts to use Internet technology to preserve national security. There are fears that there could be unwarranted intrusion and a risk of discrimination against minority groups. The FBI's Carnivore computer program is an example of the development of technology for surveillance. This system is designed to intercept Internet messages, filter them for surveillance and send them on their way.

ABOVE: Freedom of speech on the Net is limited in the interests of security

Advocates for Privacy

The Centre for Democracy and Technology (*www.ciec.org*) is one of many organizations that campaign about the government and corporate intrusion into privacy on the Internet. They give information on the intended use of new laws and technology to keep track of citizen's online activities. The Privacy Rights Clearinghouse (*www. privacyrights.org*) is a non-profit consumer education program that gives advice about disclosure of personal information to businesses and government agencies.

Pornography and the Safety of Children

Pornography is another hugely controversial issue. Attempts by governments to censor pornographic discussion groups have inadvertently cut off legitimate discussion by gay and lesbian groups. The expression of pornography is also seen as part of the right to free speech. Against these arguments are the risks posed to children by online paedophiles and the problems of unwanted exposure to undesirable material for children surfing the Web. Concerned parents can restrict their kids' browsing to approved sites and try using the filtering function in Internet Explorer.

Security and Cybercrime

Many governments have serious concerns about the use of the Internet by terrorists groups and criminals for making deals, money laundering and networking on a global scale. The US government in particular restricts the export of software that uses encryption strong enough to resist the authorities' attempts to conduct surveillance. Phillip Zimmerman's PGP (Pretty Good Privacy) is an example of a widely used encryption software that allows people to keep their messages secret.

Many types of cybercrime are practised by unscrupulous Netizens. Hacking is perpetrated by disaffected and antisocial people who want to steal credit card numbers, disrupt businesses or cause mayhem. Identity theft is another crime in which innocent people have their personal details used for fraud and crime. In 2001, the Council of Europe drew up the first international treaty on cybercrime, to combat the growing menace of hacking, infringements of copyright, computer-related fraud, child pornography and racist propaganda on the Net.

Online Shopping

Many people are concerned about using their credit cards to make purchases on the Internet, although some experts say that it does not present a significantly greater risk of fraud than when you give your credit card details over the telephone or you have your card taken out of your sight in a shop or restaurant. Here are some guidelines for shopping securely online:

1. Verify that the merchant uses the Secure Socket Layer (SSL) protocol. There are two ways to do this:

- 🖥 The address of the web page on which you submit your details should begin with https: instead of http:.
- 🖥 A small 'locked padlock' icon should appear in the bottom right-hand corner of the browser window (Internet Explorer) or bottom left-hand corner (Netscape Navigator 4.0 and later).

ABOVE: Encryption software helps Cybercriminals to keep their operations secret
ABOVE RIGHT: Secure page at www.amazon.co.uk

2. Print out and retain privacy policies, warranties, price guarantees and the like.

3. Look for the Trust-e symbol or a Better Business Bureau online seal.

4. Ensure that the merchant has a privacy policy.

5. Keep close tabs on your cards and study your bills and statements closely.

6. Destroy documents containing personal information.

7. Finally, be smart – don't shop online in Internet cafés.

Commercial Ethics

All sorts of corporations – banks, retailers, sellers of financial services – should be following best practice guidelines to help you preserve your privacy, yet many are not giving notice of their privacy policies or giving customers any control over their personal data. A survey in 2001 found that only 22 per cent of US banks gave new customers a user-friendly way to instruct them not to share their details with third parties.

You may not realize it, but when you visit many web sites, a 'cookie' is put on your hard disk without you knowing. This is a little bit of software code that tells the web site's operators about your online activities and preferences when you visit them. A problem encountered by many Internet users is junk email or spam. This is unsolicited email, often sent by unscrupulous traders trying to engage you in hopeless get-rich-quick schemes.

)))⟩ *Censorship, Children and the Net, Cookie, Credit Cards, PGP, Hacking: History, Porn on the Net: History, Security I: Basic, Security II: Advanced, Spam: History*

PRODUCT REVIEW NET

(www.productreviewnet.com)

Shopping web site. Product Review Net indexes and summarizes reviews of a huge range of products, from alkaline batteries to weight-loss programmes.

)))➤ *Shopping.com, Shopping Online, Shopping Search*

PROGRAM

Software code. A program is a self-contained set of software code that performs a task or function. Your computer's hard disk stores a wide range of programs. Simple programs that carry out a specialized task are often called utilities. Larger programs used for everyday work or leisure are often called applications. Mic-rosoft Word and Microsoft Explorer are two examples of these. The most complex program on your computer is the operating system. This operates the computer and provides the environment for all other programs to run in. Windows is the most common operating system.

)))➤ *Application, Operating System, Windows Operating System*

PROGRAM ERRORS

Programs are a list of instructions that tell the computer what to do. Written in any one of several languages, such as C, C++, Java, they are incredibly complicated. It is inevitable that errors creep in, but sometimes they only become apparent once a program is released publicly. Then a patch may be released to fix them.

)))➤ *Application, Patch*

PROPERTIES

Attributes of a file. If you use a PC running Windows, the attributes of a file or object are called its properties. You can view these and also change them. To do so, perform the following:

Select the file with a single click to highlight its name

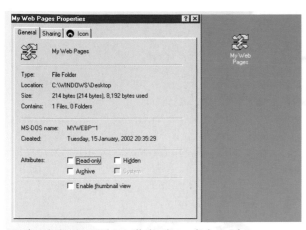

Right-click once. This will display a dialogue box with options:

- Select Properties
- Select the property you wish to change
- Close the dialogue box

)))))▶ *File*

PROTOCOL

An agreed code of behaviour. In computing, several protocols cover the rules for sending information between two devices. The protocol will cover such areas

as the type of error checking and compression used and how devices at either end of the link signal that they have sent or received information. Protocols can be set in the hardware or software. One of the most widely used is TCP/IP, which is the standard method for sending data across the Internet.

)))))▶ *Internet Connections, Network*

PROXY SERVER

A proxy server is a stand-in for the real thing. It sits between the server and the client, such as the web browser. It does this for two main purposes. The first is to improve performance – the proxy server can cache (store) information such as web pages. If they are asked for again, or requested by a different computer, the proxy server delivers them much faster than if the original page was reloaded. The second feature is security. As the proxy server sits between a LAN and the Internet it can apply filters or security rules and monitor activity to protect against hacker attacks.

)))))▶ *Server, Web Browser*

PUBLIC DOMAIN (PD)

Software that is freely available and not copyrighted by the author. Software in the public domain is freely available and users can download it, pass it on to their friends and do with it what they want. There are no restrictions on how it is used; as a result it is rare to find. More usual is freeware, which is not the same thing. Freeware is free software in which the author retains copyright. So, although there is no charge for the software you cannot do anything with it that is not expressly allowed by the author. Typically, the author will let you pass the software to other people, but not sell it or change it.

)))))▶ *Freeware, Shareware, Software*

ABOVE: Properties dialogue box of 'My Web Pages' folder
LEFT: Product Review Net offers reviews of a wide variety of products, from batteries to port

PUBLICIZING YOUR SITE

How to get noticed among the millions of sites on the Web? You could advertise, offline as much as on, but would need deep pockets. The Web works more by association. Most people will get to your site either as a link from another site or as the result of a search. To increase the chances of them finding you it is important to link up with as many relevant sites as possible. You can do this by joining a web circle (where sites on similar topics, such as web design, link to each other) or by contacting individual sites that cover related areas and suggesting reciprocal links. Search engines operate by different means, but many use spiders that scour the web to find as many pages as possible. In particular, they look for the keywords and phrases inserted as meta tags at the head of each HTML page. These tags describe the page content it contains and can improve the likelihood of your site being found by a relevant search.

))))➤ *Banner Ad, Search Directory, Search Engine, Web Authoring, Web Page: Creating I, Web Page: Creating II, Web Site, Yellow Pages*

BELOW: Quake is not an earthquake, but a popular Internet-based game and was the first big game designed to be played over the Internet

PUBLIC KEY CRYPTOGRAPHY

Encryption standard. This is an encryption system that uses two keys – one private key that is kept secret and a readily available public one. Because one key is used to lock the message (encode) and the other to unlock it (decode), it is an extremely secure method. Even if you know the public key it is not possible to work out the corresponding private one. This is the basis of a number of security systems, including digital certificates and SSL.

))))➤ *Email, Encryption, Security I: Basic*

PUBLISH

Having crafted your web site you need to publish it – that is, put it live on the Web. To do so you will need an FTP server to push your site pages up to the web server. Some web authoring programs come with a built-in FTP server. Otherwise you might have to use a stand-alone product such as CuteFTP for Windows or Fetch for the Macintosh. You will also need web space either from your ISP or from a web–hosting company.

))))➤ *FTP, Server, Upload, Web Page: Creating I, Web Page, Creating II, Web Site*

PUSH TECHNOLOGY

Broadcasting over the Net. Push technology works on the basis that the message comes to you, whether you asked for it or not. The Web is traditionally a pull technology – you send a request from your browser for a web page that is then sent to you by the server. Push technology, on the other hand, is much more like a broadcast where the information is sent out and people can tune in to view it. This could be through a news or stock prices ticker, an information channel or media player picking up a radio webcast.

))))➤ *Channel, Internet, Program, World Wide Web, WebTV*

QUAKE

Popular Internet-based game. Quake was the first big game to be designed to be played over the Internet. It has proven to be seriously addictive for gamers, who form their own clans and fight in special skins, or custom-designed outfits. Customized online versions are available at places such as QuakeWorld.

))))➤ *Games on the Net*

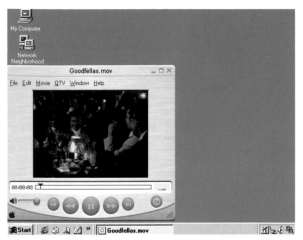

QUICKTIME

A standard format for viewing video and animation files, originally on the Apple Macintosh but now available on other platforms. It is commonly used by interactive multimedia software such as encyclopedias. The QuickTime player (or plug-in for viewing through browsers) is free and is available from the Apple site (*www.apple.com/quicktime*). It is also bundled with programs that need it to run. Quicktime files have the filename extension .mov and .qt.

)))➤ *Apple Computer, Media Players, Movies*

RADIO BUTTON

A way of selecting from a list of options when there is only one possible choice. Radio buttons are used when you have a list of options and it is only possible to select one of them. For example, when asked to select your age range from a number of different possible options. Each option has a circle by it. When selected (by clicking on it) a black dot appears inside the circle. Radio buttons are named after the old-style car radios where pushing the button for one channel automatically deselected the previous one. If you can select more than one option from a list then check boxes are used rather than radio buttons.

)))➤ *Checkbox, Input*

ABOVE: The trailer from Martin Scorsese's Goodfellas *viewed in QuickTime*

ABOVE RIGHT: CNN in RealPlayer

BOTTTOM RIGHT: Many major radio stations broadcast over the Internet

RADIO ONLINE

Radio broadcast via the Internet. Some commercial radio stations broadcast their programs over the Internet as well as by their transmitters. This means that you can log on to your favourite radio station even if you are not within its broadcast area. With Internet Explorer 5 there is a radio toolbar that gives you easy access to online radio stations. Many of the stand-alone media players now come with their own list of pre-tuned radio stations. You can choose by the type of music you like – classical, pop, rock, even talk.

)))➤ *Entertainment Web Sites, MP3, Music on the Internet*

REALAUDIO

A standard for delivering FM stereo sound quality across the Internet. The technology for streaming compressed audio is supported by the latest versions of the major browsers. A plug-in or stand-alone player, such as RealPlayer or Windows Media Player, is needed to listen to the sound files. Many radio stations broadcast over the Internet using RealAudio. A streaming media server is needed to deliver the sound from a web site. RealAudio files will have the filename extensions .ra and .ram.

)))➤ *Buffer, Media Players, Multimedia, Music on the Internet, Streaming*

REAL-TIME

Happening instantly. Real-time operating systems respond to any input immediately. Most computer operating systems are not real-time because they can take seconds, sometimes minutes, to react. There are systems where computers do need to respond instantly to any changes in information, such as air-traffic control computers tracking the position of aircrafts within a second so that they do not collide. In real-time animation, objects on the PC appear to move at the same speed as they would in real life.

))))▶ *Application, Multi-Tasking, Multithreaded, System*

RECEIVING EMAIL

One of the most pleasurable aspects of using the Internet is that moment when you have clicked to receive email and you are waiting to see who has sent you a message today. You have to be connected to the Internet to receive email, so connect in the usual way and launch your email application. The simplest way to receive email in Outlook Express for Windows is to click on the Send/Recv button on the toolbar. Outlook Express sends a request to your mail server to download all the messages waiting in your mailbox. Newly received email messages appear in the Inbox message list, displayed in bold to indicate that they have not been read.

))))▶ *Composing Email, Email, Forwarding Email, Outlook Express, Replying to Email*

RECOMMENDED SETTINGS

When installing a program, it is automatically configured with a set of recommended settings. Unless you know what you are doing it is best to leave these as they are, as they have been preset to give the maximum benefit to the most number of users.

))))▶ *Default, Properties*

REFERENCE WEB SITES

From conversion rates to definitions, if you want information there is somewhere on the Web you can find it. Want to know what xenon is, the conversion rate from kilometres to miles or what happened to your old school friends? There will be a web site you can refer to. Some are huge in their scope. Project Gutenberg

ABOVE: Real–time operating systems respond to any input immediately

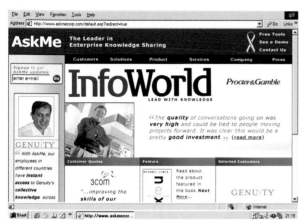

LEFT: *Browser view of* www.askme.com
BELOW: *There is plenty of relationship advice to be found on the Web*

(*www.gutenberg.net*) is an amazing attempt to put the text of most of the classic literary works online, while the About.com site (*www.about.com*) – visited by one in five Internet users every month – covers hundreds of specialist topics, from computing to wakeboarding. There are purely technical reference sites such as the Dictionary of Units (*www.ex.ac.uk/cimt/dictunit/dictunit.htm*), while online encyclopedias such as Encarta (*http://encarta.msn.co.uk*) attempt to cover the whole spectrum of human endeavour. If, however, you want a more human touch, try Ask Me (*www.askme.com*), where you can quiz an expert and get a reply by email – not instantaneous but useful. Or are you trying to catch up with old friends? Reunion sites such as *www.friendsreunited.co.uk* are springing up where people can register on their old school or college list and, for a small fee, contact others they may have lost touch with.

The only trouble in the bike shed is that some ex-pupils have made derogatory comments about their old teachers who are threatening legal action.

))))▶ *Literature Web Sites*

REGISTER.COM (*www.register.com*)

Web site offering registration for web site domain names and web site building and promotion services.

))))▶ *DNS, Domain, Name Registration*

RELATIONSHIPS: ADVICE ON

Whatever the problem there is always someone willing to give advice. As in the magazine world, relationships still tend to be categorized under subjects for women – witness iVillage.com (*www.ivillage.com/relationships*) – but they do affect both sexes. If you first want to evaluate what personality type you are then head for Close Relationships and Personality Research Web Site (*www.geocities.com/research 93*), fill in a short questionnaire and you will get feedback based on previous research. Similarly, if you want a dispassionate view on some current relationship problem go to I'm Right, You're Wrong (*www.imright.com*). Both sides post their argument online and registered users vote on the verdict.

))))▶ *Making Friends on the Internet*

REMOTE ACCESS

Network access from a distance. The ability to log into the office network from some remote location opened up the whole world of telecommuting. A liberation for some, it has proved a tyranny for others, who have no excuse for not staying in touch. All that is needed is a computer, a modem and some remote access software to dial into the network server and establish the connection. Once connected, the remote computer functions, to all extents and purposes, just as though it were connected directly to the network. However, depending on the type of connection, data transfer speeds may be much slower.

))))➤ *Remote Control, Telecommuting*

REMOTE CONTROL

Controlling a PC from afar. Not quite the TV-style remote control to operate the PC from the comfort of the couch. Rather it is a program that enables you to take control of your computer system from a remote location. Besides PC helpdesks, its main use is to enable you to access data on your home PC when you are away. It differs from remote access in that the only information sent is the keystrokes and screen updates. All the processing is done on the remotely controlled device. With remote access there is a two-way traffic between the two systems.

))))➤ *Remote Access, Telecommuting*

REMOTE RETRIEVAL

Message retrieval system. For the road warrior on the move, remote retrieval provides the easiest way to keep in touch. It enables you to call into your PC from a distant location and check for voicemail messages, emails and faxes. Messages can be played back over the phone or redirected to a PC near you. Faxes can also be redirected, either to a computer or a PC. Just so you know when to check, text messages can be sent to your mobile when mail arrives.

))))➤ *Email, Fax, Remote Access*

REPLYING TO EMAIL

If you use Outlook Express, you can reply to an email by clicking the Reply button on the toolbar. A new message window will appear with the contents of

ABOVE: Robots are programs that run automatically.
RIGHT: Browser view of www.rsi-inc.com

the sender's message included. You can either keep the sender's text and compose your message responding to the things the sender says, or you can delete it and type your message on its own. The sender's email address appears automatically in the To: box, so all you have to do is send your reply.

))))➤ *Composing Email, Email, Forwarding Emails, Outlook Express*

RESOURCE

A resource is really anything that can be used on a computer. So, a computer's memory is a resource in the same way as the more physical add-ons such as printers and scanners are. By contrast, a system resource has a more specific meaning as the data available to programs.

))))➤ *Application, Network, Software, System*

ROBOT

Automatic program. Also known as bots, these are programs that run automatically. They are particularly associated with spiders that crawl over the Web fetching web pages for search engines. These spiders follow the links from one page to another and feed them back. Large search engines have many spiders working together.

))))▶ *Internet, Search Engine*

ROUTER

Network connectors that ensure data reaches its destination by the quickest route possible. A router is really like a route planner. Routers connect two networks together, such as your local network to the Internet. Most importantly, routers check the headers on the information flowing through them to make sure it goes where it is

meant to and avoids any bottlenecks. First, it opens the header on each packet of data to see what the destination is. If it is on the same network, say within the same company, it sends it direct to the correct PC. If not, it sends it to another router closer to the destination and then that one in turn sends it further on. The number of routers or gateways a message passes through is known as the number of hops. To find the best route for the packets of data to go, the router runs a program that compares the destination address against an internal database called a routing table, which has detailed information on where packets with various IP addresses should be sent. If too many packets arrive at once they are held in an input queue, of which there may be several. If these fill then packets might be lost, in which case the TCP/IP protocol ensures they will be re-sent.

))))▶ *Network, Network Computer*

RTM

'Read the Manual'; advice, not always so politely given, to those posting time-wasting questions when they could have found the answer themselves. This is the polite version. It is often seen in chat rooms or newsgroup postings where more experienced hands feel their time is being wasted by newbies who ask silly questions that could be easily answered by looking in the manual (or more likely the FAQ list). The time-wasting question is a similar breach of netiquette as asking the same question answered elsewhere or posting messages to the wrong group.

))))▶ *Email, Netiquette, Newsgroups*

S/MIME

'Secure/MIME'; secure email attachment transfer. Using a method based on public-key encryption, S/MIME will enable people using different email clients to send secure messages to each other. A newer version of the MIME (Multipurpose Internet Mail Extensions) protocol, the main standard for converting attachments into plain ASCII text so they can be transmitted over the Internet. Secure/MIME supports messages that have been encrypted. It is based on public-key encryption technology, a system that is extremely secure and relatively simple to use. As a result, if S/MIME becomes widely adopted it will mean that even people using different email clients will be able to send secure messages to each other.

))))▶ *Email, Encryption, MIME, Security II: Advanced*

SATELLITE CONNECTION

A fast way to access the Internet for those in the remote locations that ADSL and Cable cannot reach. While ADSL brings broadband connections to many, users have to be within a certain distance from the telephone exchange. This is great for those in urban areas, but less good for those in more remote situations. The one way they can get high-speed Internet access is via satellite. It is a more expensive option as the cost of the satellite dish has to be taken into consideration as well as the service itself. While downloads are fast – received via the satellite – uploads are made through a standard dial-up connection.

))))▶ *DirectPC, High-speed Connection*

SCAMBUSTERS (*www.scambusters.com*)

Advice web site. Scambusters is devoted to offering guidance on avoiding fraud, scams, hoaxes, counterfeits and viruses.

)))⯈ *Hoaxes on the Internet, Privacy*

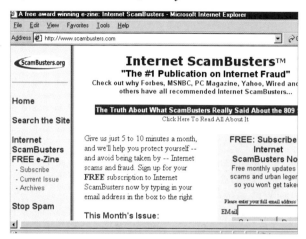

SCANNER

A device for putting images into a computer. A scanner is used to capture images, photographs and text for use in a computer. It works by using photo-electric cells to convert an image into digital data so it can be manipulated in a software program. The most common type is called a flat-bed scanner. Similar to a photocopier, it has a lid that opens to reveal a glass plate on which the item you want to scan is placed. Scanners come with their own dedicated software to run them. Many include an optional OCR (Optical Character Recognition) program that is used to 'read' a printed page and convert it into text for word processing. Many scanners allow you to scan transparencies, too.

)))⯈ *OCR, Peripherals, Printer*

SCHOOL AND THE INTERNET

For schools, the Internet is becoming an increasingly important source of general knowledge, news and educational material. In both the UK and the US, great efforts are being made to increase the number of computers in schools and make Internet access available to every child. In Britain, the government is investing heavily in networks such as the National Grid for Learning. We are still a long way from the universal 'information

superhighway' but more schools are being equipped with broadband access. This allows faster data transmission, permitting more students to browse online simultaneously and making streaming video and audio a possibility. Children lucky enough to have a computer with Internet access at home find the Internet a great help with homework and revision, and many schools are installing Internet-connected computers in libraries and study halls to bridge the gap between students who have the Internet and those who do not.

Teachers are finding that the Internet can be a valuable source of material. They can use search engines to find appropriate sites, and download text and images for use in lessons. A wealth of material is provided for this purpose by government-funded, non-profit and commercial web sites. Web sites providing learning materials for schools in the UK include Channel Four's 4Learning (*www.4learning.co.uk*) and the BBC (*www.bbc.co.uk*). Research Machines (*www.rm.com*) is a British company that specializes in providing a complete service to schools including computers, networks and software. Web sites abound in the US to serve the needs of teachers seeking resources and guidance, for example Teachers First (*www.teachersfirst.com*). Schools also find that many of the best web sites are operated by libraries, galleries and museums around the world.

Children instinctively enjoy browsing the Net and, with the direction of knowledgeable teachers, they can explore online and participate in 'edutainment'. There are several good sources of approved links to such web sites. These include the Parents Information Network (*www.pin.org.uk*) for UK sites, and Cool Sites for Kids (*www.ala.org/alsc/ children_links.html*), with links reviewed by the American Library Association, and The Kids on the Web (*www.zen. org/~brendan/kids.html*) for US sites.

Listed below is a small selection of web sites that schools may find helpful.

Dictionaries and encyclopedias

Kids can look up facts and words on sites such as Ask Oxford (*www.askoxford.com*).

Science and mathematics

Fascinating sites include NASA (*www.nasa.gov*) and Canterbury Environmental Education Centre (*www.naturegrid.org.uk*).

Art and museums

Museum of Modern Art (*www.moma.org*) and the Metropolitan Museum (*www.metmuseum.org*).

LEFT: Schools across the world can be linked through the Internet.
BELOW: Browser view of www.moma.org
BOTTOM: Whatever kids want to be when they grow up, the Internet can help

History and literature

Compare the enormous Library of Congress (*www.loc.gov*) with history teacher Andrew Field's highly rated site (*www.schoolhistory.co.uk*).

➤ ***Children and the Net I: Primary, Children and the Net II: Secondary, Education on the Internet, Kids' Web Sites, Students and the Internet***

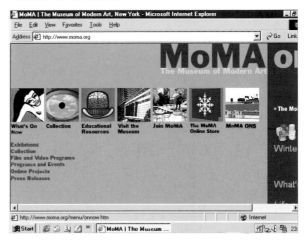

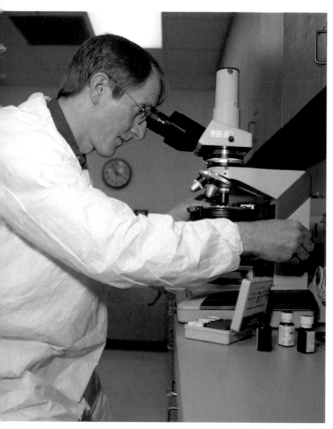

well-designed trip under the seas or through space checkout Sea and Sky (*www.seasky.org*). For ideas closer to home look at bizarre stuff you can make in your kitchen, at *www. freeweb.pdq.net/headstrong*. Whether it is how to make fake blood, or a radio with rusty razor blades, the site does not claim you will learn anything – but you may just enjoy it.

⟩⟩⟩➤ *Education on the Internet, Space Exploration Web Sites*

SCIENCE WEB SITES

Science on the Net; from determining your IQ to recipes for slime, the right scientific cook book is somewhere on the Web. Want to analyze your personality, dissect a frog, or conduct bizarre experiments in the home? All the science cook books that you need are on the Web. Intelligent enough to carry on? Check to see whether your IQ falls within the top two per cent of the population with online tests from the high IQ society Mensa (*www.mensa. org*). If not (or even if it does), go for robot wars at sites such as *www.battlebots.com*. From chemistry to physics and the environment, the Web has it all. It can be at the educational level – the interactive frog dissection (*http://curry.edschool.virginia.edu/go/frog*) is actually aimed at US high-school biology classes – or simply for those with an interest in learning a bit more about our planet. For a

SCSI

'Small Computer System Interface'; a high-speed parallel interface, commonly pronounced 'scuzzy'. A faster connection for peripheral devices than the traditional serial or parallel ports, SCSI is largely being replaced by USB connections. It is a standard for attaching peripheral devices, such as scanners, to computers. Mainly used in Apple Macintosh computers, USB connections are being introduced in preference across all PC platforms. A SCSI connection can send data

RIGHT: A SCSI connects external devices to computers

faster than a standard serial or parallel port, at up to 80 Mbs. In addition, several devices can be daisy-chained to a single SCSI port.

))))▶ **Interface, Parallel Port, Peripherals**

SEARCH DIRECTORY

An information search tool. Directories are a hierarchically structured way of presenting information on specific areas of interest. The distinction between a search directory and engine is, like many things on the Internet, becoming increasingly blurred. In general, information within a directory tends to be more structured. It is usually presented hierarchically with the main directory listings on the home page such as Business, Entertainment etc. By clicking on these you get to more specific information listed under sub-headings and you can continue to 'drill down' through these links until you reach the information you require. Probably the best-known directory is Yahoo.

))))▶ **Directory, Directory Service, Search Engine**

SEARCH ENGINE

A program that searches the Web, or any document, for keywords or phrases. Although commonly thought of as only searching the Web, a search engine is really any program that queries documents for specific terms or keywords. Enter the words or phrase you are looking for in a web search engine, such as AlltheWeb, Google or Alta Vista, and back comes a list of sites. Along

with brief details and a link comes a ranking of how likely it is to match the information you wanted. Typically, search engines work by sending out a spider that crawls the Web to find as many pages as possible. A second program then indexes the pages based on the words it finds.

))))▶ **Metasearch Program, Robot, Search Directory**

SEARCH PROVIDER

Search services for Net users; while individual web sites are searchable, search providers enable Net users to search the entire Web as well as some newsgroups. A search provider is really any system that provides search services to Internet users. In fact, the availability of freeware search software means that most web sites are searchable, although the keyword search function only works among the pages in the site. For searches across the Web it is necessary to use the traditional search engines such as Google (which also searches newsgroups) or directories such as About or Yahoo. There are also metasearch engines software that sends the query to several sites simultaneously and then removes duplicate answers and dead links from the replies.

))))▶ **Directory Service, Metasearch Program, Search Directory, Search Engine**

SECURE SERVER

A web server that uses any of the major security protocols to enable confidential information to be sent across the Web. This is particularly important for e-commerce, when customers have to be sure that their personal information or credit-card details cannot be intercepted. The most common security protocol used is SSL (Secure Socket Layer), which establishes a secure connection between two computers using a method based on public-key encryption. There are others, however, such as S-HTTP which is designed to send individual messages securely.

))))▶ **Credit-card Safety, E-commerce, Security I: Basic, Security II: Advanced**

Caption (top right):
LEFT *Browser view of* www.freeweb.pdq.net/headstrong
FAR LEFT: *The Web covers all areas of science, from robot wars to frog dissection*
BELOW: *Search results at go.com for keyword 'Beatles'*

SECURITY 1: BASIC

Protecting you and your property online. Security on the Internet is an important area of concern. It includes a wide range of issues, including online shopping with credit cards, cybercrimes and anti-social activities such as viruses and junk email, and the problem of downloads that could cause malfunctions on your computer. But do not despair: a list of recommended measures to increase your security is given below.

Security concerns

Much concern about online security centres around protecting your privacy when giving your personal and financial details to others. Many people prefer not to use their credit cards to shop on the Net. Your security can be undermined by various deliberate means: hacking, viruses, junk email (spam), and cybercrime. At other times, the security of your computer can be threatened by web sites attempting to download potentially damaging files.

What can you do?

Just as there is not a villain waiting on every street corner, neither is the Net crawling with malevolent hordes out to get you, but it makes sense to be 'street-wise' when going online.

Online shopping and forms

To protect your personal data when shopping online or filling in a form, verify that the page on which you enter and submit your details uses the Secure Socket Layer (SSL) protocol. There are two ways to check this:

1. The address of the web page should begin with https: instead of the usual http:

RIGHT: Security on the internet is an important area of concern

2. A small locked padlock icon should appear in the bottom right-hand corner of the browser window (Internet Explorer) or bottom left-hand corner (Netscape Navigator 4.0 and later)

Reputable web sites

Only do business with online traders that are accredited by one of the major security certification authorities. A reputable web enterprise will have a privacy policy document – read it carefully. Look for a box to tick that instructs the company not to divulge your personal data to any third parties.

Set up your software programs

Here are some tips for setting up the security features on two popular Microsoft applications, Internet Explorer and Outlook Express.

Internet Explorer offers a number of security options that you can set up. To access them in Internet Explorer 5 or 6 select Tools|Internet|Options|Security.

Alerts: By selecting Tools|Internet Options| Security| Custom Level, you can set up a choice of alerts. Each type of alert triggers a dialogue box to warn you when you are about to do something online that could be insecure. For example, one alert warns you that you are about to send a form that is not secure.

Certificate Authorities: Select Tools|Internet Options|Content|Certificates|Trusted Root Certification Authorities to display a list of security certificates issued by the authorized organizations that validate web sites. You can trust sites that have credentials issued by these authorities. You do have options here to view the details of certificates, delete them, enable/disable them, add passwords or reset to the default list. It is usually best to leave these as they are.

Security Zones: To increase your security further, you can use the Security Zones feature in Explorer to control the ability of web sites to download potentially damaging content on to your hard disk. You do this by setting

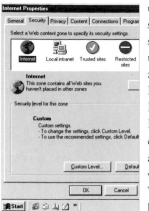

up various zones, identifying suspect web sites and specifying security levels for them. You can choose four zones of web content: Local Intranet, Trusted Sites, Internet and Restricted Sites. For each of these zones, you can add and remove the addresses of web sites about which you are concerned. You can then set a security level for each zone:

High: excludes content that could damage your computer.
Medium: warns you before running potentially damaging content.
Low: does not warn you before running potentially damaging content.
Custom: lets you specify types of permissible content (for advanced users).

Once these options are set up, every time you visit one of the specified web sites, Internet Explorer will automatically exclude, warn you about, or allow downloads on to your computer, according to your settings.

If you use Outlook Express, you can use a feature to reduce the problem of junk mail.

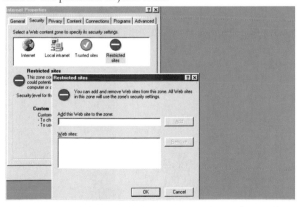

Rules: To access Rules, select Tools|Message Rules|Mail. You can set up your own rules that instruct Outlook Express how to deal with junk email. For example, you could set up a rule that instructs Outlook Express to

BELOW: Outlook Express | Tools | Messages Rules | Mail [New Mail Rule]

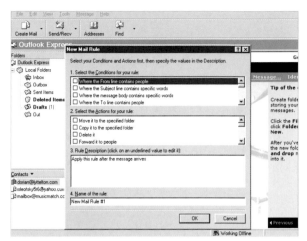

automatically delete any incoming email with '!!!GET RICH QUICK!!!' in the subject line.

Combating viruses Viruses are often distributed as attachments to emails. The best rule for combating such viruses is never open attachments from senders that you do not know. Also use a virus-checking software program and regularly visit the maker's web site to get the latest updates.

))))▶ *Credit Cards, Credit Card Safety, Internet Explorer, Junk Email, Outlook Express, Privacy, Security II: Advanced, Virus Checker*

SECURITY II: ADVANCED

Protecting yourself on the Web. Invasions of privacy, hacker attacks and intercepted information can all be protected against with the right measures of security.

The Internet was designed to help people share information but that openness is also its vulnerability. For instance, cookies can be useful for remembering user names and passwords and for delivering personalized content, but they can also be used to track users' movements in ways that raise concerns over privacy. It is possible to set your browser to refuse cookies, but you will lose the convenience they provide. Internet Passports based on standards such as the Platform for Privacy Preferences (P3P) the Internet Content and Exchange (ICE) and the Open Profiling Standard (OPS) attempt to get round this problem. The passports are stored inside the browser and allow users to declare what information they will give to web sites and what can be shared between web sites.

It is more than privacy that is under attack, though: sometimes it is the whole network. Hackers launch denial-of-service attacks, often at ISPs or high-profile sites, which cripple their servers by flooding them with traffic. DoS attacks are difficult to protect against, as the traffic is sent via legitimate networks, but hackers also attack individual computers. They gain access through programs such as Back Orifice, which you can unwittingly let on to your computer by opening an infected email. This opens a port that a hacker's port probe will detect. Through it they can take control of your computer, access and delete

files or programs etc. Online sites such as Steve Gibson's *www.grc.com* run a program that will detect what ports are open on your machine. You can further protect yourself with a personal firewall that screens the packets of data as they go to and from the Internet and blocks any that are suspicious.

There are also fears that information can be intercepted. Encrypting the data means it would look like gibberish to any unauthorized person who got hold of it. It is encryption that plays a fundamental part in ensuring that it is safe to send confidential information, such as credit-card numbers, over the Internet. The most common method is public-key encryption where there are two keys, one to encrypt the message and another to decrypt it.

Such encryption is also used to verify the identity of the sender in Digital certificates. These are issued by certification authorities – such as VeriSign – with the relevant information encoded in such a way that it uniquely identifies the sender and proves that it has not been tampered with.

))))▶ *DES, Encryption, Privacy, Security I: Basic*

ABOVE: Browser view of www.grc.com

LEFT: You never know when, or by whom, your privacy will be invaded, so it is important to protect yourself with the right security measures

SENDING EMAIL

Sending email is one of the most satisfying things you can do on the Net. It is a simple process that only requires basic typing and word-processing skills. This is how to send an email:

1. Click the Create Mail button on the mail toolbar. A new message window opens, containing the following elements: Toolbar (text editing), To: field, Cc: field, Subject: field, Formatting toolbar, Message body area.
2. Enter the email address of the person you are sending the email to in the To: field. Enter any other email addresses in the Cc: field if required.
3. Type the subject of the message in the Subject: field.
4. Type your message in the message body area.
5. Format your text using the formatting buttons, if required.
6. Click the Send button. You need to be connected to the Net in order to send the message to your mail server. To cut down on phone bills, you can compose your emails offline and go online just long enough to send them.

))))▶ *Composing Email, Email, Forwarding Email, Offline, Phone Bills: Cutting Down On, Replying to Email*

SEND TO COMMAND

A quick way to redirect files and folders and open programs to deal with them. This is one of the most convenient features in Windows. Click on a document icon and you can use the Send To command to send it to a different folder or to another program. You can also add to the list of possible Send To destinations. This is particularly useful if you want to send the document as an email or fax. Click on Send To and it opens the appropriate program. The Send To command is also a quick way to create shortcuts on the desktop or to move files.

))))▶ *Email, Fax, Windows Operating System*

SERIAL PORT

The physical connection at the back of a PC where the device is attached. The COM port, such as COM1, COM2 etc. is the connection used by software programs to connect to the device, such as an external modem. By using a serial cable two computers can be connected directly. With a serial port, data is transmitted one bit at a time, in contrast to parallel ports where several bits are transmitted simultaneously.

))))➤ *Interface, Parallel Port, Port*

SERVER

Computer-operating networked services; a computer, or software program, that provides a specific service to client software running on other computers. Everybody who connects to the Internet does so via a service provider (typically an ISP or OSP), which operates one or more servers. These are the powerful computers that are linked together to form the Internet. When you are connected to the server, your computer is technically called a client. When you click on a hyperlink to request a new web page to be displayed, or click the Send button in your email

program, you are transmitting instructions from your client computer to the server to carry out tasks on your behalf.

))))➤ *ISP, OSP, Secure Server*

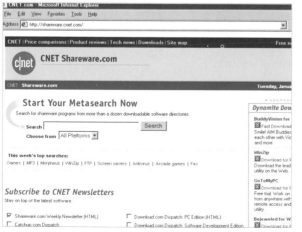

SHAREWARE

Software programs on the honour system. Shareware software programs are widely available to download and try free of charge. If you continue to use the program beyond the free trial period, you are expected to pay for it. Many very useful and popular programs are issued as shareware and it is a good idea to pay to register your copy to get updates, and to recompense the

SHOCKWAVE

A special technology developed by Macromedia that enables multimedia sound and video to run on web pages. A Shockwave file is written using an authoring tool called Director, after which it is compressed. It can be difficult to author, as it uses its own Lingo programming language, but it has a number of advantages: it supports many other formats; it can be streamed and brings CD-Rom-like interactivity to the Web; it also works across different platforms. To view it in your browser you need the Shockwave plug-in, which is available free from the Macromedia site.

))➤ *Hypermedia, Multimedia, Plug-In, Web Browser*

SHOPPER.COM

Online shopping search engine. Linked to *Computer Shopper* magazine and part of the giant CNET network, shopper.com is a search engine for buying hardware and software products online.

))➤ *E-commerce, Shopping Online, Shopping Search*

developer for his work. Shareware is often confused with freeware, open source or public-domain software, which is genuinely free and generally without any restrictions.

))➤ *Demo, Download, Finding Files on the Net, Freeware, Shareware.com, Tucows*

SHAREWARE.COM (*www.shareware.com*)

Software download web site. *Shareware.com* is a much-visited web site that searches through a vast range of programs on other shareware sites. It also offers product reviews, news and a weekly newsletter.

))➤ *Demo, Download, Finding Files on the Net, Freeware, Shareware, Tucows*

CENTRE: Shockwave enables multimedia sound and video to run on web pages
ABOVE: Shopper.com offers information and prices for a wide range of products
LEFT: Browser view of www.shareware.com

SHOPPING ONLINE

The variety of online shops reflects a lot of the Web's strengths, but precautions should be taken to ensure that extra costs and duties do not bring unwelcome surprises and that the transaction is a safe one.

1. Online shopping can take advantage of a lot of the Web's strengths. There are no geographic boundaries; you can shop as easily for Italian shoes in Italy as New York. You can personalize your purchases, such as made-to-measure clothes. It is good for the considered purchase, for those products that need a bit of research like cars, and it is easy to compare prices.

2. Web trading also has its disadvantages. You cannot try before you buy. At peak times your dial-up connection may be slow, as bad as any queues in a real-world checkout. There are additional costs besides Internet charges, such as shipping charges, which will vary depending on how quickly you want your goods delivered and where they are coming from. Import duties, sales taxes and handling charges may also be due. If you are buying from a different country your rights of redress – if anything goes wrong – may be more limited and difficult to enforce.

3. You can go to online shopping directories (such as the UK-focused *www.shopsonthenet.com*, which lists more than 21,000 online stores) to get an idea of what is available. There is a near-limitless choice – the specialist delicatessen, the store (*www.amazon.com*), the shopping mall, department stores (*www.macys.com*), auction houses (*www.qxl.com*), even the cyberspace equivalent of the classified ads (*www.loot.com*).

4. It can be nice to get someone to do the shopping for you – hence shopping bots, automated programs that search out the bargains for you. Some, such as *www.bottomdollar.com*, which describes itself as a shopping search engine, will compare prices on several sites and show what is available.

5. There is fraud online, just as there is in real-world retailing. We blithely give away our credit-card number when we are paying over the counter, or ordering over the phone, yet somehow the perceived risk of buying online is greater. In fact, the majority of problems shopping online come from disputed orders rather than sales using stolen credit-card numbers.

ABOVE: Shopping online

ABOVE RIGHT: Browser view of www.shopsonthenet.com

LEFT: The selection of goods available online is almost limitless

6. In e-commerce, as anywhere, there are some sensible precautions you can take. Only hand over personal details and credit-card numbers to sites that use secure servers where important information is sent encrypted. Be wary if the site is asking for lots of personal information. While some sites do this for their market research, answers should be optional. The only information you should have to give is that normally asked for when paying by credit card.

As in any high street a familiar name is reassuring. Even businesses that work purely online (such as amazon.com) spend a lot on marketing offline to help establish their name.

If in doubt, check it out. The site should give details of the company's real-world address and phone numbers. Contact them to get further information or to reassure yourself they are who they say they are. Never buy from a site where the only contact is an email address.

Make a screen grab and print out the web pages containing your order information.

Do not forget that if you pay by credit card and there is a problem, the credit-card company may be legally liable to make good any loss you have suffered.

7. To make the process seem more familiar most e-tailers have their online equivalent of the shopping trolley (also called basket or cart). You browse around the store and click when you want to add something to the basket. A well-designed e-commerce store will also let you remove items from the basket, change the number you want and hold the items until you are ready to pay. When you are decided on your purchases you go to the checkout.

8. At the checkout you will need to fill in the paperwork – online forms asking for details of your name, address, and credit-card information. You also choose how you want your items delivered and at what cost. The total amount is shown and at that stage you can either go ahead or withdraw if you change your mind.

9. Like their real-world counterparts, some stores are better at handling the sales process than others. At some online stores filling in the forms can be an inordinately long business. It can be difficult to get clear information about delivery options (and costs) even if the item is in stock. Sometimes there is no acknowledgement of what has been ordered. Most good stores will email you details of your purchases and even provide a reference number for tracking where your order is in the system.

10. There should also be a link telling you what the company's returns policy is, if the goods are not as described or are damaged in some way, along with details of any guarantees or warranties attached to your purchases.

))))➤ *E-commerce, shopper.com, Shopping Search*

SHOPPING SEARCH (www.shoppingsearch.com)

Shopping search web site. This site searches through a number of other shopping sites to compile lists of the best prices on a range of products including electronic goods, furniture and pet supplies.

))))▶ *E-commerce, shopper.com, Shopping Online*

SHORTCUTS

Icon or quick route to a file. In Windows, a shortcut is an icon placed on the desktop that l inks to a file, folder or program. The shortcut has the same icon as the original file except for a tiny arrow added to the bottom left-hand corner. It is not a duplicate file, but a pointer to that file. The equivalent on an Apple Mac is called an alias. In Windows, you can also use shortcut keys. These are key combinations that work like shortcuts. You can assign a shortcut key combination to a file, folder or program.

))))▶ *File, Folder, Icons, Program, Windows Operating System*

SIGNATURE

Digital signatures used to replace handwritten ones or text files with contact details in order to bring a new level of confidence to secure communications. While a signature may simply be that – a scanned image of your handwritten signature or a text file with your contact details – it can also be a digital signature. Such signatures add digital codes to messages that guarantee that the sender is not only the person they claim to be, but also that the message has not been tampered with during transmission. To prevent digital signatures being forged they are encrypted, usually using a method called public-key encryption.

))))▶ *Email, Password, Sending Email, Usenet*

SIGNATURE FILE

An add-on to the end of an email message containing contact details, company information or sometimes even a thought for the day. Signature files are short text files automatically inserted at the bottom of emails or newsgroup postings. After the usual contact details users often include a favourite quote or philosophical saying. Less loftily, it may include company mission statements, legal disclaimers or even product promotions. It is possible to set up several signature files, for example one for personal use and one that follows the company's standard format.

))))▶ *Email, File, Password, Sending Email, Usenet*

SITE MANAGEMENT

The maintenance of a web site once it has been created. This can involve a multitude of skills. Not only is there the technical maintenance of the web server, it is also important to update the site regularly so there is new content to attract users. This might involve editing web pages as well as incorporating a system of checks to ensure that pages are cross-browser compatible and that there are no missing or broken links.

))))▶ *Hyperlink, Web Page, Webmaster, Web Site*

---

digital signature - a searchSecurity definition - see also: e-signature - Microsoft Internet Explorer

File   Edit   View   Favorites   Tools   Help

Address http://searchsecurity.techtarget.com/sDefinition/0,,sid14_gci211953,00.html   ▾ ⏎ Go

digital signature   powered by ◎ whatis?com

A digital signature (not to be confused with a digital certificate) is an electronic signature that can be used to authenticate the identity of the sender of a message or the signer of a document, and possibly to ensure that the original content of the message or document that has been sent is unchanged. Digital signatures are easily transportable, cannot be imitated by someone else, and can be automatically time-stamped. The ability to ensure that the original signed message arrived means that the sender cannot easily repudiate it later.

A digital signature can be used with any kind of message, whether it is encrypted or not, simply so that the receiver can be sure of the sender's identity and that the message arrived intact. A digital certificate contains the digital signature of the certificate-issuing authority so that anyone can verify that the certificate is real.

How It Works

Decisions 2002
>New Newsletters: Fi
& Virus Tips
>Top Security Predic
2002
>Top Security News

▭ Email this page t
friend

Information Sec
Solutions

CryptoSwift H

◎ Internet

SLIP

'Serial Line Internet Protocol'; a method for connecting to the Internet using a dial-up connection via a modem. This is now being replaced by the newer and more reliable Point-to-Point Protocol (PPP), which is more sophisticated and has the capacity to re-send any packages that have been garbled, which frequently happens with bad telephone lines. Some service providers still support both protocols, but PPP is the more popular. SLIP can only transport data using TCP/IP, whereas PPP can carry data using different protocols, such as IPX or Appletalk, at the same time on the same connection.

)))➡ *Modem V: Technical, Network, PPP, Serial Port*

SMILEYS AND EMOTICONS

Graphics created using text characters to suggest an emotion. When you get an email or look at a posting in a newsgroup it is sometimes difficult to tell when someone is being serious or joking. To help out a research scientist suggested using small text glyphs to show people's feelings. Thus the smiley :-) was born and a whole vocabulary made up of the punctuation characters and spaces used in plain text has followed. Smileys are also dubbed 'emoticons', short for 'emotional icons' but they now cover much more than feelings. The original plain text icons are best viewed with the head slightly tilted to the left (or you might end up puzzled ?:-/).

)))➡ *ASCII Art, Chat, Email, Newsgroups*

ABOVE- Maintaining a web site can require a team effort
LEFT: Article on digital signatures at http://searchsecurity.techtarget.com

SMTP

'Simple Mail Transfer Protocol'; the standard set of rules for sending email. SMTP is the system used for sending messages between servers and from your PC to the mail server. The messages are then retrieved from the server using either the POP3 protocol or the more powerful IMAP. This is why when you set up your email client, such as Outlook Express, you normally have to specify the address of both your POP (or IMAP) server and the SMTP server. Often these will be different, in the form *pop.ispname.com* and *smtp.ispname.com*

))))➤ *Email, IP, POP3, Sending Email*

SOCKET

The standard method of linking programs to the protocols that enable them to connect to the Internet. While your computer uses the rules within TCP/IP to connect to the Internet, it also needs software that enables the PC to handle and understand that protocol. The link between the two is called a socket, or TCP/IP stack. Despite its name, which suggests some sort of hardware, it is software. The software for PCs is called Winsock (short for Windows Sockets) and for Macs it is MacTCP. They both provide a standard way for Internet client programs, such as a browser, to work with the Internet connection program controlled by the operating system.

))))➤ *Internet, UNIX, Windows Operating System, Winsock*

SOFTWARE GUIDES

There are many software download sites, so competition is increasing to make them more meaningful. Magazine publishers have the advantage that they can link to software reviews from their hard-copy titles (*www.zdnet.com*). Nearly all sites give rankings based on user ratings, as well as publishing user reviews (*www.download.com*). One of the selling features of Tucows (*www.tucows.com*) is that it has mirror sites around the world, so download time can be improved by using a local site. At Software Vault they ensure the downloads they host are up-to-date by polling authors nightly for the latest information.

))))➤ *download.com, Search Engine, shareware.com, Software, Tucows*

SOFTWARE NEEDED TO CONNECT TO THE INTERNET

Internet software programs. You are most likely to use a computer and a modem to make use of the Internet. These items are called hardware. But you also need something else – software. If your computer is a PC running Windows you are in luck, because all the software you need to connect to the Internet comes with the Windows operating system. The various software programs are listed below.

Communications software

Before going online, you must first set up your connection by configuring the communications software. This software works

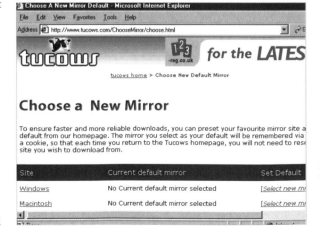

BELOW: *Choose a mirror site at* www.tucows.com *to speed up your download*

with the modem to transfer data to and from other computers on the Internet. Many ISPs or OSPs will provide you with a disk that installs its own software and easy-to-follow instructions on the setting up procedure. If no disk is supplied, you should use Windows' Internet Connection Wizard to enter the connection details manually. You need to use this software each time you connect to the Net.

Browser

The browser is the software program you use to browse web pages on the World Wide Web. The inventor of the pioneering browser program Mosaic went on to launch the popular Netscape browser that helped to popularize the Web. The most commonly used browser now is Microsoft's Internet Explorer. This comes with the Windows operating system. When you first launch your browser, it displays your home page. To visit other pages you can type in another web site's address in the Address field and click the Go button, or simply click on a hyperlink.

Email

This is the other main software program that you will use on the Internet. An email software program allows you to send and receive email messages. Commonly used email programs include Microsoft's Outlook Express (which comes with Windows) and Eudora. An email program provides a range of standard features to make it easy to use. You can create a new message, reply to a message sent to you, forward a message on to a third party or delete unwanted messages. Another standard feature is an address book that allows you to maintain a database of email addresses of your contacts.

OSPs

Some of the most popular OSPs supply their own software for the Internet, incorporating a browser and email and other services such as instant messaging. AOL is a well-known OSP.

)))➤ *AOL, Connecting to the Internet I: Basic, Hardware Needed to Connect to the Internet, Internet Connections, ISP, OSP*

SOFTWARE: PURCHASING

The increasing use of broadband connections to the home, both ADSL and cable, have made online software purchasing a much more attractive proposition. The high-speed connections mean programs can be downloaded in around a tenth of the time it would have taken previously. Accordingly, many software companies, such as Symantec, sell downloadable versions of their software online, as do mail order companies such as Jungle (*www.jungle.com*). There is an obvious saving in post and packing charges for the user, although there is still the option to buy a boxed copy for delivery.

))))➤ *E-commerce, shopper.com, Shopping Search*

SOUND CARD

Audio circuit board. A sound card is a circuit board that plugs into an expansion slot inside your PC. Using an analogue-to-digital/digital-to-analogue converter, a sound card can record audio files and replay them so that they are heard through your PC's loudspeakers. It can also generate analogue sounds, such as musical notes, using the digital-to-analogue converter or an FM synthesis chip. Musicians use sound cards to control MIDI instruments.

))))➤ *Audio File, Sound File*

SOUND FILE

A file stored on disk that contains sound data. This can be of two types:, a digitized analogue sound signal or notes for a MIDI instrument. Under the first method the continuous audio signal is 'sampled' thousands of times per second and the results are stored digitally. The higher the sampling rate, the better quality of sound and the larger the file. With MIDI sound, no actual sound samples are sent, the synthesizer simply sends the instructions that tell the sound board how to reproduce the sound.

))))➤ *Audio File, MIDI, MP3, Sound Card, WAVE (WAV) File, WMA*

SOUND RECORDER

A simple to operate sound-recording program that comes with the Windows operating system. Want to add your own sounds to Windows or to a document? Try Sound Recorder, a basic but easy to use

sound-recording program that is packaged with Windows. It not only allows you to record sounds (if you have a microphone), but also to mix, play and edit them. You will still need a sound card and speakers on your PC for playback. The program can be accessed from the Enter-tainment folder in the Accessories section of the Start menu.

))))➤ *Audio File, Sound Card, Sound File*

SPACE EXPLORATION WEB SITES

Travelling through space in Cyberspace. The final frontier has been passed several times by US and Russian space missions, but it still contains many mysteries. The main source of information for all things in space is NASA. The top level of their site at *www.nasa.gov* provides links to their many missions and discoveries. But this just fronts a whole labyrinth of databases covering such delights as a daily image from space and the solar-system simulator (*http://space.jpl.nasa.gov*), where you select your options and create a colour image of your favourite planet. To get your own view of space you can send requests to a robotic telescope (*www.telescope.org/rti/*) to look at a particular area.

))))➤ *Science Web Sites*

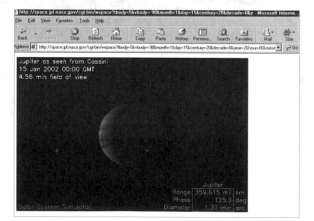

SPAM

Unwanted email. Spam is the scourge of email. It is the online equivalent of junk mail. It offers the same unsolicited diet of ads pushing everything from losing weight and getting rich quick to buying a degree. Certain email services, such as AOL, have made attempts to reduce the amount of spam travelling through their servers. You can attempt to block it, by setting up keyword or address filters in your email client, but these are rarely completely successful. Spam still gets everywhere, not only wasting people's time with unwanted mail but also eating up a lot of bandwidth. There is nothing more annoying than logging on to your ISP's mail server and finding that the lengthy download was all junk. Because the Internet is public there is little that can be done, although you should be wary of which sites you hand your email address to. Some people find it useful to have separate email accounts – one for business or friends and another to use when signing up to newsletters or promotions.

))))➤ *Email, Filtering, Junk Email, Spam: History of*

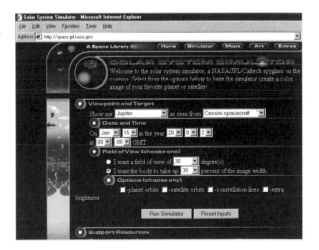

ABOVE: You can make your own journey into space, courtesy of the Web
LEFT: Browser view of http://space.jpl.nasa.gov; *Jupiter as seen from Cassini, 15 January 2002*

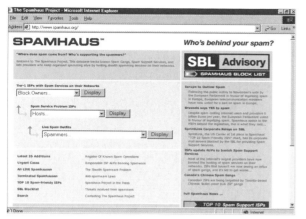

SPAM: HISTORY OF

The story of junk email. Spam is the jargon word for junk email, which is unsolicited email sent in bulk by unscrupulous people. Spam also refers to the same article being repeatedly posted a high number of times to one or more newsgroups.

The identity of the person who coined the term is not known, although it has been attributed to programmers in the early 1990s. The source name, however is well-known: it comes from the tinned luncheon meat product made by Hormel Foods. Originally infuriated by the linking of their famous food product with a notorious form of Net abuse, they now accept the situation. Hormel claim that the blame rests with the British comedy troupe Monty Python and their television sketch in which a group of Vikings sing a chorus of 'SPAM, SPAM, SPAM...' in an intrusive and repetitious manner in an attempt to drown out other conversation. The link being that junk email is seen as drowning out normal discourse on the Internet.

One spam-sending company whose name lives in web infamy is the Arizona law firm Canter & Siegel, who sent bulk postings advertisements to Usenet groups. Their idea backfired when they were 'flamed' (inundated with emails from multiple senders) by thousands of irate newsgroup members and could not filter out genuine responses from the avalanche of hate mail that clogged their server.

The problem of spam has not gone away and a number of web sites, such as Samspace (*www.samspace.org*) and Spamhaus (*www.spamhaus.org*), have sprung up to offer software tools and advice for combating spam.

))))▶ *Email, Junk Email, Spam*

SPECIFYING DESTINATION FOLDER FOR DOWNLOAD

It is a good idea to set up a special folder for all downloads, to make sure they do not get lost. Call the folder Downloads and when the file transfer starts select this as the destination folder. That way you will know where the program is, otherwise you will have to hunt through your folders to locate the missing file.

))))▶ *Directory, Download, Navigation*

SPORT ON THE NET

Sports information on the Web. A fan's paradise, the Net lets you see, follow and talk about your team, however lowly they are. Many local sports clubs have set up their own web sites and even discussion boards as a handy way for members to keep in touch. They are small-scale versions of similar fanzines and official web sites are *de rigueur* for any major club or sport. Sport is also a powerful driver for e-commerce. Football (soccer) clubs such as the celebrated English team Manchester United have as many fans around the world as they do in their home country, all wanting their replica team strip. As broadband coverage increases, more sports events will be webcast, but already fans can tune into streaming radio for live coverage of important games. The Web is also the ultimate quiz answer book. Whether it is from the cricketing pages of Wisden, the Association of Football Statisticians or the pages of NFL.com you will find the answer to that niggling question. This is also the place you can find out what the rules of darts are or indeed what is wakeboarding (for the uninitiated it is waterskiing on a board…).

))))➤ *Games on the Net*

SPREADSHEET

Calculation file or software program. A spreadsheet is a special type of file that is most frequently used for doing numerical calculations and designing reports and tables. The software program that produces such a file is called a spreadsheet program, and the most popular one is Microsoft Excel. When you create a new spreadsheet file, a window filled with a simple grid opens. The grid is composed of columns identified by letters along the top (A, B, C and so on) and rows identified by numbers (1, 2, 3 etc.) along the left margin. Each rectangle in the grid is called a cell. You can type both words and numbers into cells, but the real power of a spreadsheet lies in its ability to manipulate numbers.

You could, for example, create a cash-flow document for logging the number of products you sell month by month. Down the first column, you could type the names of the products, a different one on each row: Apples, Pears, Lemons, for example. Then, at the top of 12 columns, you could type in the months of the year: January, February, March, and so on. You could then enter the number of each product sold in the appropriate cell. You could use the calculating ability of the spreadsheet to display not only how many products were sold each month, but also how many of each type of product were sold in the year.

If you run a business, you might find it useful to set up a spreadsheet to make invoices. You could, for example, type the name and address of your business and the name of the person to whom you are sending the invoice. On separate rows you could type the products or services you sell, the number of units sold, the price per unit and the total price. At the bottom you could enter a calculation to display the total amount due.

Spreadsheets such as Excel also have powerful graphical functions. You can use these to produce colourful charts and graphs from your data. These are useful when producing reports or presentations. Excel has formatting buttons similar to those found in Word. These can be used to format a spreadsheet to make it easier to read on screen and create a good impression when printed. You could, for example, make your column headings bold and negative numbers red. As with a word-processing file, you can save a spreadsheet file and print it.

))))➤ *Application, Office Suite*

LEFT: There are plenty of web sites to entertain sports fans
FAR LEFT: Browser view of www.spamhaus.org

SSL (SECURE SOCKET LAYER)

'Secure Socket Layer'; a protocol used for sending encrypted documents securely via the Internet. It works by using public key encryption to enable one computer to check the identity of another. Many web sites use the protocol when asking for confidential information, such as credit-card numbers. Web pages that use an SSL connection start with https: instead of http:.

))))▶ *Security II: Advanced, Web Server*

STOCKBROKERS ONLINE

Across time zones and stock exchanges online brokers enable you to trade shares in real-time. This is your chance to keep up with the day traders – or even to be one. The global nature of the Internet makes it particularly useful for trading in stocks around the world. If you have the stamina you could trade on markets across different time zones. Under new investment schemes it is even possible to buy shares on foreign exchanges in a single currency, such as sterling.

To trade shares online you will need the services of a broker. As you deal in real-time, with confirmation of your trade direct to your screen, share prices in the trading area will be shown live. Some stockbrokers also provide share-price tickers that sit on your desktop scrolling through the (usually delayed) prices of stocks in your portfolio.

Most brokers offer execution-only trading – that is they will not give investment advice but will simply carry out any requests. There is usually no shortage of advice elsewhere on the site, though, with access to news, broker forecasts, research, charts and even investment tips from the press. While some brokers charge a flat-rate fee for each trade regardless of the number of shares involved, others will charge a percentage.

))))▶ *Banking and Finance on the Net, Banking and Finance Web Sites, Business Web Sites*

STORING FILES ON THE NET

Online file storage. Storing files online is not only secure, but it also enables access from anywhere there is an Internet connection. In an increasingly mobile world the chances are you can be logging on to the Internet from any number of places – a customer's premises, Internet café and so on. Inevitably the urgent file you want will be inaccessible on the hard drive of your PC at home. By storing files on the Net they can be

ABOVE: Browser view of www.freedrive.com
LEFT: Stockbrokers in the days before the Internet

accessed from any machine. This is a good solution for sharing or accessing frequently used files or for backing up data. Files can be securely transferred and access can be password protected.

)))**➤** *Directory, FreeDrive, Upload, Web Site*

STREAMING AUDIO/VIDEO

Sound or video files that play in real-time rather than having to be fully downloaded first. Probably the best example of this is online radio. For it to work properly it might need a plug-in, such as RealAudio, which has become the de facto standard for audio data on the Internet. As the streamed sound or video is delivered to the PC it is passed to the program (the player or plug-in) that processes it and displays it. If the program receives the data quicker than it can handle it, it is stored in a buffer.

)))**➤** *Buffer, Download, Hypermedia, Plug-In, RealAudio*

STRING

Any series of characters that are treated by the PC as a group. This is different from a name in that it does not have to stand for something else as it is not representing an object. It might just be given that name by a programmer to make it easy to refer to that string. A string is usually shown by being enclosed within single or double quote marks. For example, Bookends would be a name, but 'bookends' would just represent a string of characters.

)))**➤** *Boolean Modifier, Input*

STUDENTS AND THE INTERNET

The Internet for learners. With computers and Internet access widely available in schools and colleges, students are finding that the Internet is becoming an indispensable resource for their education and leisure. They use the Internet for research and revision, accessing libraries and other universities, making contacts with other students, distance-learning courses, and for a host of leisure activities including music downloads, chat and entertainment listings.

The Internet is also the best place to do research. It gives students access to the world's best libraries, art galleries, museums and science establishments. They can search through databases of articles and look up facts to aid them in writing essays and revising for exams. The Net

makes it possible for students in different parts of the world to collaborate on projects, share information and publish their findings. Educational establishments were among the earliest members of the Internet and their often-excellent web sites are a valuable source of information for students comparing courses and colleges. On the negative side, a tiny minority of students are unfortunately tempted to use the technology to copy other people's work, but anti-plagiarism software is deployed to catch them out.

A growing number of colleges offer distance-learning courses. These use web technology to offer tutorials online without requiring students to be in the same place as their tutors. Distance courses are either synchronous or asynchronous. Synchronous courses can use video conferencing or interactive TV to allow student and teacher to participate in real-time. The more common asynchronous courses allow students to work at their own pace with web-based tutorials, some allowing the sending of students' answers and tutors' feedback via email. These technologies are opening up education to more people and are ideal for those who are working and studying at the same time.

Students do not only use the Web for work, of course. They enjoy using it for leisure, too. The craze for downloading MP3 music files caused many American college web-masters considerable headaches, such was the load placed on college servers as students downloaded their favourite music for hours on end. Email, chat and instant messaging are all popular with students, as are the sites offering the latest information on movies, clubs, music and the arts.

)))**➤** *Children and the Net II: Secondary, Education and the Internet, Kids' Web Sites, School and the Internet*

ABOVE: The Internet has become an invaluable resource for students

STUFFIT

A file compression utility. Originally developed for the Macintosh, StuffIt now works across most major platforms, including Windows and Linux, and most compressed file types, including .sit and .zip. By removing redundant information it is possible to compress files up to 98 per cent of their original size and speed transmissions via the Internet, email or company network.

))))➤ *Archive, Compression, WinZip*

SURFING

Browsing the Web. Surfing is another word for browsing the World Wide Web, particularly the activity of quickly jumping around many web sites. This is done by clicking on the hyperlinks on web pages in order to view other web pages or sites. This sort of browsing can be compared to zapping between channels on a cable television, as the surfer moves through the Web without any particular destination in mind. Surfing is linked to the

idea of the Web as cyberspace, the three-dimensional virtual world first mooted by William Gibson in his highly influential 1984 novel *Neuromancer*.

))))➤ *Browser, Cyber Café, Cyberspace, HIT, Internet, World Wide Web*

SWITCHING ISPS

Be careful when switching ISPs as it will usually involve changing your email address as well, and you will have to send the new details to all your friends and contacts.

))))➤ *ISP*

SYNCHRONIZING PAGES

Updating stored web pages. You may store web pages from sites with a lot of detail, or that you refer to often, on your hard drive so you can browse them offline. If you do, you need to go online occasionally to check you have the latest versions. This is known as synchronization. In Internet Explorer it is accessed by Synchronize on the Tools menu. You can set which pages to synchronize and when. Synchronization can be done automatically when you log on, or to a schedule, or in the background when the computer is not busy on other things.

))))➤ *Internet Explorer, Web Page*

SYSTEM

Computer controlling software. System refers to a computer and its associated peripheral devices. It can also mean the operating system – the software that controls the operation of a computer and provides the environment for all the other software programs to work in. The most commonly used operating system is Microsoft Windows.

))))➤ *Computer, Operating System, Peripherals, Software, Windows Operating System*

TAGS, HTML

Elements of the mark-up language HTML used to create the structure and layout of a web page. Typically, a command on a web page that sets out how

LEFT: Surfing the Web is the cyberspace equivalent of channel hopping

that part of the document should be formatted. On the Web, tags are also used to set up hypertext links that enable you to move between pages at the click of a mouse. There are hundreds of tags within HTML. The tags appear within pointed brackets and usually need to be followed by a closing bracket. So, <i>this</i> would italicize this.

))))➤ *HTML, Hypertext, Web Page*

TCP/IP

Two protocols in one, it stands for transmission control protocol/Internet protocol. This is the standard method for sending information over the Internet. It works by splitting the messages sent into small packets of data which are reassembled at the other end. The IP element covers the way information is addressed to make sure it reaches the right destination. What this system does not do is make any connection between the sender and where the message is going. This is done by the TCP, which establishes the connection between computers and tracks the data to make sure it is delivered intact and in the right order.

))))➤ *IP, Network, Protocol*

TELECOMMUNICATIONS WEB SITES

The Internet has become the core channel of communication for most people. Besides email, there is now instant messaging, web faxing, chat, video conferencing and much more. There are a number of sites

to help you keep up with this electronic chatter. Services such as J2 (*www.j2.com*) and efax (*www.efax.com*) will send faxes. They will also forward to you, as an email attachment, any faxes received, as well as your voicemail. If you want to make sure you are not waking anyone up, check out dialling codes and time zones from one country to another with *www.whitepages.com.au/time.shtml*

))))➤ *Computing Web Sites, Science Web Sites*

ABOVE: Browser view of www.whitepages.com/ intl_sites.pl

TELECOMMUTING

The term was first coined back in the 1970s, when it was more of a wish than a practical possibility. Now, many of us are well equipped to work on a PC at home, linked by modem to the office. The work we do, the messages and data, does the commuting rather faster than we can. Many people are more productive working at home, but managers are still wary of it. Some tele-commuters also feel socially isolated from activities at the office.

))) *Home and Internet, Network, Remote Access, Remote Control*

TELECONFERENCING

Talk-based conferences held over a phone or network connection. With a webcam added to the PC, these are now largely being replaced by videoconfer-ences. Teleconferencing is a great way to span geography and time zones for those who really must have a meeting. Teleconferences are talk-based meetings held via a telephone or over a network. Depending on the system

used, dozens of people can be involved in the conference call. However, with the low-cost solution of a webcam added to the PC, the teleconference is being eclipsed by the videoconference. This enables the group to do more than talk as they can actually see each other – they can also share files and applications.

))) *Network, Videoconferencing*

TELNET

Telnet is a handy tool that lets you log on to a remote computer via the Internet. Your computer effectively becomes a dumb terminal linked to this host computer. Several clients can access the host at any one time, but guests will usually have to log on. Given the variety of platforms used by the host computers – UNIX, Windows etc. – the text-based system works by terminal emulation, whereby your computer emulates (pretends to be) a similar type. Telnet is a useful way to control web servers remotely.

))) *IP, Remote Access, Terminal*

TEMPLATE

The standard format for a document; a set way of laying out a particular document, such as an invoice or a letter. Also known as style sheets, templates cover the page size, the position of the margins, the choice of fonts, what text is in bold etc. They also standardize the kind of information to be included, such as addresses, contact details or logos and where they should go. They are handy as they give a consistent look to documents and are more efficient as they do not have to be set up from scratch each time they are needed.

))) *File, Input*

TEMPORARY INTERNET FILES

Offline storage of web pages, in effect the cache, where Internet Explorer stores web pages that you visit. When you request the same web address again, the browser will check the cache and load it from there rather than reload the page from the Net. This way, surfing is

LEFT: Telecommuting is less time-consuming than the usual method of travelling to work

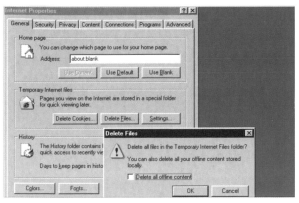

speeded up. These temporary Internet folders also provide your History and enable you to browse the files offline. They should be cleared periodically to free up space and speed up browsing.

)))➤ *Cache, Internet Explorer*

TERMINAL

Computer monitor and keyboard. A terminal describes a combination of computer keyboard and display screen. A dumb terminal has no processing capabilities and only works when connected to another computer, typically a server or mainframe. In networking, a terminal is a dumb terminal, personal computer or workstation connected to a mainframe or server. A personal computer can run terminal emulation software in order to communicate with Internet servers designed for use by terminals only.

)))➤ *Computer, Network, Remote Access, Server*

TEXT FILE

A basic type of digital document. A text file is a basic form of digital document that usually contains only the characters included in a standard set, called ASCII ('ass-key'), an acronym for the American Standard Code for Information Interchange. This is the standard code for representing text and is commonly used to encode email messages. A text file is also often called a 'text-only' file. This means a version of a word-processing file that contains the basic text and punctuation but has all the formatting removed. You can generate a text file in Windows using Wordpad or on a Mac using SimpleText.

)))➤ *ASCII, File, Unicode*

THREAD

A string of messages all related to the same topic. So, for example, if a subscriber to a collectors' newsgroup posted a query about Wedgwood pottery, all replies would be part of the same thread. Each newsgroup will have several, even hundreds of, new threads daily covering different topics. You start a new thread by posting a message on a new topic. One of the features of newsreader software is to sort messages into their different threads so they can be read together.

)))➤ *Newsgroup, Post, Usenet*

ABOVE: Conferences can be held via a telephone or a network connection
ABOVE LEFT: Internet Explorer \ Properties \ Temporary Internet Files: Delete Files

THUMBNAIL

 A miniature version of an image or document. In Windows Explorer you can view your files and folders as thumbnails. Some web pages also have thumbnails of images. These download quicker than the full-sized picture. Sometimes, you can access the bigger image if you click on the thumbnail. In PDF files on the Web, such as a user manual for a software program, each page may be represented by a thumbnail. A quick way to navigate to the page you want is by clicking on the appropriate thumbnail image.

))))➤ *Graphics File, Icons*

TIFF

'Tagged Image File Format'; graphics file format. One of the most widely used file formats for graphical images. It is advisable to save scanned images as TIFF files before converting them into GIF or JPEG files for the Web. Files in the TIFF format usually have the extension .tif.

))))➤ *BMP, Graphics File, Picture Formats*

TILE

A way of arranging Windows and background images so they do not overlap each other. Kitchen tiles or bathroom tiles are not laid to overlap each other; in the same way, if you open a series of windows on your desktop and arrange them so they do not overlap, they are tiled. (Windows that do overlap are called cascading windows.) Similarly, on the desktop or a web page, background images are often used. The picture may be repeated several times to fill the space available. If it is arranged so as not to overlap it is tiled.

))))➤ *Background, Wallpaper, Windows*

TIME-RELATED WEB SITES

Given the erratic timing on your PC's clock it might be time to synchronize it with something more reliable, such as an atomic clock. You can do this with the freeware Atomic Clock

Sync (*www.worldtimeserver.com/atomic-clock*). Just as conveniently the same site gives you access to a list of the local time in towns across the world, so there is no excuse for phoning your pals in Broken Hill, Australia in the middle of the night. For the morbid who feel time slipping away they can clock the countdown to meeting the grim reaper at *www.deathclock.com*.

))))➤ *Calendar*

TOP-LEVEL DOMAIN (TLD)

See Zone

TRANSPORT WEB SITES

The real trainspotter's bible is the NMRA Directory of World Wide Rail sites at *www.cwrr.com/nmra/rroffic.html*. In fact it is more of a siding for web sites about railway modelling, but it does have good links to the big-brother train companies. If you prefer to check on the going rate of a Piper Chieftain aircraft go to Aircraft Shopper (*www.aso.com*). Alternatively, for something closer to the ground, DealerNet gives you the spec for the latest cars, trailers and boats across America or to pick up that used car bargain in Britain head to Exchange and Mart (*www.exchangeandmart.co.uk*).

TRAVEL, FLIGHT AND HOLIDAYS ON THE INTERNET

Tourism via the Web. Whether it is a last-minute holiday or a regular trip, the Web is a vast resource of information and cheap deals. It is ironic that while virtual meeting rooms and video conferencing may have cut back on business travel, the time saved by bored office workers is often used to log on to the Net to plan their next holiday. The Web is the premium resource for travel information, from last-minute holidays to the time of the last bus. Whether it is by boat, plane or train, travel planners, online reservation systems and availability checkers are all just a browser away.

RIGHT: You could find your dream holiday on the Internet
FAR RIGHT: Browser view of www.timeout.com
LEFT: Browser view of www.deathclock.com

For a start, you can check the destination with online guides, such as the Time Out tourist guides (*www.timeout.co.uk*), the Rough Guides (*www.rough-guides.com*) or the more encyclopedic CIA World Factbook (*www.odci.gov/cia/publications/pubs.html*). Do not forget to stock up with the paperback version ordered through online book stores such as the Adventurous Traveler Bookstore (*www.gorp.com/atbook.htm*). Check the reviews and availability of hotels through online reservation services, such as the European-based Hotel Net (*www.u-net.com/hotelnet/*) or Travelocity (*www.travelocity.com*), which links into the giant SABRE network and also features online reservations for air travel, hire cars and holidays. Like many of the one-stop shops, such as the UK-based w*ww.deckchair.com*, it will compare flight costs to get the cheapest available.

In fact costs online – for airlines at least – are usually cheaper. Making reservations through the Web cuts down on administration costs, which is reflected by the lower charges for e-tickets. No-frills airlines, such as Easyjet, also offer discounts for booking online. If you do not like the price, set your own with *www.priceline.com* and see if you are lucky.

Once at your destination and you need a map, try Maps on US (*www.mapsonus.com*), which offers local maps in the US or travel directions for how to get from one location to another. Similar route planners are available in the UK with the two main motoring organizations the AA (*www.theaa.co.uk*) and the RAC (*www.rac.co.uk*). For anorak-style motorists there is the cultish game of checking how seldom the two routes are the same.

To get all the flight and holiday services you need under one cyber-roof there are travel supermarkets such as *Expedia.co.uk* (*Expedia.com* in the US). Besides booking the trip itself, this is the place to log on if you need to double check flight times, order travel money, arrange insurance, calculate prices in different currencies, or make sure you have met the necessary passport/visa requirements. After all that organizing you will need a holiday!

))⯈ *Shopping Online*

TROJAN HORSE

In computing, these are software time-bombs. Rogue programmers make their mischief by sending software as seemingly innocuous attachments which, once

TROLL

Someone who deliberately posts a message to a newsgroup or mailing list in order to anger people and upset them enough to start a flame war. Named after the ugly mythical creatures, trolls have no real interest in the subject under discussion, they just like being disruptive.

))))➤ *Flame, Hoaxes on the Internet, Newsgroup*

TROUBLESHOOTING

Rectifying faults. Troubleshooting means finding out why something is not working correctly on your computer. The best approach to troubleshooting is to work calmly and logically through the possible causes of the problem. Here is a summary of recommended troubleshooting actions.

1. Computer Crash

Note any error messages on the screen and re-start your computer and try the task again. If the problem persists, consult appropriate Help menus, FAQs or seek assistance.

2. Error Messages

This is a message from the computer telling you that something has gone wrong. Here are some common causes of error messages on the Internet:

Web site is not found.
Solution: Check your typing of the URL and click the Go button again.

A hyperlink to a web page is 'broken'.
Solution: try typing only the basic URL and finding the page on the site yourself.

opened, can take over your machine and delete data. The only way to deal with them is to have up-to-date anti-virus software that also protects your email.

))))➤ *Anti-virus software, Virus Checker*

RIGHT: Troubleshooting shouldn't involve shooting your computer in frustration

You have lost the connection to your ISP.
Solution: check your connection is working and try again.

The server of your intended web site is busy.
Solution: try again later.

3. Help
Consult the main Help menu accessible from your desktop or within the relevant software program.

4. FAQs
Read the Frequently Asked Questions provided by your service provider or associated with your software program.

5. Technical Support
Contact the technical support department of your service provider.

))))➤ *Error Codes, FAQ, Help Menu*

TRUMPET WINSOCK
Communications software program. Trumpet Winsock is a popular Winsock program for early versions of Windows (3.x). The function of a Winsock program is to allow a computer to communicate with other computers on the Internet using the TCP/IP protocol.

))))➤ *Communications software, TCP/IP, Windows Operating System, Winsock*

TRUSTED BRAND NAMES
Unless you feel technically confident, it is best to avoid that bargain basement-priced PC and go for a well-known brand; they may not be the cheapest but they will usually offer better support – including online technical advice – and warranties covering their products if anything goes wrong.

))))➤ *Computers: Purchasing Online, Shopping Online*

TUCOWS (www.tucows.com)
Download web site. One of the most popular download web sites on the Net, Tucows offers a vast range of shareware, demos and freeware for Windows and Mac.

))))➤ *Download.com, Finding Files on the Net*

UART
Communications buffer. A buffer for serial port and modem communications, the UART has proven at times to be a transmission bottleneck. Short for universal asynchronous receiver-transmitter the u-art, as it is pronounced, is a chip for handling the serial ports on a computer. Internal modems also have their own UART. The chip is a buffer that receives data from the ports or modem and stores it ready for access by the processor. It does the same thing for data going the other way. It works by asynchronous communication, because the data flows intermittently rather than in a steady stream. It can also be something of a bottleneck if the buffer cannot keep up with the transmission speeds of some of the fast external modems.

))))➤ *Chip, Modem V: Technical*

UL MARKS
Look for a UL mark as a sign that your computer product has been checked and approved by the Underwriters Laboratories for meeting safety standards.

))))➤ *Trusted Brand Names*

ABOVE LEFT: Start | Help | Troubleshooting

ULTIMA ONLINE (www.uo.com)

Games web site. This site presents a virtual world in which multiple players can immerse themselves and engage in fantasy role-playing.

))))▶ *Games on the Net*

UNICODE

An extended format for storing text. Unicode uses double the number of bits to represent each character and as such it can handle a much wider range of languages than the ASCII format. While ASCII can only show 192 different characters, Unicode can represent more than 65,000 individual characters. This might be considered a bit excessive for standard English and European languages, but it is necessary for other languages such as Greek, Chinese, Japanese and Korean. Because of this it may eventually replace ASCII as the standard text format.

))))▶ *ASCII, File, Text File*

UNITED COMPUTER EXCHANGE (www.uce.com)

Computer sales web site. A global clearing house for buyer and sellers of new and used computer equipment.

))))▶ *Computers: Purchasing Online*

UNIX

A computer operating system; although less user-friendly than Windows, UNIX is increasing in popularity as an operating system through its open-source version, Linux.

UNIX is a very different type of operating system from Windows. It will run on almost any computer, from PCs to minicomputers and large mainframes. It is more command-based and is therefore more complicated to use than Windows. It is a multi-user, multi-tasking operating system that comes in several different versions. Currently, the most popular is Linux, because it is part of the open

source movement where anyone can access the code (free of charge) that makes it work and modify it.

))))▶ *Multi-Tasking, Multithreaded, Operating System*

UNTRUSTED SITES

When downloading files or programs from the Internet it is important to be cautious if the site is not one you know well. It is always advisable to have anti-virus protection. Be especially careful if there are no contact details or information on the site about the people who run it.

))))▶ *Security I: Basic, Security II: Advanced*

UPGRADE

Modernize a computer. To upgrade your computer hardware or software means to replace an existing item with a newer version that accomplishes the same task, or to add new features. Memory chips, sound cards and internal modems are among the commonly upgraded components inside personal computers. Peripherals such as printers and modems can be upgraded, too. Software is easily upgraded by downloading the latest version or inserting a CD and following the on-screen prompts to install it. Always check that an upgrade is compatible with your computer before buying and installing it.

)))▶ **Computer, Peripherals, System**

UPLOAD

File transfer. Upload means to copy a file from your computer's hard disk on to another computer on the Internet. If you design your own web page, you must upload to your ISP's server in order for it to be available for everyone else on the Web to look at. Uploading is the opposite of downloading, which is the transferring of a file from a web site to your computer.

)))▶ **Download, Web Site**

URI

Universal (or 'Uniform') Resource Identifier. The generic term for all types of names and addresses that refer to objects on the World Wide Web. The most common kind of URI is an URL.

)))▶ **URL**

URL

'Uniform Resource Locator'; a web address. An URL ('U-R-L' or 'earl') is short for Uniform Resource Locator. It is a jargon term meaning web address. It tells your server where to locate a specific file on the World Wide Web – this could be a web page, or even a particular image within a page. A typical URL – *http://foundry.co.uk/home.html* – includes the following elements:

http://:The protocol used to transfer data over the Web
foundry.co.uk: The domain name of the web site
/home.html: The name of the file that describes the home page

)))▶ **Address, Domain, Internet, Protocol, Web Page, Web Site, World Wide Web**

URN

Uniform Resource Name'; a new address scheme for the Internet which identifies web pages by name rather than by location. Under the more familiar web naming system of URLs, the address specifies the network location where the page is stored. As a result, if a page is moved to a different computer and the referring URL is not changed the link becomes broken. To combat this, the Internet Engineering Task Force (IETF) is working on a new scheme, the Uniform Resource Name, or URN, where resources on the Internet will be identified by their name, rather than by where they are located.

)))▶ **Address: Internet, Web Page, Web Site, World Wide Web**

FAR LEFT: If you imagine yourself as a hero, and want to indulge in fantasy role playing, click on www.uo.com
LEFT: Browser view of www.foundry.co.uk

USB

'Universal Serial Bus'; a plug-and-play interface. The USB is set to become just that – universal. It is expected to replace conventional serial and parallel ports completely. Among its advantages as a high-speed connection between a computer and peripherals, such as a scanner, is the fact that it supports plug-and-play. This means you can plug devices in and they work without having to install adapter cards or change settings. What is more, the devices are hot swappable – you can plug them in or take them out while the computer is running. USB's support for plug-and-play and hot swapping means that it is likely to take over as the preferred way to connect peripheral devices to a computer.

)))➤ *Computer, Interface, System*

USENET

A global discussion forum. Usenet is a global bulletin board, accessed through the Internet or online services, where anyone can join in conversations on thousands of subjects. Each collection of postings on a particular topic is called a newsgroup. To join in a newsgroup you need a reader (such as Outlook Express), access to which is built into many browsers. The reader lets you view the different discussion threads and post your own contribution. When a message is posted, Usenet servers distribute them to other sites that carry that newsgroup. Not all sites carry all newsgroups.

)))➤ *Discussion Groups, Forums, Newsgroups*

USERNAMES

The shorter the username the better it is, as typing in a long name several times a day can become a real chore.

)))➤ *Name Registration, Password*

UUENCODE/UUDECODE

File conversion format. Uuencode is a standard format for converting email attachments from binary files into ASCII text for sending over the Internet.

As email messages are sent across the Internet in plain ASCII text, any binary-file attachment, such as a picture, spreadsheet or program, needs to be converted first. One standard method for doing this is BinHex (particularly for Macintosh files), another is uuencode. This stands for Unix-to-Unix encode but its use has widened to cover the transfer of files across many other platforms, including Windows and Macintosh. Nearly all email programs support uuencoding for converting the binary code into the seven-bit ASCII characters that can be sent over the Internet and uudecoding for reassembling the converted attachments.

)))➤ *ASCII, Binary File, Email, Encryption, Text Files, Usenet*

VAPORWARE

The computer world's version of the Bermuda Triangle. Brand new products, hardware and software are announced, but then vanish from the industry's radar screen, never to be seen again. Often it is just the result of a marketing ploy to undermine a rival's actual new product announcement.

)))➤ *Pirated Software, Software*

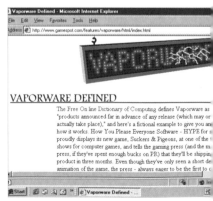

LEFT: Usenet is a forum for discussion and covers all topics of conversation

VDO MAIL

A video email program. One of the first email clients for producing video emails. Now with a web cam and your PC it is easy to create a video message that can be sent via most email clients. The video files can be sent as attachments in the same way as a spreadsheet or a text document. There are also specific programs for recording video email messages, such as Video-Express, which use streaming technology rather than having to download multimedia attachments.

)))▶ *Program, Video Mail*

VERONICA

Index to Gopher files. Very Easy Rodent-Oriented Net-wide Index to Computerized Archives. Veronica offers a keyword search of most types of data supported by the Gopher protocol.

)))▶ *Gopher, Internet in the 1980s: History*

VIDEO

Electronic moving pictures. Video refers to visual images in electronic form for recording and playing

back on a screen. Images recorded using analogue video technology such as VHS can be converted by modern personal computers into digital video. With suitable software, digital video can be edited on personal computers, too. 'Streaming' is a widely used technique for delivering video over the Web using software such as RealPlayer or Quick Time. Complete movies are released as digital video on DVD.

)))▶ *DVD, Movies, Streaming Audio/Video, VDO Mail, Video Capture, Video Mail, Video conferencing*

VIDEO CAPTURE

Recording digital video. Video capture is the recording of video images using digital technology. This can be achieved by using a digital video camera or webcam to capture the images. This digital data is then transferred to your computer by connecting the camera by cable to the appropriate port on the computer and using digital video editing software to record the video data on to the hard disk. Digital video files are very large and arc usually stored on CDs or DVDs.

)))▶ *DVD, Streaming Audio/Video, VDO Mail, Video Mail, Video conferencing*

VIDEO CONFERENCING

Internet-based meetings; with the use of video conferencing, people all over the world can meet online and share applications, with the use of their PCs. A boon for the reluctant traveller, video conferencing has given birth to the virtual meeting room. By linking up video, audio or computer equipment through a network, people scattered around different geographic locations can talk and see each other. They can also share applications and write on a common whiteboard. To take advantage of this technology you will need a webcam fitted to your PC. While most teleconferencing applications work over high-quality private networks, there are also Internet-based applications such as Microsoft's NetMeeting.

)))▶ *Teleconferencing, VDO Mail, Video Capture, Video Mail*

LEFT: In the virtual meeting room you can talk to international clients without having to travel to the otherside of the world

VIDEO MAIL

 Attaching video to an email. If you have a video camera or a webcam, and software such as VDOMail for Windows, then you can make a video file and send it as an attachment to an email. Even when compressed, video files are large and a video mail could take a very long time to send and receive. Some web sites such as Video Mail Studio (*www.videomailstudio.com*) offer a service to send streaming video with an email.

))))▶ *Stream Audio/Video, VDO Mail, Video conferencing*

VIEWER

Software for viewing video. A viewer is a software program that allows you to view video on your computer monitor. RealPlayer is a widely used media viewer. It is a plug-in program that automatically launches inside your browser window when you click to view a RealPlayer file. Intel is another

manufacturer of a streaming media viewer plug-in. The main viewers are Windows Media Player and Quick Time Player.

))))▶ *Plug-in, Streaming Audio/Video, Video*

VIRTUAL REALITY

3-D digital environment. Virtual reality, or VR, is the three-dimensional electronic representation of a real or fictional environment. The idea of VR was highly influenced by the invention of 'cyberspace' by William Gibson in his 1984 novel *Neuromancer*. Cyberspace is an incredibly complex 3D graphical representation of all the world's data. Ten years after the novel's publication, two innovators, Mark Pesce and Tony Parisi, were inspired to propose a way of encoding graphical information so that a web browser could show a 3D space that could be moved around in. It is called VRML (Virtual Reality Modelling Language).

))))▶ *Cyberspace, Browser, VRML*

TOP: Video Mail Studio previewing a video
ABOVE: Viewer is software for viewing images

VIRUS

Disruptive software program. A virus infects other software programs by embedding itself in them. Some viruses are timed to perform mischievous or harmful actions such as writing messages on the screen or even deleting all the data on a hard drive. Viruses distributed as email attachments are frequently targeted at Microsoft users.

))))➤ *Virus checker*

VIRUS CHECKER

Anti-virus software. A virus checker is a software program that checks all files being used by a computer for harmful viruses. A virus checker checks files

from all sources: floppy disks, CDs, downloads from web sites and, most problematic of all, emails. Always check for updates on your virus checker's web site, as a virus checker cannot detect viruses invented after its release date.

))))➤ *Virus*

VOICEMAIL

Software that turns your PC and modem into a telephone answering service handling voice calls and faxes. This is a mixed blessing, it can either be a good way to screen calls, or a nightmare if you are trying to get hold of someone urgently. Voicemail software basically turns your PC into a fullyfledged answering service. Using your modem – which needs to be voice capable – it answers the telephone, plays a recorded greeting and stores messages on the hard drive. It can also distinguish between voice calls and data (faxes) and respond accordingly. It is possible to set up a number of separate mailboxes for each person using a particular connection.

))))➤ *Fax on Demand, Modem I: Introduction, Phone Dialer*

VRML

'Virtual Reality Modelling Language'; the language used to create 3-D worlds on the web; this needs a special viewer to interpret the files. This is where you can walk through a building, such as an art gallery, or travel through space. VRML files are simply text files with the geometric instructions to enable

the computer to build the virtual world. To create its look graphics files are 'painted' on and need to be downloaded with the VRML files. VRML files have the extension .wrl ('world'). To view them you need a VRML-enabled browser or plug-in.

))))➤ *Virtual Reality*

ABOVE: VRML files are used to create virtual worlds on the Internet

VT-100

Video terminal. Manufactured by Digital Equipment Corporation (DEC), the VT-100 was the definitive video terminal in the early 1980s. VT-100s were dumb terminals that were connected to mainframe computers via networks.

))))➤ *Internet in the 1980s: History, Terminal*

WAIS

'Wide Area Information Servers'. Distributed information retrieval system. WAIS is a system for retrieving documents using keywords. Other information retrieval systems include Gopher and World Wide Web.

))))➤ *Gopher, World Wide Web*

WALLPAPER

The background to your desktop. Originally it was just still images in graphics files, such as GIFs or JPEGs that could be added to bring a splash of colour to the screen, but with Windows' Active Desktop it is possible to add your favourite web page, or pages, and position them where you want on the screen. You can even set up a synchronization schedule so that the latest version of the page is regularly downloaded.

))))➤ *Background, Control Panel, Windows*

WAREZ

Pirated software. Many commercial software programs are protected against copying by needing the correct registration or serial number in order to run. Hackers who crack the codes will post the complete, pirated programs with copy-protection removed to the Web for download. Pirated software like this (usually games) is called warez or appz.

))))➤ *Pirated Software, Software*

WAVE (WAV) FILE

Audio file format; the standard file format used by Windows for storing sounds as waveforms. The files have the extension .wav. Some sound cards use WaveTable synthesis for generating sound electronically on a PC. This means that rather than using modulators to create sounds, they use actual samples of real instruments.

))))➤ *Music on the Internet, Audio File, MP3, Sound File, WMA*

WEATHER ONLINE

As regular a topic of conversation for the Brits as the drizzle over Dartmoor, there is no getting away from it on the Web. Every portal has its weather service, with localized forecasts. But for the heavy downpours go to *www.intellicast .com*, where you will find international forecasts as well as regularly updated satellite feeds, personal allergy profiles and weather planners. For the more official view on what is happening to our weather, the UN division responsible for monitoring our climate is the World Meteorological Organization at *www.wmo.ch*.

))))➤ *Nature Web Sites, News Online*

WEB

 See World Wide Web

WEB100 (www.web100.com)

Ratings web site. Web100 measures the hits on the world's web sites hourly and displays them in charts.

))))➤ *Web Site, World Wide Web*

WEB AUTHORING

Designing and creating web pages using HTML. It is possible to do this with no more than a basic text program such as Notepad – in fact the purists believe this is the best way. But there are also web authoring programs, such as Macromedia's Dreamweaver and Adobe's GoLive, that not only help you design the pages but also manage the site. These authoring tools let you arrange the text and graphics on the page without having to type a single HTML tag. Inevitably, however, you will need to tweak something, so it is useful to know a little HTML.

))))➤ *HotDog, Microsoft Front Page, Netscape Composer, Web Page: Creating I:, Web Page: Creating II*

WEB-BASED EMAIL

Online email service. This service is great for the traveller, as it is possible to access an email account and contact list from any computer. All you need is your username and password. Most web-based email providers, such as Yahoo, Hotmail or BT Internet offer similar services: you can send and receive mails with attachments (although the size that is accepted may be limited). However, they usually only offer limited storage space and you have to be online to access your messages. Web-based email accounts are also a hot target for Spammers.

)))))➤ *Hotmail*

WEB-BASED FAXING

Rather than clogging up your modem faxing when you could be surfing, try web-faxing. Your faxes are sent to a web server, which sends it on to the fax number requested. Faxes sent to you are delivered by email. Most web-fax services are very reliable with the basic services free.

)))))➤ *Fax*

WEB BROWSER

Software program for browsing the Web. You need a web browser to browse the World Wide Web. The world's most popular browser is Microsoft's Internet Explorer. Other popular browsers are made by Netscape and Opera. A typical web browser includes the following features:

- Navigation buttons such as Next and Previous, which take you to the next and previous web pages visited
- Address field, into which you type the address of the web site you wish to visit
- Main window in which web pages are displayed

A web browser allows you to click on hyperlinks to jump between different web pages.

)))))➤ *Browser, Hyperlink, Internet Explorer, Netscape Navigator, World Wide Web*

WEBCAM

PC-mounted video camera. Webcams are simply small video cameras that plug into your PC. Usually mounted on top of the monitor, they can be used – with the appropriate software – for videoconferencing. But they can be pointed anywhere and are often used as video feeds to people's web sites. They can capture anything – from whether the office coffee pot is full, to a view of Niagara Falls. Some cams appear to be sending live video images, in fact they are a series of snapshots sent every few seconds that give the illusion of a moving picture.

)))))➤ *Teleconferencing, VDO Mail, Video Capture, Videoconferencing, Video Mail*

WEBCRAWLER (*www.webcrawler.com*)

Search engine. Webcrawler offers a searchable index of web pages, news and photos that is organized into topics.

)))))➤ *Search Engine*

WEBMASTER

The person who manages a web site. The scope of the job is about as varied as the number of web sites available: it can be planning and designing the web site or creating and managing the updating of the web pages. On bigger sites, the webmaster is more likely to be responsible for the technical maintenance of the site, that is making sure the web server is running properly, the site is secure and any downtime is minimized. That is why there is often an email link to the webmaster to report a problem when a page does not load correctly or a link is broken.

)))))➤ *Site Management, Web Authoring, Web Page: Creating I, Web Page: Creating II, Web Site*

WEB PAGE

Page on a web site. A web page is what appears in your browser window when you visit a web site. Web pages are created using HTML, a set of codes for designing text and images for displaying in a web browser. The first web page you will see when visiting a web site is the home page. This typically has a banner at the top like a masthead on a newspaper, a menu of options in the left-hand column and a central area with text and images. Web pages contain hyperlinks that take you to other web pages when you click on them.

)))))➤ *Browser, Home Page, HTML, Hyperlink, Web Site, World Wide Web*

WEB PAGE: CREATING I

Creating web pages involves careful planning and some knowledge of HTML, whether you intend to use an HTML editor or a WYSIWYG authoring tool. Here is some advice on how to go about creating a basic web page.

1. Whether it is for a school reunion, family history or the society for the collection of fruit stickers, it is not difficult to build a web page. There are a lot of tools, many free, to help you do it. In fact, you can create simple web pages using a word processor such as Microsoft Word. Alternatively, some ISPs, such as MSN, provide a simple step-by-step wizard to build an online site or picture gallery.

2. Take time and plan the site – to decide on its purpose, prepare or source the content needed and gather the material together.

3. Decide on the structure of the site. Will it be a tree structure, where information is arranged hierarchically – that is, you go from general information at the top, the home page, to more specific data on the pages (branches) further down? Or will it be linear, where you simply click from one page to the next? Or, as often seems the case even when it is not intended, will it be totally random?

4. The basic web page is created in HTML, which is rather like road signs for the Web. The HTML tags tell the browser software how to display and handle the information or objects contained within them. The benefit of HTML is that it is pure text (ASCII only) so it can be read by software running on any platform, whether it is Windows, UNIX or Macintosh.

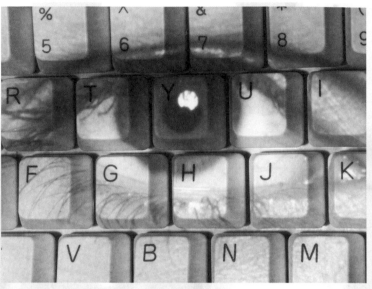

5. Each HTML document has two main parts: the head, which contains general information about the file and scripts that need to be run etc.; and the body, which is the content that will appear in the browser window.

6. There are literally hundreds of HTML tags, but they can be divided into two main types – structural tags, which define the different elements on the page (headings, paragraphs, tables, images, and so on) and style tags, which say how the text within those labels should be presented, such as in bold or italic, in large or small type etc. Each HTML tag has several parts. For example, <font size="4">Applies to text here</font>. Font is the start tag that tells the browser where a particular style or element begins. This may have an attribute attached that gives the browser extra information about the tag. Here it is size="4" which gives the relative size it should be. The text that the tag applies to sits between the start and the end tags. Most HTML tags have an end tag, which is the same as the start tag with a slash character (/) before it.

ABOVE: Using one large single image on your web page can dramatically increase the time it takes to download

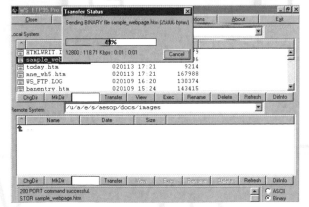

for the Macintosh, you still have to know how to write HTML by hand, but they can make the process quicker and more efficient. With the what-you-see-is-what-you-get (WYSIWYG) style tools such as Microsoft's FrontPage or Macromedia's Dreamweaver, the coding is taken care of, letting you place elements on the page visually. They are more like page-layout programs, although it is still useful to know a little HTML in order to do any tweaking needed.

8. When you put text on a web page any formatting that it may have had will be lost. The only way to mark it up is by using the HTML tags. It obviously enhances the page to add graphics, but too many pictures or a single image that is too big can increase download time dramatically. A slow-loading page is the prime reason users give up and move to another site.

9. One of the fundamental ideas behind the Web when it was first created by Tim Berners-Lee was to link documents on different networks to make it easier for researchers to share their work. These hyperlinks can be a highlighted word, an icon, or a picture. Click on the link and you move to a different web page that may be part of the same site on the same server (referred to as a relative link), or on a completely different site on a server on the other side of the World (an absolute link).

10. When finished the pages need to be moved to the ISP's web server where they are being hosted. An FTP program is needed to connect via a dial-up connection to the ISP's server. Normally you will need a user name and password to log on to the directory where you will put the HTML pages and any graphic files that go with it. You can then check the published pages by typing into the browser the URL given by your ISP.

)))) ➤ *HotDog, HTML, Hypertext, Microsoft Front Page, Netscape Composer, Web Authoring, Web Page: Creating II*

TOP: Source code for sample web page viewed in a simple HTML editor
MIDDLE: The sample web page as it appears in Internet Explorer – notice that the URL for the hyperlink at the bottom appears in the Status bar
BOTTOM: Uploading a web page to web site, using WS_FTP

7. Because HTML documents are just plain text files, they can be created using simple text editors such as Notepad. However, the process is a lot easier if you use either an HTML editor or a web-authoring tool. With an HTML editor, such as HomeSite for Windows or BBEdit

WEB PAGE: CREATING II

A static web page can become a dynamic one using the latest DHTML-based technologies. But support for them is variable, so you will need to test your pages in a variety of situations to check that they look and work as you planned them.

1. The ordinary HTML-based web page is static. Like a page from a newspaper, once published it will not change. There is a basic interactivity, in which the page responds to input from the user. Click on a link and the page you are looking at changes. But for animation, or to search a database, or purchase online, deeper coding is needed.

2. Dynamic HTML (DHTML) takes the ordinary static web page and enables it to change on-the-fly. For example, an animation of a car driving across the browser window can action several seconds after the page downloads. Although it is given a single name it is made up of a combination of technologies that can either work together or by themselves. These include HTML, or a client-side scripting language such as Javascript and CSS (cascading style sheets).

3. Cascading style sheets, more commonly called style sheets, are templates for formatting the way elements appear on the page. For example, you can set a style for links when active or when they have been clicked, for text, for lists and so on. The advantage of style sheets over HTML markup is that rather than tag each element individually you can create a central style sheet for all web pages. Therefore you can specify that you want all headlines to be of a specific point size

and colour. If you later decide to change the colour, you do not need to alter each page, you simply alter the style sheet and it is applied throughout the site. There can be several style sheets for a site that are set up in a hierarchical order. The 'cascade' sets rules for which style in the hierarchy has precedence and overrides another.

4. Client-side scripting languages such as Javascript are the main engine for DHTML. These scripts, which are written directly within the HTML code, perform the actions. So, in rollovers they change the colour of the background when a mouse moves across a word or swaps one image for another.

5. While DHTML enables web pages to be more interactive and flexible, bigger changes are likely to come from XML (eXtended Markup Language). What it does is separate the content on a page from the way it is presented. Whereas HTML looks at structure and style together, XML simply looks at the structure. For example, putting a news story on the web page XML would tag the headline, the writer's byline, the introductory paragraph and the body text. Other technologies, such as style sheets, determine how each of those tags should be formatted. The advantage of this is that you can take the same content and deliver it in different ways – such as in HTML for a web-site or via WAP for a mobile phone – without the effort and expense of having separately created pages for each device. Even with a web site it makes it easier to redesign the site without having to redo each page.

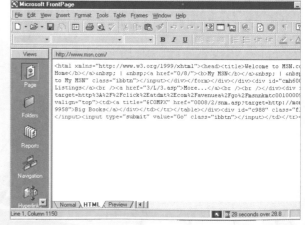

6. The rapid changes in web technologies create difficulties as newer features will not be supported by all browsers on all platforms. Part of the process of creating a web page is identifying who your typical audience is likely to be and designing a site that will be viewable by the majority of users. So, for example, an HTML tag like <blink> is supported in Netscape browsers but not Internet Explorer. Even when supported by one make of browser, it will not be supported by all versions. CSS support is generally available only in later versions of the main browsers. Similarly the implementation of the Java virtual machine is different between Netscape and Microsoft, which means that scripts might not run – or run as intended – in all browsers.

7. The net result is that the only way of making sure your web pages look and work as you planned them is to test them. You should view the pages at different resolutions. The higher the resolution the more information on screen. But web designers have to base the size of their pages on the 'average' screen resolution of their potential users, which currently is 800 x 600. You should also view the pages in different browsers as each web browser has its own peculiarities. The two most popular web browsers are Microsoft's Internet Explorer and Netscape's Navigator, but there are a steady band of supporters for the slim-line browser, Opera. Even the same browser on different

platforms will change the way your pages look. For example, fonts viewed on the Macintosh will appear a point size smaller than on the PC.

8. While it is easy to test your site in a couple of browsers most people might not have the time or resources to view their site on different platforms or at different resolutions. There are sites, such as *www. netmechanic.com*, that will do it for you and take a snapshot of the screen so you can see how your page looks in different situations.

⟩⟩⟩▶ *HotDog, HTML, Hypertext, Microsoft Front Page, Netscape Composer, Web Authoring, Web Page: Creating I*

WEB SERVER

Software that serves up web pages and carries out other browser requests. Every web site sits on a host computer. The operating system for this server – which can be UNIX, Windows or Macintosh – controls the communications over the Internet. In addition there is web-server software, which sits on the host computer and serves up the web pages using the HyperText Transfer Protocol (HTTP). It also carries out any other browser requests, such as conducting a search in a database. This is done by the server sending a request to run the mini-program that returns the results, which are then sent to the browser with the web page.

)))➤ *ISP, OSP, Server, Web Site, World Wide Web*

WEB SITE

Collection of web pages. A web site is a collection of web pages linked together by hyperlinks, enabling a visitor to navigate from page to page. When visiting a web site, the first page you see is the home page. This typically displays an introduction to the site and a menu of options. You can click on the options to view the various sections of the site. You visit a web site by typing its address (or URL) in the Address field of your browser. The World Wide Web contains millions of web sites, built for almost every purpose imaginable: from entertainment and education to business and the arts.

)))➤ *Browser, Hyperlink, Home Page, Publish, Site Management, URL, Web Page, World Wide Web*

WEBTV

The way to surf the Net from your TV. Home shopping, banking and interactive services are all keen to exploit the potential of getting people on the Web without a PC. Typically WebTV-style products consist of a small box connecting the TV and phone line. When something is viewed on the TV it is possible to dial through the phone line and connect to the Web site or some other service simply by pressing the remote.

ABOVE: The home page of a web site usually leads to a series of other linked pages, often indicated by graphics and text to produce a lively effect
FAR RIGHT: Finding someone is made easier with a white page directory

However, pages designed for the Web can look very odd on TV and there is still some way to go before the TV is surfer friendly.

)))➤ *Channel, Push Technology, Film and TV Web Sites*

WEIRD WEB SITES

Strange sites on the Internet. Crazy laws, crazy people, crazy stories – welcome to the weird World Wide Web. For stories with a disturbing and often shocking (be warned) twist there is the truly bizarre Bizarre Magazine (*www.bizarremag.com*). For those who take their weirdness a bit more seriously the Fortean Times (*www.forteantimes.com*) is the 'journal of strange phenomena' that looks for a

plausible explanation. For those who think the law is an ass there is proof at *www.dumblaws.com*, while if you think your neighbour is an ass for passing off an urban myth as one of his funny stories then Snopes (*www.snopes. com*) can help by carefully debunking the myth and explaining the truth.

))))▶ *Cruel Site of the Day, Web Site*

WHITE PAGES

People search directory. Whereas yellow-page directories are lists of businesses and commercial companies, white pages are directories of individuals. Usually they carry contact details, such as phone numbers and street addresses as well as email addresses. There are several 'white page' style directories on the Web, such as

whowere.com and BigFoot. These use a standard for organizing directory databases called LDAP (Lightweight Directory Access Protocol), which makes the whole process easier to organize. Unfortunately, with millions of people with email addresses on the Internet no one directory will have everyone listed.

))))▶ *Directory, Directory Service, LDAP, Search Directory*

WHOWHERE (*www.whowhere.lycos.com*)

People-search web site. WhoWhere is one of the premier sites for searching for people by name, email address, phone number and in public records. It also gives a wealth of people-related guides on celebrities and others.

))))▶ *Directory Service, Finding People on the Net, Search Engine*

WILD CARD

Search support. Search engines would be a lot more frustrating to use if they did not support wild cards. These are symbols you can use to stand for missing characters. For example, an asterisk (*) can be used as a wild card to stand for several missing letters, while a question mark just represents a single doubtful character. You can also use wild cards when searching for file types. So, myst*.* will find any file of any type that starts with those letters while myst*.xls will only find spreadsheet programs that start with myst.

))))▶ *Boolean Modifier, Search Engine*

WINDOWS

Onscreen work areas. Windows are the rectangular work areas used to contain documents, software programs and folders within a personal computer's Graphical User Interface (GUI). Windows is also the name of the widely used operating system made by Microsoft. Windows are a principal feature of both Mac and Microsoft Windows interfaces. They have a top title bar displaying the name of the window's contents, buttons to resize and close the windows, and are often bounded by scroll bars used to move around inside a window.

))))▶ *Folders, GUI, Mac, Windows Operating System*

WINDOWS MESSAGING

Sending messages via a computer. Email, fax, voicemail, instant messaging – it is becoming increasingly difficult to stay out of touch. Previously, you may have had an email client and possibly some fax

ABOVE: Searching for images is made much easier by using wild cards
RIGHT: Microsoft's new Windows OS, XP, is featured on their web site
ABOVE RIGHT: In the PC and software community Bill Gates, the founder of Microsoft, is a figure revered for his ideas and determination

software, each with its own mailbox and address book. Now, through the Windows messaging system, they can work together, along with other programs. So you have a single client interface from which you can view your faxes, organize your voicemail, see all your email messages, read newsgroup postings, access a variety of phonebooks and may be even start a chat session.

))))➤ *Email, Fax, Network, Windows Operating System*

WINDOWS OPERATING SYSTEM

Operating system. Windows is the name of the world's most widely used operating system for IBM-compatible personal computers. Based on the pioneering Apple Macintosh interface, it was launched in 1985 by Microsoft as the replacement for the old DOS operating system, which obliged users to type in commands to control the computer. Windows is a Graphical User Interface (GUI) system. It displays a representation of a desktop on the computer screen, menus from which programs can be selected, icons that represent objects, which when clicked on using a mouse, open to reveal rectangular windows. These windows that give the operating system its name can contain documents, software programs or folders.

The latest version is Windows XP. This boasts a new user interface intended to make it easier to find what you need and enhanced software to make the computer more reliable. Windows XP's new or enhanced features include:

Windows Media Player for Windows XP – a program for finding, playing, organizing and storing digital media such as video and audio.

Network Setup Wizard – this utility makes it easier to connect the computers and peripheral devices in your home and share data.

Windows Messenger – a communications and collaboration tool that offers instant messaging, voice and video conferencing, and application sharing.

Help and Support Centre – this helps you to recover from problems and get help and support when you need it.

))))➤ *GUI, Macintosh, Operating System, PCs: Introduction, Windows*

WINFAXPRO

Fax software. One of the best-known fax software programs, its makers Symantec have developed it into a personal messaging centre. Integrated with the Windows Messaging system it is possible to view email messages and personal folders alongside your faxes and voicemail messages. What is more, you can access your Windows contact books so you do not need to re-enter individual contact information into different phonebooks for faxes etc. It comes with a number of templates for standard messages, a cover-page designer, and voicemail software.

))))➤ *Fax, Program*

WINMODEM

Unlikely with modern PCs, but make sure your faxmodem is not a WinModem, which uses software to emulate a fax machine and is not very reliable.

))))➤ *Fax Modem*

WINSOCK

Communications software. Winsock is short for Windows Socket. The function of a Winsock program is to allow a personal computer to communicate with other computers on the Internet using the TCP/IP protocol.

))))▶ *Socket, Trumpet Winsock*

WINZIP

File compression utility. WinZip is one of the most popular programs for handling ZIP files in Windows. The ZIP files are archives used for distributing or storing several files together. The files are usually compressed to save space and reduce download time. WinZip will unzip this file – that is, open the ZIP archive, extract the different files stored in it, decompress them and store them in separate new files. To protect

ABOVE: *A Wizard can help you solve your problems*
LEFT: *Contents of the Windows drive archived in a ZIP file as viewed in WinZip*

against any nasty viruses lurking in the ZIP file, WinZip can link up to most virus scanners. WinZip can also create archives, in order to keep related files together and compress them to save space.

))))▶ *Archive, Compression, Stuffit*

WIZARD

Helpful utility program. A wizard is a software program in Windows that gives guidance in accomplishing a task or solving a problem. An example is the Network Setup Wizard, which helps you set up a network to connect computers and peripheral devices.

))))▶ *Automation, Utility*

WIZARD FOR DETECTING MODEM

The Install New Modem wizard, launched from the Modems control panel, will automatically search for your modem and guide you through the installation of the necessary drivers.

))))▶ *Modem, Wizard*

WMA

'Windows Media Audio'; sound file format that offers similar sound quality to MP3 at a reduced file size. This is the Windows Media Player format for storing sound files. Some analysts believe it sounds as good as MP3 files, even though it records at half the bit rate. As a result you can get the same quality as MP3 at

only one-third of the size. Consequently, download time is less and it eases the pressure on storage space. Sound files saved in the Windows Media Audio format will have .wma as the file extension.

))➤ *Compression, Hypermedia, Media, Sound File*

WORD PROCESSOR

Application for producing documents. A word processor is a software program for typing, editing and formatting words in order to produce documents. The most popular word processing application is Microsoft Word, although the key principles of word processing apply to all such applications.

To create a new document, click File|New, and enter your text. At this stage your text is in a basic form, but you can improve its appearance by using the formatting capabilities of a word processor. For each element you want to change, you must select it first. To make a heading stand out, for example, you first select it by dragging the mouse pointer along the relevant line. The heading will appear highlighted by a colour. You can then format it by clicking on one of the formatting buttons, such as bold, italic or underline. The appearance of a single word or an entire document can be changed using this technique.

Perhaps the most useful feature of a word processor is its ability to edit text you have already typed. The simplest way to delete and retype a few words is to press the

ABOVE: It is difficult to imagine reverting back to the old typewriter when word processing allows us to type, edit and format our work on screen

Backspace key repeatedly until you have deleted the unwanted words and then type the new ones. If you want to make more major changes to your text, a word processor offers a more powerful feature: Cut and Paste. For example, you could swap the order of two paragraphs. To do this, select the first paragraph by dragging the mouse pointer diagonally from the start to the end of the paragraph, then click Edit|Cut on the menu. Position your mouse pointer where you want the paragraph to move to and click Edit|Paste. The paragraph will now appear in the new position.

Another very useful feature of a word processor is the spell-checker. It is a good idea to use it before saving or printing your document. To use the spell-checker in Word for Windows, click Tools|Spelling and Grammar. The Spelling and Grammar dialog box will appear and Word will highlight every incorrect word and allow you to change it.

Having prepared your document to your satisfaction, you should save it on to your hard disk by clicking File|Save and typing in a useful name for the document. You will probably also wish to print it. To do this, select File|Print.

))➤ *Application, Office Suite, WYSIWYG*

WORLD WIDE WEB

The World Wide Web, or 'Web' for short, is a global network of linked information resources called web sites stored on computers. The Web is a place where businesses, institutions and individuals can display information about their products, knowledge, or their lives. Anyone with a computer equipped with browser software and connected to the Internet can view this information. The Web offers new ways to shop, enjoy entertainment and keep up with events. Perhaps more importantly, it allows friends to keep in touch and communities to interact.

1. The Web dates from 1989, when British physicist and computer scientist Tim Berners-Lee first proposed a global network of linked hypertext while working at CERN. In 1991, he released the first web server and client software, and interest in the idea grew rapidly. The release in 1993 of Mosaic, the first web browser with a graphical user interface (GUI), changed all that. It was the beginning of a phenomenal surge in interest that has made the Web a vital part of the lives of millions around the world.

2. Although many people mistakenly think so, the World Wide Web is not the same thing as the Internet. The Internet, or 'Net', is an international network of computers permanently joined together by high-speed cables and dedicated computers called servers. The Web is one of the applications that is built on the Internet's technology. However, it is by far the most important aspect of the Internet.

3. Perhaps the most remarkable thing about the Web is the people who use it. Access to the Web is growing rapidly day by day, and is naturally most advanced in developed countries. It has become a resource open to all walks of life. Students find it invaluable for research, travellers can check on fares, kids can enjoy games, business people can track stock prices in real time. The Web is also having a profound influence on globalization as communities in far flung parts of the world see how others live and can communicate with them.

ABOVE: People from all walks of life can use, enjoy and learn from the Internet
RIGHT: Cartoon on the NASDAQ Crash at the Bennett Cartoon
(Archivew.claybennett.com/pages/nasdaq.html)

4. To access the Web, you must connect a computer to the Internet. Although new devices such as interactive televisions, PDAs and games consoles are gaining importance, access is made by many people using their personal computer. When connected, the personal computer is called the client, and is linked to a server computer operated by a service provider. This server computer is directly linked to all the other servers that store the Web's vast collection of web sites. It sends data back and forth between the client computer, displaying web pages and responding to mouse-clicks made by the user.

5. The set of rules that clients and servers use to talk to each other is called a protocol. The Web uses a protocol called HTTP – HyperText Transfer Protocol. You will see these letters at the start of every web address in the Address box on your browser. It is the protocol that defines how hypertext information is delivered across the Web, and determines what actions web servers should take in response to instructions given by clicking in a browser.

6. The Web is composed of an enormous number of web sites. A web site is a collection of web pages linked together by hyperlinks, enabling a visitor to navigate from page to page. When visiting a web site, the first page you see is the home page. This typically displays an introduction to the site and a menu of options. You can click on the options to view the various sections of the site. You visit a web site by typing its address (or URL) in the Address field of your browser.

7. A web page is the document that appears in your browser window when you visit a web site. Web pages are created using HTML ('HyperText Markup Language'), a set of rules and codes for designing text and images for displaying in a web browser. The instructions that tell the browser how to display the page are encoded within the document itself and are called HTML tags. The browser knows how to interpret the HTML tags, so the web page appears on the user's screen as the web designer intended.

8. Possibly the most powerful attribute of the Web is its hyperlinks. A hyperlink is a method for linking web pages. To use a hyperlink on a web page, click on it once and the hyperlink takes you to another place in the same page or, perhaps, to a web page in another web site. If the hyperlink is a word or a phrase, it will probably be underlined and when your mouse pointer is over it, it will change into a hand, to let you know that it is 'hot'. A hyperlink can also be a graphic, and the part of the screen in which you click to activate it is called a 'hotspot'.

Clicking around on hyperlinks to explore the Web is called browsing or surfing. The more you surf, the more you will be amazed at how much there is on the World

Wide Web. And with new web sites being added every day, you will never run out of places to go!

))))➤ *Address, Browser, GUI, HTML, HTTP, Hyperlink, Internet, Surfing, URL, Web page, Web site*

WORLD WIDE WEB: HISTORY

The story of the Web. The World Wide Web was the brainchild of British physicist and computer scientist Tim Berners-Lee, who began working on hypertext systems in the early 1980s. In 1991, while working at CERN, Berners-Lee released the first web server and client software. Interest in the idea grew rapidly following the release in 1993 of Marc Andreesen's browser, Mosaic, the first Internet program with a graphical user interface (GUI). Its author went on to develop the hugely popular Netscape Navigator browser. In 1995, Microsoft entered the fray with its own browser, Internet Explorer, which eventually triumphed over Netscape.

The late 1990s saw an astonishing rise in the Web's popularity as millions browsed, looking for information, entertainment and things to buy. The rush to cash in on the Net's commercial promise led to unprecedented investment in new technologies and a new kind of business dubbed 'dotcoms'. Millions of dollars were made by early investors, and millions more were lost as the bubble eventually burst with the crash of technology stocks on the Nasdaq index in March 2001.

))))➤ *Browser, CERN, Internet Explorer, Internet in the 1980s: History, Internet in the 1990s: History, Mosaic, Netscape Navigator*

WS_FTP

File transfer program. The acknowledged standard for downloading and uploading files from the Internet is the File Transfer Protocol (FTP). It is particularly good for handling big files. While ordinary web pages and the small image files displayed in them can easily be handled by the HyperText Transfer Protocol (HTTP) used by browsers, something more robust is needed for transferring big graphics files or programs. Using an FTP client, such as WS_FTP, is not only faster but you can resume the transfer from where you left off, should the connection be broken. The FTP client software establishes a connection between the local PC and the remote FTP server and displays a directory of each in separate windows. Then it is a simple case of transferring one from the other. To maximize speed multiple connections can be set up so you can browse the FTP site while downloading files. The latest version of WS-FTP also supports SSL (Secure Sockets Layer) encryption if there are confidential files that need to be transferred over the Internet. While many browsers can also act as FTP clients they do not have the same extensive features as standalone FTP client programs such as WS_FTP.

)))➤ *File Transfer, FTP Search, FTP Server*

WYSIWYG

Type of software display. WYSIWYG (pronounced 'wizzywig') is an acronym for What You See Is What You Get. It describes a type of display used by word-processing or desktop publishing programs, which allows you to see your document on the screen as it will appear when printed. For example, if you format a line of text in a WYSIWYG program so that it is bold, it will appear as bold on the screen. It is made possible by a Graphical User Interface (GUI) such as used on Macs and Windows PCs.

)))➤ *GUI, Mac, Windows Operating System, Word Processor*

X.400

Email addressing system. The bureaucratic sounding X.400 is just that, a weighty standard defined in hundreds of pages by the International Telecommunications Union (ITU) in Switzerland. It covers how to address and transport email messages, whether they are being sent over a TCP/IP connection or via a dial-up line.

)))➤ *Email, IP, Sending Email*

X.500

Global directory standard. This is a standard from the International Telecommunications Union (ITU) in Switzerland, the same people who produced X.400. This one defines how global directories should be structured to produce a white-pages style model to look up people's email addresses. The directories are hierarchically organized by country, state, city etc.

)))➤ *Directory Service, Email, IP, Sending Email, White Pages*

XMODEM

Data transmission protocol. Developed in the 1970s, Xmodem is a simple protocol for using telephone lines to transfer data between computers. It works by sending a checksum with a block of data and then waiting for acknowledgement that it has been received at the other end. Most modems support Xmodem, but it is only effective at slow speeds.

)))➤ *Dial-up Connection, File Transfer, Protocol, Zmodem*

YAHOO! (*www.yahoo.com*)

Search directory web site. Yahoo is the most popular search service on the Web. Since its launch in 1994, it has enjoyed a good reputation for helping people find information easily. Yahoo is an enormous directory of over one million web sites, compiled and categorized by a large team of editors. Yahoo supplements its results with those from Google, so that if a search fails to find a match within Yahoo's own listings, matches from Google are displayed.

)))➤ *Portal, Search Directory, Search Engine*

YAHOO AUCTION (auctions.yahoo.com)

Auction web site. Yahoo Auctions is one of the Web's many popular sites for browsing, selling and buying all kinds of goods and curios.

)))) **Auctions Online**

YAHOO DAILY NEWS
(dailynews.yahoo.com)

News web site. Yahoo Daily News is a popular destination, particularly with users of the Yahoo! search engine (www.yahoo.com). It offers a regularly updated source of ncws on world events, stock markets and popular culture.

)))) **News Online**

YELLOW PAGES

Online business directories. While white pages are directories where you can look up details of people online, yellow pages are business directories. They are giant databases that can be searched to find companies either by type of business or location. Among the best known are Yell in the UK and SuperPages.com in the US.

)))) **Publicizing Your Site, Directory Service, Search Directory**

ZIP FILE

Compression file format. Shareware programs in particular are often saved on the Internet as ZIP files, so that they will be quicker to download. The files, compressed using the popular ZIP format, usually have .zip as the file extension. Once the zipped file has been downloaded it needs to be 'unzipped' before it can be run. Utilities such as WinZip (for Windows) or StuffIt Expander (for the Mac) can decompress these files. Alternatively, the zipped file may have been saved as a self-extracting file that can be unzipped simply by double-clicking.

)))) **Archive, Compression, WinZip**

ZMODEM

A fast, efficient protocol enabling two computers to communicate over phone lines, now largely replaced by PPP. Zmodem is a faster, more efficient version of the Xmodem protocol for transferring data between computers over a telephone line. It is faster because, unlike Xmodem, it does not wait for the receiving modem to send back confirmation that the data arrived successfully. It relies on the modem itself to provide error correction. Consequently, it sends blocks of data in rapid succession. In a further enhancement over Xmodem, should transmission be interrupted the transfer can resume where it finished off, without having to re-send earlier information. However, it is rarely used now that computers use the Point-to-Point Protocol (PPP) to connect to the Internet.

)))) **Dial-up connection, File Transfer, Protocol, Xmodem**

ZONE

Part of web site URL. The end part of a web site's URL or address, which shows the type of organization hosting the computer (such as .gov for government or .com for commercial) or the country code where the URL has been registered. You can choose any zone available, which is why Tuvalu (.tv) has become very popular.

)))) **Address, Domain, Hostname, URL**

LEFT: Guitars are amongst the many different items whcih can be bought and sold on the Internet through auction sites

150 USEFUL WEB SITES

FIND IT!

Search engines and directories are the virtual librarians of the Net – except that these librarians are also super-scavengers with an astounding store of knowledge at their disposal. They can find whatever you're looking for and each have their own strengths and weaknesses. Here, in alphabetical order, are the best of the bunch…

1. A-Zfind (*www.a-zfind.com* **)**
A-Zfind is a directory and reference site. The content of the results of an A-Zfind keyword search consists of web pages that have been critically reviewed by A-Zfind's staff – i.e. intelligent human beings rather than search robots. As an extra bonus, rather than taking you to a site's home page, A-Zfind will go to contents pages which are more helpful for browsing and navigating.

2. AltaVista (*www.altavista.com* **)**
AltaVista, aka The Search Company, one of the oldest search engines on the Web (launched 1995), with a large index of web pages and a wide range of powerful searching commands, is one of the most popular search sites on the Net. As well as searches for images, video, MP3/Audio and news, it also offers a set of specialized search tools.

3. All the Tests (*www.allthetests.com* **)**
A novel slant on the search engine, All the Tests helps you find any kind of test on the Web, ranging from memory

tests and IQ profiles, to health, personality, knowledge, relationship, career tests and more. You can also publish your own tests or quizzes either with All the Tests or – with their 'interactive quiz design' – on your own home page.

4. All the Web (*www.alltheweb.com* **)**
All the Web not only allows you to search for an exact phrase in 'all the web, all the time', as its motto states, but in a large number of different languages. The search results include a selection of 'FAST topics' that save you from having to dredge through sometimes lengthy lists to find what you're looking for.

5. Ask Jeeves (*www.askjeeves.com* **)**
With Ask Jeeves, you can type your question in plain English and it will answer with links to web sites chosen from their human-compiled database. Of course, you can't expect even the most intelligent of butlers to know the answer to every question…

6. Copernic (*www.copernic.com* **)**
Copernic operates as a standalone program and, unlike other multiple search engines such as MetaCrawler, it not only queries search engines and directories but also

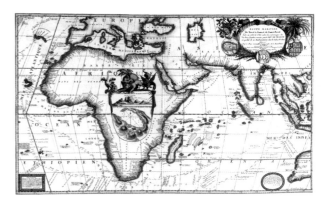

Usenet archives and email databases. After filtering out duplicates, it displays the results on one page, retrieving them for offline browsing.

7. Dogpile (*www.dogpile.com*)

As a 'metasearcher' Dogpile can query multiple search engines simultaneously ('You pick the engines. We do the searching.') Among the databases it trawls are: GoTo, AltaVista, LookSmart and Yahoo! An efficient method of finding your stuff in one go without having to plough through several different engines.

8. Google (*www.google.com*)

A relative newcomer, Google has rapidly become the search engine of choice because of its unfussy, efficient performance and its ability to cope with the trickiest of keyword searches. It has a large database and is highly effective in ranking results by popularity (known as 'relevance').

9. Google Groups (*http://groups.google.com*)

A new service from Google, allowing you to search thousands of newsgroups. With Google Groups you can choose popular discussion groups, such as those listed in the categories alt, biz, comp, rec and misc.

10. Google Picture Searcher (*http://images.google.com*)

While the number of pictures to be found on the Web multiplies daily, finding the right image can be time-consuming. Google's new picture searcher takes care of this. Just enter a keyword and a variety of matching GIGs or JPEGs will instantly be located. You can also see the original page that contained the picture.

11. Hotbot (*www.hotbot.com*)

A favourite of many researchers, Hotbot has advanced search filters, including date, languages and words to exclude, which help to refine your search.

12. MetaCrawler (*www.metacrawler.com*)

Probably the best of the 'metasearchers' (multiple search engines that search the indexes of other search engines), although MetaCrawler has a limit of 30 hits per site.

13. Northern Light (*www.northernlight.com*)

A favourite search engine among researchers, Northern Light features a large index of the Web and organizes pages into topics. It also offers 'special collection' sets of documents from over 7,000 publications, newswires, magazines and databases. Searching these documents is free, but there's a charge to view them.

14. Open Directory Project (*http://dmoz.org*)

Labelled 'the largest human edited directory of the Web', the Open Directory Project – or DMOZ – is 'constructed and maintained by a vast, global community of volunteer editors' (at the time of writing, 45,622 of them). Its aim is to provide a 'definitive catalog of the Web'. Various search engines make use of ODP data.

15. Yahoo! (*http://uk.yahoo.com*)

The original – and still most popular – directory, whose content is compiled and categorized by a large team of editors. If you have a site, you decide the Yahoo! category you would like it to appear in (although of course Yahoo! reserves the right not to include it). Yahoo supplements its results with those from Google; if a search fails to find a match within Yahoo's own listings, matches from Google are displayed. Yahoo! has also developed in the last few years into a major portal.

THESE BOOKS ARE MADE FOR WALKING...

Since Amazon's spectacular breakthrough – in massive turnover of units rather than actual profit – bookselling online has become big Internet business. In 2002 Amazon was even able to announce to the seriously depressed dotcom world that for the first time it had actually made a modest net profit, promising great things to come. In theory there's a perfect fit between the demand for reading material online and its supply by willing booksellers. It also makes good sense in other ways: a book does not vary according to the shop in which it's bought and you can read reviews and even sample excerpts online. Furthermore, Net suppliers' low overheads translate into substantial discounts. Of course the delivery speed can be a problem... So check out our selection of online bookstores...

1. Alphabet Street (*www.alphabetstreet.infront.co.uk*)
Alphabet Street, one of the smaller online bookstores, offers 30 per cent discount off its Top Ten books – not a bad inducement to shop here. Items are shipped within 24 hours and, like Amazon, the Street provides a simple one-mouse click ordering process for regular users. Once you get to trust the security of a particular site, such as this one or that of Amazon, this fast ordering approach – cutting out the tedious, fiddly and time-wasting re-entry of personal details – has great advantages. In spite of its relatively small presence on the Net, Alphabet Street boasts a huge range of books. Other sections include Music, DVDs, Games, Videos and Streetwise – a free entertainment magazine.

2. Amazon (*www.amazon.co.uk*)
The original online bookstore – and still perhaps the best – Amazon.com began selling books online in July 1995 and has since expanded its product range to include CDs, videos, DVDs, toys and electronics. An estimated 29 million shoppers make Amazon probably the world's biggest shopping web site. Amazon offers excellent book reviews, smart recommendations (based on your previous buying patterns, though some people may find this aspect obtrusive and irritating) and loads of special offers. Ordering is simple and efficient, and Amazon keep customers informed of the status of their orders by email.

3. Blackwell's (*www.blackwell.com*)
While the prices at Oxford-based Blackwell's are not particularly cheap, it offers free delivery. Sections include a Student Learning Site and Headfiller (which puts together booklists from every student course in the

country) and a particularly good, searchable Rare Books 'department'.

4. Bol (*www.bol.com*)
The approach of Bol (Books Online, aka 'The Other One', i.e. the one that isn't Amazon) to bookselling is simplicity and efficiency: short reviews and descriptions, a basic style that will appeal to many buyers who already know what they want and use Bol for its vast range of titles, good prices and a reliable ordering process. Bol also provides music, DVD/video, games and software sections.

5. Swotbooks (*www.swotbooks.com*)
As its name implies, Swotbooks specialize in academic textbooks, both new and secondhand (you can buy and sell them), though you can also purchase regular mass-market trade books here – and the prices can be highly competitive. 'Low cost books for clever dicks' is Swotbooks motto.

6. WH Smith Online (*www.whsmith.co.uk*)
Once just the most ubiquitous UK high-street newsagent and bookshop, WH Smith has well and truly entered the Internet fray with bags of discounts, special offers, reviews, interviews, extracts, competitions, e-books and an online literary prize. All orders over £40 are delivered free. WH Smith also provides music, DVD/video, games, adventure, stationery and magazine sections, as well as features such as 'Education Zone'.

7. ABE Books (*www.abebooks.com*)
One of the best sites for second-hand books. Although based in Canada, shipping is relatively cheap at approximately £4.

BEST OF THE REST

8. Alibris (*www.alibris.com*)

Another online second-hand bookstore – excellent for rare first editions and even signed copies at decent prices.

9. Antiquarian Booksellers' Association (*www.abainternational.com*)

A must for lovers of rare books, maps, prints, manuscripts, letters and ephemera.

10. The Book Place (*www.thebookplace.com*)

Apart from functioning as an online bookstore where you can browse subjects, the Book Place claims to have every text for every Open University course.

12. Justbooks (*www.justbooks.co.uk*)

Justbooks allows you to buy and sell out-of-print, rare, used and antiquarian books. There are links to this impressive service from Bol, WH Smith and Swotbooks.

13. Student Book World (*www.studentbookworld.com*)

Another student bookstore listing 1.2 million books at its site (including every British book in print) and offering bargain textbooks and trade books. It 'aims to offer all books at discounted prices, some at discounts of up to 30 per cent'.

14. Talking Book Shop (*www.talkingbooks.co.uk*)

Specialists, obviously, in audiobooks; as is the Talking Book Club (www.talkingbookclub.co.uk) where for an annual fee of £7.50 you can rent audiobooks (£5 each, regardless of length).

11. Crime Bookshop (*www.crimebookshop.co.uk*)

A site for crime fiction aficionados, affiliated to Bol and Amazon, i.e. the links are supplied by the big guns, and associate founder Guy Clapperton receives 5 per cent of the retail price of each Amazon book sold – and 7 per cent from Bol.

15. Tesco (*www.tesco.com*)

The supermarket scores highly as an online bookseller by offering attractive discounts on bestsellers – the Top 50 at a guaranteed 10 per cent less than Amazon and WH Smith.

ON YOUR MARKS...

The Internet – as you will discover below – could almost have been invented as the natural medium for sports coverage. The beauty of the Web is that it can combine live real-time reportage with archival data in a way that is unique to this no-holds-barred medium. So here is a selection of the best sports sites. Get set … go!

1. Football 365 (*www.football365.com*)

For soccer fanatics everywhere, this is the ultimate site. It's packed with footie news, gossip, betting, live commentary, statistics, video clips and even downloadable ringtones for your mobile.

2. Freeserve's Sport (*www.freeserve.com/sport*)

As one of the major portals, Freeserve covers a full range of sporting activities on its Sport pages, including an auction site where you can bid for (or sell) tickets for major sports events or find bargains in sporting equipment. And Freeserve's Sports Directory enables a keyword search for any sport under the sun (assuming, of course, that it's also on the Net!). Action sports covered include BMX, canoeing/kayaking, scuba diving, snowboarding, skating, windsurfing and skydiving.

3. Sporting Life (*www.sportinglife.com*)

Leeds-based Sporting Life, originating from the eponymous newspaper, claims to be the UK's most popular multi-sports web site. Its contents include separate pages for Football, World Cup, Racing, Cricket, Rugby Union, Six Nations, Rugby League, Formula One, Golf, Tennis, Boxing, NFL, Snooker, Winter Olympics … and many other sports. There is also a 'Betting Zone', a sports radio station, a fanzine, sports results, sports diary and calendar – and, of course, competitions a plenty. (Note: another site, www.sportal.co.uk, the UK sports portal, is in fact administered by Sporting Life and is virtually identical.)

4. Sports.com (*www.sports.com/en*)

Type 'www.sports.com' and you'll be sent to 'www.sports.com/en' – the UK arm of www.sportsline.com, the US version. In fact Sports.com includes a number of international sites, including French, German, Spanish and Italian. At Sports.com, apart from the usual variety of sports pages, users can participate in polls, view archival sporting pix and make bets. There are also contests, games and fantasy leagues. Content can also be delivered to WAP and handheld devices and you can even click to see Sports.com on a WAP emulator.

LET ME ENTERTAIN YOU

When it's time to relax and let your hair down, the Internet offers a cornucopia of leisure and entertainments sites. Here are just a few...

5. Aloud.com (*www.aloud.com*)

'All the Live Event Tickets You Can Buy Online' is the proud boast of Aloud.com. You can search by artist, town or genre for any commercial music gigs or festivals in the UK. Other features include: 'Win A Kiss', live reviews, ticket ordering and tracking, and a free list of gigs sent by email.

6. Kissogram (*www.kissogram.com.au*)

If you're having a good day, send a virtual kissogram – not just animated lips but trembling butts and lickograms. As the site exhorts, 'Be part of the latest b-craze to hit the world (wide web). Email a kiss, a mamogram, an ozogram or the real thing, 'Send it now! Something for everyone ... free, non fattening and there is no exchange of body fluids.'

7. SceneOne (*www.sceneone.co.uk/s1/home*)

An all-embracing entertainment site with sections on Cinema, Television (listings for both terrestrial and digital channels), Radio, CDs, Gigs, Theatre, Comedy, Books, DVD/Video, Auctions, Showbiz News and info on forthcoming festivals. You can purchase tickets online. SceneOne, which describes itself as 'the UK's leading entertainment guide from Flextech Interactive', claims to be the first service in this country to go live on all current digital platforms – Internet, television and mobile phone. As an interactive TV service (courtesy of Cable & Wireless and Sky Digital) viewers can purchase tickets via their remote control.

8. Ticketmaster (*www.ticketmaster.co.uk*)

The site for purchasing tickets online, Ticketmaster greets you on its opening page with the main up-and-coming live events in various categories – Music, Theatre, Sports, Attractions, Performing Arts – with messages such as 'on sale today', 'new', 'last chance' or – depressingly, 'currently not available'. Ticketmaster sells over 80,000 tickets a month and includes 36,000 events in its database. Beat that, you touts!

9. Time Out (*www.timeout.com*)

Although originally a London-based 'what's on' events magazine, the online version of Time Out is truly international, with city guides to the world's top 33 cities. As it says on its home page 'We review thousands of the best restaurants, clubs and bars, assess the hotels and show you the finest sights and shows. Wherever you're going, we have the lowdown on this month's hottest events.' The cities are divided into three categories: Europe, USA and Rest of the World. And of course you can buy tickets online for theatres, gigs and restaurants.

10. Whatsonstage (*www.whatsonstage.com*)

This national information service for the performing arts (its motto is 'The Home of British Theatre') includes a ticket booking service, theatre news (with pages such as 'Openings' and 'Closings') and gossip ('The Goss'), reviews of West End and regional plays, and a discussion forum. Other features include 'The Big Debate'and the WOS awards with categories including Best Actor, Best Actress, Best New Musical and Best Comedy. There's also news from across the Pond ('New York Nights') and an Interactive Play.

READ ALL ABOUT IT

The Internet has allowed the traditional press to compete on far more equal terms with television when it comes to breaking news. Here's a round-up of how they're doing…

1. FT.com (Financial Times) (*www.ft.com*)

Those who remember the FT as the grey and sombre broadsheet of high finance will need to think again when they see the web site. Of course financial news in real time still dominates, but just click on the News button and there's a plethora of headline links, from 'world news' from each continent to 'people in the news' and 'discussion on the news', a forum for discussion groups. At the time of writing, there were 42 replies to the subject of 'Milosevic in the dock'. The FT is free, though you have to register to access some sections of the site. There's also a searchable database of some 2,000 publications.

2. Guardian Unlimited (*www.guardian.co.uk*)

Guardian Unlimited brands itself 'The UK's most popular newspaper web site' and this may well be the case. Breaking news is updated every two hours. Its special reports are a particular strength and in its coverage of, for instance, the war on terrorism it has come into its own. As the web site name implies, it's all free, so there's the added joy of a new Steve Bell cartoon in full colour on your monitor every morning! Sections include: Popup headlines, UK latest, World latest, Arts latest, Audio reports, World dispatch, Net news, Special reports, The issue explained, Columnists, News quiz, The wrap (a digest of the best of the rest of the daily press), The informer (lunchtime news service delivered free every weekday at 2 p.m.), The weblog (GU's pick of noteworthy reads online), Picture gallery and Net notes. There are also many other features, such as Diary and Letters; resources such as Search the archive and TV listings; and interactive pages such as Talkboards, Live online, Quiz room and – of course - Crossword.

3. The Independent.co.uk (*www.independent.co.uk*)

A rather more highbrow affair than its competitors – with relatively few pictures and a curious grey and yellow graphic design – the online Independent tends to emphasize opinion rather than breaking news. Main sections are divided into News, Sport, Argument, Education, Money, Travel and – the fun part – Enjoyment. The last of these contains, apart from the obligatory Crosswords section, 'e-break' which includes lyric and caption competitions and brain teasers.

4. The Sun Online (*www.thesun.co.uk*)

The online version of the Sun is, if anything, more subdued and less sensationalistic than its tabloid counterpart, though it makes liberal use of pictures and graphics – and retains its traditional Page 3 (to access the selection of videos of Page 3 lovelies you pay a premium rate for a special dialler). Elsewhere there is ample coverage of breaking news and domestic and world news, though the Sun's populist slant, as always, peeps through the murkiest complexities of the real world.

5. The Telegraph.co.uk (*www.telegraph.co.uk*)

Formerly known as Electronic Telegraph, the online version of the Daily Telegraph has an excellent range of breaking news coverage and in-depth analysis, and a stunning array of links. In terms of pure news reportage this is the cream of the crop of online British news sites, but there is also an exhaustive list of sections – Arts, Books, Business news, Crossword Society, Education, Family, Fantasy football, Fashion, Gardening, Health, Horoscopes, Jobs, Law reports, Letters & Feedback, Money, Motoring, News, Obituaries, Opinion, Outdoors, Personal finance, Promotions, Property, Science, Shopping, Sport, Technology, Travel, Weather, Wine – and other features such as Business file, Connected, Global network, Internet for schools, Juiced (its student web site) and Press Office.

6. Times Online (*www.thetimes.co.uk*)

The design of the online version of the august newspaper is still undergoing changes, but it has managed to retain the right balance between the traditional authoritative broadsheet format and a sense of being contemporary and on the ball. There is a healthy mix of breaking news (and Times Services include email or mobile phone text updates) and features: Breaking News, Britain, World, Sport, Business, Your Money, Comment, Sports Book, Travel, Shopping, Classifieds, Law, Games, Crossword, Talking Point, Times 2 (leisure features), Appointments, Films, First night reviews, Theatre, Food & Drink, Television & Radio, Arts, Property, Motoring, Health, Creme (mainly for women), Fashion & Style, Education, Weekend, Play, From the Archive, Promotions etc.

BEST OF THE REST

Australia
7. The Age (*www.theage.com.au*)
8. The Australian (*www.news.com.au*)
9. Sydney Morning Herald (*www.smh.com.au*)

Britain
10. Daily Mail (*www.dailymail.co.uk*)
11. Evening Standard (*www.thisislondon.co.uk*)
12. Express (*www.express.co.uk*)

USA
13. Boston Globe (*www.globe.com*)
14. Chicago News Network (*www.chicago-news.com*)
15. LA Times (*www.latimes.com*)

16. New York Times (*www.nytmes.com*)
17. USA Today (*www.usatoday.com*)
18. Village Voice (*www.villagevoice.com*)
19. Washington Post (*www.washingtonpost.com*)

Rest of the world
20. The Hindu (*www.hinduonline.com*)
21. Irish Times (*www.irish-times.com*)
22. Jerusalem Post (*www.jpost.com*)
23. La Stampa (*www.lastampa.it*)
24. Le Monde (*www.lemonde.fr*)
25. South China Morning Post (*www.scmp.com*)
26. St Petersburg Times (*www.sptimes.ru*)
27. Times of India (*www.timesofindia.com*)
28. Toronto Star (*www.thestar.com*)

Newswires: breaking news
29. ABC (*www.abcnews.com*)
30. BBC (*www.news.bbc.co.uk*)
31. CBS (*www.cbs.com*)
32. CNN (*www.cnn.com*)
33. ITN (*www.itn.co.uk*)
34. NBC (*www.msnbc.com*)
35. Reuters (*www.reuters.com*)

ARE YOU THE WEAKEST LINK?

Even if you're not planning to go on Who Wants to Be a Millionaire? or The Weakest Link – or secretly getting into training for Trivial Pursuits at Xmas – having reference info at your fingertips is generally useful and sometimes indispensable. With our rundown of some of the best reference sites on the Web, there's no more need to phone a friend – except of course to say hello…

1. Babelfish (*http://babelfish.altavista.com*)
The name was coined by Douglas Adams in *The Hitch Hiker's Guide to the Galaxy*, 'The practical upshot of all this is that if you stick a Babel fish in your ear you can understand anything said to you in any form of language.' Which is more or less what AltaVista Babelfish does for you, except that the fish doesn't go in your ear. Instead, you can type up to 150 words for translation (into and out of any one of eight languages) or specify a web page for translation. It's all powered by a system called SYSTRAN and though in theory it's fiendishly clever, the results may read a little oddly. Babelfish works most effectively for a few words or phrases, though it may still help to keep a dictionary handy – or at least consult one online.

2. British Library Public Catalogue (BLPC) (*http://blpc.bl.uk/*)
An excellent – and free – bibliographical service from the British Library, allowing you to search their catalogue which has been developed over 250 years and contains no less than 150 million items! Even if you only know the name of an author, or just a book title, it will probably yield all the bibliographical data you need. You can order documents or, if a book is in the BL's collection, view it in the London Reading Rooms.

3. Encarta Online (*www.encarta.msn.co.uk/reference*)
The online version of Microsoft's reference CD. For public use (without owning the CD) you can perform a keyword search of the Encyclopedia, Encarta World English Dictionary or Multilingual Dictionary (translating to and from French, Spanish, German and Italian) or browse categories and use other resources, such as guides and quizzes. Although Encarta is not as comprehensive as the Encyclopedia Britannica, if your search is successful a complete article will appear rather than merely the opening paragraph that Enc Brit supplies to non-subscribers. On the other hand, Encarta does provide a more comprehensive service, called Online Deluxe; to access it you have to own the Encarta Deluxe Encyclopedia or Encarta Reference Library CDs.

4. Encyclopedia Britannica (*www.britannica.com*)
In spite of its name and history, the online version of the Enc Brit has a distinctly American bias. On the home page you enter a keyword search either from Britannica.com or the Encyclopedia, or Dictionary or Thesaurus. Results are displayed in two columns, one specific to EB (you have to subscribe to view all but the opening paragraph), while the other column's results are gleaned from the 'Web's best sites'. You may browse Britannica by subject or alphabetically, or browse the Britannica Atlas. There are galleries celebrating over two

The chances are, of course, that none of the data in these additional fields, apart from the phone number, will be present, in which case you're invited to add them to UK Phonebook's database. You can also access a map of the relevant area, choosing its scale.

7. Webopaedia (*www.pcwebopaedia.com*)
Everything you always wanted to know about the Net but were afraid to ask. Webopaedia, a subsidiary of Internet.com, contains a comprehensive dictionary and search engine dealing with computer and Internet terminology. On the opening page you'll find a list of recently added bits of jargon. These included, at the time of writing, 'pulsing zombie' and 'virus signature' (to discover their meaning, you'll have to consult Webopaedia). You'll also find 'Term of the Day', 'Top 15 Terms' and 'Webopaedia Jobs' where you can search for 'hot IT jobs in your area' from over 100,000 – yes 100,000 – listings.

BEST OF THE REST
8. Academic Info (*www.academicinfo.net*)
9. Allexperts.com (*www.allexperts.com*)
10. Biography (*www.biography.com*)
11. Info Please (*www.infoplease.com*)
12. Online Dictionaries
(*www.bucknell.edu/~rbeard/diction.html*)
Links to 800 dictionaries in 160 languages
13. Ordnance Survey (*www.ordsvy.gov.uk*)
14. Study Web (*www.studyweb.com*)
15. Symbols (*www.symbols.com*)

centuries of Britannica, highlights and special features. Britannica is still probably the single most comprehensive source of reference information on and off the Net.

5. Thesaurus.com (*www.thesaurus.com*)
The online version of Roget's Thesaurus, allied to Dictionary.com (*www.dictionary.com*), Thesaurus.com allows you to look up synonyms or antonyms, or browse by headword or category. The keyword lookup gives you the choice of consulting either the dictionary or the thesaurus. There are also resources such as Cool Tools, a daily crossword and word search puzzles, a translator and writing resources (grammar, usage and style guides; writing tips and other resources).

6. UK Phonebook (*www.ukphonebook.com*)
A highly useful resource, UK Phonebook, using data from BT, enables you to locate business and residential numbers. After entering a name and, if known, town or village, click on a resulting address and a phone number will be supplied, together with relevant web site, email, second phone number, mobile number and fax number.

LEAVIN' ON A JET PLANE...

Finally, a bumper crop of useful travel and transport web sites. There are so many fantastic sites in this category that we've saved the best – and most – till last. Finding out more about them is just a click away, so let your fingers do the walking until your boot-heels go a wanderin'…

The guides

First the major online travel guides – indispensable at the dreaming and planning stages – and on your travels, in which case you'll probably be accessing them from an Internet café, somewhere far away…

1. Lonely Planet (*www.lonelyplanet.com*)
A beautifully organized site, with a text version for those in a hurry. The graphic version has vivid icons, packing you off to Lonely Planet's sections: The Thorn Tree (talk to other travellers – bulletin board for those with itchy feet); Scoop (travel news and features, updated weekly – 'We promise our newsreaders go without trousers'); Ekno (complete communications kit for travellers); On the Road (travel lit from RG's Journeys series – tall and true tales from authors on the road); Postcards (find out what other travellers are saying about the world – save time, money and mayhem); Propaganda (order a Lonely Planet guide); Health ('survival kit to staying healthy (or at least upright) on the road'); SubWay (tastiest travel sites on the Web); FAQ; Upgrades ('reboot your guidebook'); and Talk2Us.

2. Moon Travel Guides (*www.moon.com*)
'What sets this series apart? Moon Handbooks reach beyond the obvious and allow you to capture the true spirit of your destination – even before you head out the door.' Read excerpts, and in some cases the full text, of Moon's acclaimed travel guides and newsletter, written by seasoned travellers and packed with practical advice and in-depth coverage of regional arts, culture, history and social issues.

3. Rough Guides (*http://travel.roughguides.com*)
At first sight Rough Guides.com appears more of a portal, with separate areas for Music, Catalog, etc. However, delve into the travel section and you'll be in more familiar Rough Guide territory. The opening page greets you with a map of the world; click on this or use the search boxes to select a destination. Enter, say, Cambodia and there's a main article on the country with links to Best of Cambodia, Basics, History, Books, Language, Explore Cambodia. Like the Rough Guide books, the site dispenses with frills and gets down to what you need to know.

BEST OF THE REST

Air couriers
4. Air Courier Association (*www.aircourier.org*)
5. Airhitch (*www.airhitch.org*)
6. IAATC Air Courier (*www.courier.org*)

Discount/last-minute flights
7. Bargain Holidays (UK) (*www.bargainholidays.com/*)
8. Best Fares (*www.bestfares.com*)
9. Cheap Flights (UK) (*www.cheapflights.co.uk/*)
10. Internet Air Fares (US) (*www.air-fare.com/*)
11. Itravel.com (worldwide) (*www.Itravel.com*)
12. Lastminute.com (UK) (*www.lastminute.com*)
13. Lastminutetravel.com (*www.lastminutetravel.com*)
14. Lowestfare.com (US) (*www.lowestfare.com/*)
15. TravelHub (US) (*www.travelhub.com/*)

Government health advice/warnings
16. Australia (*www.dfat.gov.au*)
17. General health info for travellers (*www.cdc.gov/travel*)
18. UK (*www.fco.gov.uk*)
19. US (*http://travel.state.gov/travel_warnings.html*)

Major travel services
Use for research, accommodation and travel tips rather than cheap fares and customer service:
20. Biztravel (US) (*www.biztravel.com*)
21. Expedia (Australia) (*www.expedia.com.au*)
22. Expedia (UK) (*www.expedia.co.uk*)
23. Expedia (US) (*www.expedia.com*)
24. ITN (US/worldwide) (*www.itn.com*)
25. Preview Travel (US) (*www.previewtravel.com*)

26. Travel.com.au (Australia) (*www.travel.com.au*)
27. Travelocity (worldwide) (*www.travelocity.com*)
28. Travel Select (worldwide) (*www.travelselect.co.uk*)

Reverse auction sites

Bid on a destination and wait for a bid:
29. Priceline.com (*www.priceline.com*)
30. Travelbids (*www.travelbids.com*)

Travel: miscellaneous

31. AA (Automobile Association: UK) (*www.theaa.com*)
Useful travel features; details of AA services.
32. A2Btravel.com (*www.a2btravel.com/*)
Travel into, around and out of the UK.
33. Air Traveler's Handbook
(*www.cs.cmu.edu/afs/cs/user/mkant/Public/Travel/airfare.html*)
Comprehensive annotated links to air travel and general travel resources.
34. Arab Net (*www.arab.net*)
North African and Middle Eastern: peoples, geography, economy, history and culture.
35. Art of Travel (*www.artoftravel.com*)
See the world on $25 a day.
36. ATM Locators (*www.visa.com/pd/atm/*), (*www.mastercard/com/atm*)
Find an ATM; remain solvent abroad.
37. Bed & Breakfast Channel (*www.bbchannel.com*)
Special B&B deals worldwide.
38. Currency Converter (*http://quote.yahoo.com/m3?u*)
39. Epicurious Travel (*http://travel.epicurious.com*)
Tips from Traveler magazine, including World Events calendar.
40. Europe through the Back Door
(*www.ricksteves.com*)
41. Eurostar (*www.eurostar.com*)
For Channel Tunnel users everywhere.
42. Eurotrip (*www.eurotrip.com*)
Backpacking through Europe.
43. Excite Travel (*www.city.net*)
Links to global community, health and tourist information.
44. Fielding's Danger Finder
(*www.fieldingtravel.com/df/*)

Adventure holidays – lots of dangerous things to do and dangerous places to visit, accompanied by copious warnings.
45. Find a Grave (*www.findgrave.com*)
Check out where celebs are buried.
46. Fit for Travel (*www.fitfortravel*)
NHS medical guide to travelling abroad.
47. Hostels.com (*www.hostels.com*)
48. Hotel Discount (*www.hoteldiscount.com*)
49. Infiltration (*www.infiltration.org*)
'Infiltration offers a mix of the practice and theory of urban exploration in areas not designed for public usage.'
50. International Home Exchange
(*www.homexchange.com*)
51. Journeywoman (*www.journeywoman.com*)
Sisters are doing it for themselves…
52. Mapblast (*www.mapblast.com*)
53. Mapquest (*www.mapquest.com*)
54. Streetmap (*http://www.streetmap.co.uk/*)
55. Tourism Offices Worldwide (*www.towd.com*)
56. Travlang (*www.travlang.com*)
Learn the language of your destination country.
57. Travel-Library.com (*www.travel-library.com*)
Personal travelogues, trip reports, worldwide tourist information.
58. The Virtual Tourist (*www.vtourist.com*)
More links to global tourist information.
59. The World Traveler Book & Maps
(*www.travelbookshop.com*)
You can order guides here from a wide range of travel literature.
60. Yahoo Travel Section
(*www.yahoo.com/Recreation/Travel/*)
Links to thousands of travel/regional sites.

TOP ISPS

CHOOSING AN ISP

For more on ISPs, see page 89. When choosing an ISP, bear in mind that if you choose to connect via satellite, cable, DSL or ISDN, your ISP will probably be restricted to one or two companies that operate in your area. If, however, you choose a dial-up connection, you are likely to have a much wider choice. Do some research before choosing an ISP: read internet magazines, consult friends, consider your requirements. Here are some suggested criteria:

- **Ease of connection** Ideally, choose an ISP that gives you a free CD that automatically installs the software you need and simplifies the set-up procedure on your computer.
- **Technical support** Assess an ISP's reputation for giving technical support, both online and by telephone, preferably by free-phone number.
- **Quality of service** You can only truly assess the speed and reliability of an ISP's connection by trying it out.

TOP 50 ISPS

TOP 10 ISPS (BY SUBSCRIBERS)

The following were the ten most popular ISPs in the UK at the end of 2001 (figures supplied by ISP Review). Positions depended on the number of subscribers, shown in millions.

1.	Tiscali	1.60
2.	AOL	1.50
3.	BTInternet	1.30
4.	Freeserve	1.10
5.	Supanet	0.83
6.	ic24	0.79
7.	Tiny Online	0.70
8.	NTL	0.68
9.	Breathe	0.63
10.	Line One	0.43

INTERNATIONAL ISPS

1. AOL

Web site address:	www.aol.co.uk/.com
Contact phone no:	0800 279 1234
Point of presence:	Worldwide
Set-up cost:	Free
Monthly cost:	Cheap
Email accounts:	7
Free web space:	35 mb
Cost of support calls:	Free

Main features: Unmetered service with access to AOL extras; some problems but overall a good service although terminating connection after 40 minutes has occasionally been reported.

AOL is one of the world's two biggest OSPs; it has grown from providing limited online services in 1985 to serving a worldwide membership of 31 million. As well as giving its members Internet access, AOL offers a host of other proprietary services. It has been a pioneer in simplifying Internet access for a wide audience and its software is designed so that members do not need any other software; a web browser for surfing the Net and an email function are built in. Although many of its features – such as chat rooms, shopping and message boards – can be found on other web sites, AOL offers a combination of services that put most rival ISP's in the shade:

AIM (AOL Instant Messenger) Hugely popular feature allowing members to send messages to each other in real time

Buddy List Tells members when their friends are online

ICQ Allows members to communicate with friends as they surf

Mapquest Route planner and street finder (USA only)

Moviefone Service for finding and booking movies (USA only)

AOL now provides cheap unmetered access.

2. Compuserve

Web site address:	www.compuserve.com
Contact phone no:	0870 6000 800

Point of presence: ....Worldwide
Set-up cost: ....Free
Monthly cost: ....Moderate
Email accounts: 7
Free web space: ....10 mb
Cost of support calls: ....National rate
Main features: Access at local rates, first month's subscription free.

Compuserve offers members a host of services and channels in addition to connecting them to the Internet. Founded in 1969, the company was one of the Web's pioneers of online services, most notably for being the first to offer email and technical support. Now owned by America Online, Inc., Compuserve focuses on adult and professional users, offering services such as Corporate Business Accounts. They provide resources for business users who use the system to conduct commercial research and keep up to date with the latest business developments. In addition to email and instant messaging (IM), subscribers can also make use of Web Centers that provide stock-market quotes and customized news feeds. Compuserve now makes many of these services available to all Internet users via its web site. A number of specialized services aimed at particular business sectors are offered. These include American Lawyer Media, a portal page tailored for lawyers; a custom service for the American

International Group to cater for insurance brokers; and Airline Crew Services which provides online access and support to many airlines such as British Airways and Virgin Atlantic.

3. Microsoft Network (MSN Freeweb)

Web site address: ....www.msn.com
Contact phone no: 0870 601 1000
Point of presence: ....Worldwide
Set-up cost: ....Free
Monthly cost: ....Moderate
Email accounts: ....web-based
Free web space: ....none
Cost of support calls: ....national rate
Main features: Email addresses via Hotmail; relatively expensive in terms of services which are limited; however, there is good technical support and connection speeds can be fast.

Microsoft's MSN web site is one of the most popular web sites and a main rival to the AOL service. It functions both as an OSP and a portal. Subscribers in the US can connect to the Internet using MSN as an OSP, with a choice of dial-up or faster DSL connections. MSN is also a portal for all users of the Internet that offers a host of features and content including MSN Messenger, Hotmail, search, shopping, chat and news.

UK ISPS: UNMETERED ACCESS

The following ISPs allow unmetered access to the Internet. In other words, after paying your monthly rental and any other one-off costs, your connection is free and you don't need to pay for any phone calls – an attractive option if you plan to be online frequently…

* 'Support costs' refers to the cost of phone calls for Technical Support at the time of publishing.

Name and URL	Cost per month	BT line required	Unmetered availability	Web space (mb)	Newsgroups	Support costs*
4. BT Connect *www.btclickforbusiness.com* tel: 0800 800 001	Expensive	Yes	24 hrs	20	Yes	Local rate
BT's unmetered service with free calls all the time. Very popular, but lots of complaints						
5. BT Internet AnyTime *www.btinternet.com* tel: 0800 800 001	Cheap	Yes	24 hrs	50	Yes	Premium
BT's unmetered service with free calls all the time. Very popular, but lots of complaints						
6. Business Unmetered Business User 24 *www.business-unmetered.com* tel: 0870 0102 472	Moderate	Yes	24 hrs	10	Yes	Premium
This is the UK Fantastic-backed business version of 0800Dial						

Name and URL	Cost per month	BT line required	Unmetered availability	Web space (mb)	Newsgroups	Support costs*
7. ClaraNET Free Time AnyTime *www.clara.net* tel: 0845 355 1000	Cheap	Yes	24 hrs	50	Yes	Local rate
Always rates highly in terms of customer satisfaction; fast, strong 24/7 option; good choice of packages; no apparent cut-off						
8. Demon Premier Connect Plus *www.demon.net* tel: 0800 0279 200	Expensive	Yes	24 hrs	20	Yes	Local rate
9. Eclipse Internet *www.eclipse.net.uk* tel: 01392 333302	Cheap	Yes	24 hrs	10	Yes	Standard BT
Old BT Surftime system; average price; limited services; good support; good speeds						
10. Force9 Connect 15 *www.force9.co.uk* tel: 0845 1400250	Cheap	Yes	24 hrs	250	Yes	National rate
PlusNet associate; good price; average services; average speeds; good support						
11. Freechariot FC Unlimited *www.freechariot.co.uk* tel: 0870 7419111	Cheap	Yes	24 hrs	10	Yes	Premium
12. Free-Online Connect 15 *www.free-online.co.uk* tel: 0845 140 0030	Cheap	Yes	24 hrs	250	Yes	National rate
13. Freeserve Anytime *www.freeserve.com* tel: 0870 872 0099	Cheap	Yes	24 hrs	15	Yes	Premium
Variable speeds and support						
14. ic24 *www.ic24.co.uk* tel: 0870 909 0925	Cheap	Yes	24 hrs	20	Yes	Premium
Brand new unmetered 24/7 access package; however, speeds are slow; average services; poor support						
15. ntlworld *www.ntlworld.com* tel: 0800 952 4343	Free	No	24 hrs	10	Yes	Premium
Cheaper if you also have the ntl telephone service; winners of Future UK Internet Awards; note: monthly cost is £0.00 because Internet connection is a free extra in the basic cable package; you pay a monthly subscription for cable TV						
16. PlusNet Connect 15 *www.plus.net* tel: 0845 140 0200	Cheap	Yes	24 hrs	250	Yes	National rate
Cheap; they used to be strict on over-use but now there are no bandwidth limits; average support						
17. Supanet *www.supanet.com* tel: 0800 915 8185	Cheap	Yes	24 hrs	20	Yes	Premium
Reliable service; allows you to stay online for over four hours each time; 12 month contract; have had some problems; standard ISP						
18. SurfAnyTimeGold *www.surfanytime.co.uk* tel: 0141 548 8010	Moderate	Yes	24 hrs	10	Yes	Premium
Little-known company, but a neat service; good value for 24/7 unmetered access						
19. Tiscali Anytime *www.tiscali.co.uk* tel: 0845 660 1010	Cheap	Yes	24 hrs	25	Yes	Premium
Huge multinational ISP; should provide rock-solid service; good packages, average prices; comprises: LineOne, WOL, LibertySurf and several other ISPs						

Name and URL	Cost per month	BT line required	Unmetered availability	Web space (mb)	Newsgroups	Support costs*
20. TotalServeUltimateSurf24/7 *www.totalserve.co.uk* tel: 0906 3020174	Moderate	Yes	24 hrs	10	Yes	Premium
21. **Virgin.net** *www.virgin.net* tel: 0500 558 800	Cheap	No	24 hrs	10	Yes	Premium or Monthly Payment

Virgin's 24/7 access package was launched in late October 2001

BROADBAND AND ADSL SERVICES

With super-fast, always-on access, this for most home users is going to be the most expensive option. Of course, if a dial-up connection has previously sent your phone bills rocketing, then even with the addition of the one-off cost you may find you save money by choosing broadband.

Name and URL	Cost per month	Type of access	One-off fee	Email addresses	Web space (mb)	News groups
22. **BT Openworld (consumer)** *www.btopenworld.com* tel: 0870 241 4567	Moderate	ADSL	Moderate	10	20	n.a.
23. **ClaraDSL Solo** *www.clara.net* tel: 0845 355 1000	Moderate	ADSL	Moderate	Unlimited	50	Yes
Always rates highly in terms of customer satisfaction; fast; good choice of packages						
24. **Demon (consumer)** *www.demon.net* tel: 0800 0279 200	Moderate	ADSL	Moderate	Unlimited	20	Yes
25. **Firstnet 500** *www.firstnet.net.uk* tel: 0113 292 7700	Expensive	ADSL	Expensive	Unlimited	20	Yes
26. **Force9 ADSL Home** *www.force9.co.uk* tel: 0845 140 0250	Moderate	ADSL	Moderate	Unlimited	250	Yes
27. **Free-Online ADSL Home** *www.free-online.co.uk* tel: 0845 140 0030	Moderate	ADSL	Moderate	Unlimited	250	Yes
28. **HomeChoice (consumer)** *www.homechoice.co.uk* tel: n.a.	Cheap	ADSL	Cheap	Unlimited	20	Yes
29. **Iomart CopperBurst 500 USB** *www.iomartdsl.com* tel: 0845 272 0052	Expensive	ADSL	Expensive	Unlimited	25	Yes
30. **MacUnlimited (formerly AppleOnline) (consumer)** *www.macunlimited.net* tel: 08707 444411	Moderate	ADSL	Moderate	Unlimited	25	Yes
31. **MetroNet (consumer)** *www.metronet.co.uk* tel: 020 8426 4446	Moderate	ADSL	Moderate	5	20	Yes
32. **NTL** *www.ntl.co.uk* tel: 0800 052 2351	Cheap	Cable	Moderate	5	10	Yes
33. **Pipex Home Professional** *www.dsl.pipex.net* tel: 0870 600 4454	Moderate	ADSL	Moderate	12	50	Yes
34. **PlusNet ADSL Home** *www.plus.net* tel: 0845 140 0200	Moderate	ADSL	£176.25	Moderate	250	Yes
35. **World Online (consumer)** *www.worldonline.co.uk/adsl* tel: 0845 660 1001	Moderate	ADSL	Moderate	Unlimited	25	Yes

WHAT IS BROADBAND?

Broadband is a class of data communications methods. Most computer communications use baseband transmission methods: digital transmission with only one signal per wire. Newer, faster transmission methods use broadband transmission, where a single wire carries several signals at once. Cable TV, for example, uses broadband transmission, which is why you can use a cable modem and get TV and Internet access at the same time. Your other broadband choices when connecting from home are several varieties of DSL (Digital Subscriber Line), in which both data and regular telephone traffic are carried, simultaneously, over a regular home telephone line. There are also wireless connections, perhaps the broadest band of all.

Cable modems

If your local TV cable company provides cable modem service, that's probably your best bet, both for speed – cable modem service is by far the fastest (unless it's vastly oversubscribed) – and for cost – it's generally a lot cheaper than other broadband alternatives. Cable modems are different from normal dialin modems. Cable modems are always external, connected on one side to your TV cable and on the other side to an Ethernet card in your personal computer. The cable company may call the Ethernet card a NIC (Network Interface Card); they will probably provide and/or install it, but they might ask you to do it yourself or have it done. This all sounds complicated, but your cable company will send a technician, or perhaps two, to your home. They will probably do most of the work of installing and setting up your cable modem and configuring your personal computer to use it. Cable modem transmission speeds vary – there's a lot of throughput, but it's not all yours; you share it with your neighbors. Thus, the number of other connections on your line matters. Nevertheless cable modems are still very fast!

DSL (Digital Subscriber Line)

DSL (Digital Subscriber Line) is relatively new as a choice for Internet connections in the home. Its speeds are comparable to cable modems and it has some advantages over them, but it also has disadvantages. First, the advantages: assuming you've got an ordinary telephone line, you've already got the wiring required for DSL in your home. DSL services may be available in your area but if not your ISP can supply it remotely. ADSL (Asymmetric DSL) is the most common form of DSL. ADSL requires the installation of a splitter in your home, which generally means two service calls to get it going – one for the phone and another for the computer. If you can't get cable modem service and are out of range for ADSL, you should look into IDSL, which is DSL running on ISDN lines (see below). It supports much longer wires.

ISDN and wireless: the old and the new

ISDN (Integrated Services Digital Network) runs over standard copper telephone wires (like DSL). ISDN was actually a simple innovation. The telephone network is already almost entirely digital, the only exception being the line between the customer and the local exchange. ISDN makes this last segment digital as well. ISDN allows telephone wires to carry two B-channels (bearer channels) of voice or data at the same time at 64 Kbps each, 128 Kbps if both are used for data. Compared to 56 Kbps dialin connections on one hand and the 20 or more times faster cable modems on the other, there's little practical use for ISDN any more. And there's also wireless. Don't expect to get it any time soon, but it is on its way. It's competitive in speed, too, in the megabit (Mbps) range.

PAY ISPS

When you're paying for your phone calls, you may prefer an ISP that charges a (modest) monthly fee to ensure you get the best service. These are the ISPs who (in theory at least) should be providing the best technical support and are concerned with the highest quality access. Here's our pick…

* 'Support costs' refers to the cost of phone calls for Technical Support at the time of publishing.

Name and URL	Cost per month	Email addresses	Web space (mb)	Support costs	V 90	128K ISDN
36. Cablenet	Cheap	Unlimited	50	Standard BT	Yes	No
www.cablenet.net						
tel: 01424 830900						
37. CIX	Cheap	Unlimited	5	Local rate	Yes	Yes
www.cix.co.uk						
tel: 0845 355 9999						
38. Demon	Moderate	Unlimited	20	Local rate	Yes	Yes
www.demon.net						
tel: 0800 0279 200						

20Mb homepage space, unlimited personal email addresses, subscription to @Demon magazine included

Name and URL	Cost per month	Email addresses	Web space (mb)	Support costs	V 90	128K ISDN
39. **Direct Connection** *www.dircon.net* tel: 0800 072 0000	Cheap	Unlimited	20	Local rate	Yes	Yes
40. **Easynet** *www.easynet.co.uk* tel: 0800 053 4343	Moderate	Unlimited	Unlimited	Local rate	Yes	No
41 **Pipex Dial** *www.dial.pipex.com* **Offers a mass of different choices (DialTime), realistic (heavy) prices, good performance, good services; good support** tel: 0870 600 4454	Moderate/Expensive	12	50	National rate	Yes	Yes
42. **U-NET** *www.u-net.net* tel: 0800 0 365 247 **Average services; good support; fast speeds**	Moderate	Unlimited	25	Local rate	Yes	Yes

FREE ISPS

Finally, these are the free ISPs. You pay them no subscription; they charge you only for local call phone rates.

Name and URL	Email addresses	Web space (mb)	News groups	Support costs	V 90	128K ISDN
43. **BT Internet** *www.btinternet.com* tel: 0870 241 4567 See p. 000	5	10	Yes	Premium	Yes	Yes
44. **ClaraNET** *www.clara.net* tel: 0845 355 1000 **Always rates highly in terms of customer satisfaction; fast; good choice of packages**	Unlimited	10	Yes	Local rate	Yes	Yes
45. **Line One** *www.lineone.net* tel: 0845 660 1001 **Good support; fast; but limited services**	5	50	Yes	Premium	Yes	No
46. **Netscape Online** *www.netscapeonline.co.uk* tel: 0800 279 1234 Subsidiary of AOL	Unlimited	20	Yes	Premium	Yes	No
47. **Tiny Online** *www.tinyonline.net* tel: 0845 660 1001 **Now partly owned by Tiscali; good support; fast; limited services**	5	15	Yes	Premium	Yes	No
48. **VirginNet** *www.virgin.net* tel: 0500 558 800 **Reliable with plenty of free web space; good but expensive support calls**	5	10	Yes	Premium or Monthly Payment	Yes	No
49. **Waitrose** *www.waitrose.com* tel: 0800 188 884 **Average speeds; good support; good services; online food ordering**	Unlimited	20	Yes	Free	Yes	No
50. **World Online Tiscali Classic** *www.worldonline.co.uk* tel: 0800 542 1717 **Very fast; good support; average services**	Unlimited	25	Yes	Premium	Yes	No

BIBLIOGRAPHY

Alexander, Ric, (ed.), *Cyber-Killers*, Orion, UK

Anuff, Joey, Cox, Ana Marie and Colon, Terry, *Suck: Worst Case Scenarios*

Ater, Mark P. and Ater, Betty, *Internet User's Handbook 2001*, McFarland & Company, 2001

Baron, Chris and Wll, Bob, *Drag 'n' Drop CGI Enhance Your Web Site Without Programming*, Addison-Wesley, US, 1999

Barron, Bill and Elsworth, Jill, *The Internet Unleashed*, SAMS, 1999

Bates, Alan, *Advanced Web Skills*, Dorling Kindersley, 2000

Bradley, Phil, *The Advanced Internet Searcher's Handbook*, Library Association Publishing, 2001

Castells, Manuel, *The Internet Galaxy*, Oxford University Press, 2001

Collin, Simon, *The Virgin Guide to the Internet*, Publisher: Ted Smart, 1999

Cooper, Brian, Milner, Annalisa and Worsley, Tim, *Essential Internet Guide*, UK, 2000

Comer, Douglas and Droms, Ralph, *Computer Networks and Internets*, Prentice Hall, 2001

Davis, Ziff, *How to Use Netscape Navigator*, Ziff-Davis Press Development Group, 1997

Gentry, Lorna, Brookes, Kelli and Bond, Jill, *New Rider's Official Internet and World Wide Web Yellow Pages*, New Riders, US, 1999

Harn, Harley, *Internet and Web Yellow Pages*, McGraw-Hill, US, 1999

England, Janice, *Practical Computing for Beginners*, Roperpenberthy Publishing, 2001

Engst, Adam, *The Internet Stater Kit*, Hayden, US, 1999

Flanders, Vincent and Willis, Michael, *Web Pages that Suck*, Sybex, US, 1999

Graham, Ian S., *HTML 4.0 Sourcebook*, John Wiley & Sons, US, 1999

Hale, Constance, *WiredStyle*, HardWired, US, 1999

Harris, G., *Internet for Beginners*, Paragon Publishing Ltd., 2000

Hughes, Lisa and Benton, Tim, *The Internet*, Hodder, UK, 1999

Hyman, Michael, *PC Roadkill*, IDG, US, 1999

Ingham, Linda, *Grandma's Guide to the Internet*, Willow Island Editions, 2000

Internet Users' Reference: 2002 Edition, Addison Wesley, 2000

James, Jeff, *The Internet and Multiplayer and Gaming Bible*, St Martin's Press, US, 1999

Junor, Bill, *Internet: the User's Guide for Everyone*, Branden Publishing Co., 1995

Kennedy, Angus, *The Mini Rough Guide Website Directory*, Rough Guides, 2001

Kalbag, Asha, *World Wide Web for Beginners*, Usborne Publishing Ltd., 1997

Kennedy, Angus, *The Rough Guide to the Internet*, Rough Guides, London, 2001

Lewis, Chris, *101 Essential Tips Using the Internet*, Dorling Kindersley, UK, 1997

Levine, John R., *The Internet for Dummies*, Hungry Minds Inc., 2000

Littman, Jonathan, *The Fugitive Game*, Little Brown, US, 1999

Mandel, Thomas and Van der Leun, Gerard, *Rules of the Net*, Hyperion, US, 1999

Miller, Michael, *Absolute Beginner's Guide to Computers and the Internet*, Que, 2002

Morris, Kenneth M., *User's Guide to the Information Age*, Light Bulb Press, 1999

Mueller, Scott, *Upgrading and Repairing PCs*, Que, US, 1999

Multi-Media, Dorling Kindersley, UK, 1996

Naughton, John, *A Brief History of the Future*, Orion Paperbacks, 2000

Negropponte, Nicholas, *Being Digital*, Knopf, US, 1999

Neilson, Jackob and Tahir, Marie, *Homepage Usability*, New Riders, 2001

Platt, Charles, *Anarachy Online: Net Sex Net Crime*, Harper Prism, US, 1999

Reader's Digest Beginner's Guide to Home Computing, The Reader's Digest Association Limited, UK, 1998

Randall, Neil, *The Soul of the Internet*, Thomson, US, 1999

Rosenfold, Louis and Morville, Peter, *Information Architecture for the World Wide Web*, O'Reilly & Assoc., US, 1999

Selkirk, Errol, *Computers for Beginners*, Writers and Readers, 1995

Shelly, Gary B., Forsythe, Steven G. and Cashman, Thomas J., *Netscape Navigator 6*, Course Technology, 2001

Simpson, Paul, *The Rough Guide to Shopping Online*, Rough Guides, 2001

Steinmetz, Ralf and Nahrstedt, *Multimedia*, Prentice Hall, 2002

Treays, R., *Computers for Beginners*, Usborne Publishing Ltd., 1997

Wingate, Phillipa, *Internet for Beginners*, Usborne Publishing Ltd., 1997

Wolf, Michaelm *Burn Rate*, Simon & Schuster, US, 1999

Zeff, Robbin and Aronson, Brad, *Advertising on the Internet*, John Wiley & Sons, US, 1999

ACKNOWLEDGEMENTS

AUTHOR BIOGRAPHIES

Roger Laing
Advanced, Hot Tip, Intermediate, Technical
A writer and journalist, Roger Laing has edited several online publications, including sites backed by major IT companies, such as Lotus and Microsoft. He has also written and edited various books and magazines about PCs, the Internet, Web Design and Information Technology. He has an M.A. in Experimental Psychology from Oxford University.

Martin Noble
Technical Consultant
Martin Noble is an Oxford-based writer/editor whose published novels include *Private Shulz, Who Framed Roger Rabbit, Tin Men, Ruthless People* and *Trance Mission.* He has written biographies on Ewan McGregor and Leonardo DiCaprio, and advised on several Internet-related books, including *Get Online.*

Ian Powling
Basic, History of the Net, Hot Web Site
Ian Powling has a background in music, film, multimedia and publishing. He now works as a content architect, helping people in business and education with the design and content of their web sites.

PICTURE CREDITS

All pictures are courtesy of Foundry Arts except:

Hulton Archive: 15 (t); 32 (r); 33 (l); 93 (r); 94 (r); 135 (b); 145 (r); 148 (t); 178 (b)

Mary Evans Picture Library: 17 (r); 21 (t); 27 (t); 29; 31 (r); 46 (l); 67 (b); 95 (r); 108 (t); 113 (l); 123 (r); 124 (r); 170 (l); 178 (l,r); 180(t); 196 (t)

Topham Picturepoint: 40 (t); 62 (b); 65 (r); 69 (t); 76 (t,b); 78 (t); 88 (t); 96 (r); 97 (r); 98 (l); 99 (r); 100 (t); 102 (r); 116 (t); 118 (b,t); 119 (l); 120 (l); 138 (l); 140 (l); 144 (l); 146 (t); 151 (t); 152 (b); 183 (l)

INDEX